Tales of Transit

American Studies

AMERICAN STUDIES publishes monographs and edited volumes on American history, society, politics, and culture. The series is a forum for groundbreaking approaches and areas of research, as well as pioneering scholarship that adds new insights into relatively established fields in the study of America.

Series Editors:
Derek Rubin and Jaap Verheul
Utrecht University

Published in this series

Derek Rubin and Jaap Verheul (eds.)
American Multiculturalism after 9/11: Transatlantic Perspectives
2009 (ISBN 978 90 8964 144 1)

Sebastian Reyn
Atlantis Lost: The American Experience with de Gaulle, 1958-1969
2010 (ISBN 978 90 8964 214 1)

Anna Pochmara
The Making of the New Negro: Black Authorship, Masculinity, and Sexuality in the Harlem Renaissance
2011 (ISBN 978 90 8964 319 3)

Tales of Transit

Narrative Migrant Spaces in Atlantic
Perspective, 1850-1950

Michael Boyden,
Hans Krabbendam, and
Liselotte Vandenbussche (eds.)

Amsterdam University Press

Cover illustration: Emigrants on deposit (Stadsarchief Rotterdam).

Cover design: Neon, design and communications | Sabine Mannel
Lay-out: JAPES, Amsterdam, the Netherlands

ISBN   978 90 8964 528 9
e-ISBN 978 90 4851 875 3 (pdf)
e-ISBN 978 90 4851 876 0 (ePub)
NUR   763

© M. Boyden, H. Krabbendam, L. Vandenbussche / Amsterdam University Press,
2013

Table of Contents

Acknowledgements

This book grew out of an international conference that was held at the Felix Archive, Antwerp, in June 2010. The conference was a joint organization of research groups at the universities of Ghent, Antwerp and Leuven, the Roosevelt Study Center in Middelburg, and the Red Star Line Museum in Antwerp. We received additional financial support from the Research Foundation – Flanders, the American Embassy in Brussels, the Belgian Luxembourg American Studies Association, and the Fox Family Foundation. The production costs of this collection were covered by the Roosevelt Study Center and the research fund of Ghent University College. We are grateful to the anonymous reviewers of Amsterdam University Press for their valuable feedback on the manuscript, and to the editors of Amsterdam University press for seeing it into print. We also would like to thank Mrs Michael Strange for help with proofreading and Miss Erika Van Leeuwen for creating the index.

The Editors

Introduction

Michael Boyden, Hans Krabbendam, and Liselotte Vandenbussche

Recent publications in transatlantic studies emphasize the exchange of influences and movements across bodies of water, which are approached as areas of connections rather than separation.[1] Transportation historians have begun to deepen the dynamic character and the reciprocal nature of the transatlantic passage of migrants. The enchanting myth of poor migrants pushed from their homes, pulled by shady promises, and in the middle victimized by greedy skippers is counterbalanced by the experiences of more active travelers.[2] These revisionist historians place the providers of services and customers in the context of trade, which often involves a profitable exchange for all parties involved: entrepreneurs, agents and middlemen, and sometimes also the travelers. The power relations seem uneven, but ship owners and travelers both took risks and depended on each other. The migrants needed reliable transportation, but they usually had a variety of options. They actively negotiated to obtain permits to leave their country and enter a new one, sometimes re-evaluating their options during transit. The shipping companies sought profits within the confines of a growing net of legislation and regulation. They had to handle the fluctuating flow of customers, which followed economic circumstances. During economic downturns, the companies had to find alternatives for survival such as diversifying their passengers by tapping into the tourist market. They relied heavily on advertising, and a strong network of agents could recover some of their losses by transporting return migrants home. At the same time, the companies encountered ever closer supervision by the states, which took initiatives to limit the spread of misleading information and to enforce health checks before and after the transatlantic voyage.[3]

Another prominent strand in transatlantic studies has explored the connections between translation and migration, including both travel and exile. Translation and postcolonial scholars tend to approach migrants as "translated beings" whose physical movement from one locale to another often entails a movement between languages and cultures.[4] Drawing on frequently cited formulations of "third spaces" and "contact zones," the plethora of books and articles on this topic usually stress the in-betweenness of the migrant: his or her being a part of several cultures at once, even while belonging to none.[5] Rather than approaching translation as an egalitarian transfer between cultures, these publications highlight the power differentials and identity stakes involved in translation processes. As Anne Malena observed, most studies of this kind (including the contributions to her special issue) display a marked bias in favor of "the literary side of things." They focus on (self-)translations of canonized literary genres rather than unpublished migrant letters or transcriptions of actual exchanges taking place at border crossings, immigration stations, or doctor's offices.[6] This privileging of established literary sources may lead to an overestimation of the agency of migrants, resulting in somewhat romanticized claims concerning translation as an instrument for attaining "inclusive forms of citizenship."[7] At their best, however, these postcolonial and translation studies approaches may supplement the perspective of migration historians. Their focus of attention is on the complex dynamics of linguistic exchanges, which reveal how migrants are continuously involved in not just translating the host culture for themselves, but also translating themselves for the relatives at home. As several essays in this volume show, transit places play a crucial role in such translation situations.

A third group of researchers has extended insights developed in the fields of ethnography and anthropology to the migrant experience. The German-French anthropologist Arnold van Gennep coined the term "rites of passage" as a metaphor to describe ritualized movements of separation, transition, and incorporation. He based this analytical model on the territorial passage across a border between two nations. Writing a century ago, he was probably insufficiently aware of the increasing importance of borders. In 1909 he stated: "Except in the few countries where a passport is still in use, a person in these days may pass freely from one civilized region to another."[8] Within a decade this optimistic idea would be completely reversed since, as we know, the open door of the United States was shut in the early 1920s. Nevertheless, the connection between rituals and travel may prove a fruitful one.[9] Van Gennep divided rituals into those before, during, and after passing a threshold. In relation to migrants, the focus is on symbolic gestures, including religious rites, which travelers created or were subjected to during their passage. As several contributions in this volume illustrate, rituals were enacted in places of transit to assuage tensions caused by the process of uprooting and transplantation. They functioned as a means of (often imperfectly) casting off an inherited identity and creating a new one for oneself in the host culture. The increasing regulation of the sector stimulated new cultural patterns that came close to rituals. Even bureaucratic and medical procedures, which companies and state authorities used for controlling migration movements, had a ritual side to them.

Conceptualizing the migration experience in terms of rites of passage is also relevant in other respects. The repetitious dimension of rituals may alert us to the fact that migration has never been, and probably never will be, a unique and irreversible undertaking. A significant part of the transatlantic travelers crossed repeatedly. Scholars have estimated that between a quarter and a third of all European emigrants returned to their native lands in the period between 1840 and 1920. Inspired by recent examples of transnational migration, social scientists

MICHAEL BOYDEN, HANS KRABBENDAM, AND LISELOTTE VANDENBUSSCHE have pointed out the positive contribution made by returning migrants to their regions of origin. This insight adds to the tales of transit in both directions and allows us to approach return migration not only in terms of failure or retirement but as an extension of a process of transformation in the former homeland. Returning migrants have contributed new designs for home building, new products and production methods, new kind of jobs, and new religious expressions in their countries of origin.[10]

Tales of Transit brings together several of the above perspectives (migration and transportation history, translation and literary studies, cultural anthropology) by focusing on the role of transit places in Atlantic migration flows during the period 1850-1950. Although research on Euro-Atlantic migration may seem saturated by now, remarkably little thoroughgoing research has been devoted to the pivotal position of such transit places or zones (docks, inspection offices, railway stations, customs houses, migrant hotels, ships' decks, churches, etc.). Most studies still approach the Atlantic passage from the perspective of either the receiving or the sending societies, and the gravitational pull of national institutions and traditions makes it difficult to collect sufficient archival materials or statistical data about those who were merely "passing through." In this way, migrants who returned home, went back and forth, or got stranded in transit usually pass below the radar of migration research or are not considered relevant. The essays collected in this volume, each in different ways, take transit as their central focus. We have divided them into three sections, although some of the concerns and themes sketched above are present throughout the volume. The first section, "Rethinking Atlantic Migration," is social historical in scope and questions received notions of the so-called "huddled masses" who crossed the ocean around the turn of the twentieth century. The second section, "Off the Beaten Track," deals with personal testimonies of migrants who chose less common (or less researched) destinations in Latin America and the (translational) problems they encountered there, but also in their communication with their former homeland. The third and final section is entitled "Liminal Spaces" and pays particular attention to the rituals by which migrants as well as their spokespersons and descendants have made sense of their in-betweenness in literary and journalistic endeavors. As a ritual of transition, all migration is in a sense return migration.

Rethinking Atlantic Migration

The first set of essays in this volume presents new insights from historical research on Atlantic migration between 1850 and 1950. The essays challenge the persistent idea that the Atlantic migration was predominantly a one-way passage, whereby migrants were driven from their lands in Europe and, after an agonizing and never-to-be-repeated passage in steerage, built a new life in America. In contrast to this view, the essays collected here describe the migration process as a series of micro-level decisions. Migrants made these decisions as active agents in response to technological, political, and economic upheaval, information spread by railroad companies, shipping companies, and various other intermediary agents, and in response to the interconnected web of government regulations which contained many loopholes. The stereotyped image of the transatlantic ordeal needs to be understood in relation to other seasonal migratory patterns in the Euro-Atlantic space. The journey itself was seldom one-way, and the endpoint remained unstable, as migrants would reconsider their options after a time in the host society, travel on to another country, or go back home. Even those who never returned frequently went home as tourists or went to welcome the ships in the harbor to ritually express their emotional attachment to their homeland, if not its political institutions, and to transmit this attachment to their offspring.

In "Central Eastern Europeans in the Euro-Atlantic Migration System Before the First World War," Adam Walaszek reminds us of the crucial connection with interior European destinations. The railroads were indispensable for Central Eastern Europeans to find their way to Western ports. Moreover, these people were used to moving around. Millions of them had been seasonal workers, who simply extended their search to find work to include transatlantic destinations, offering attractive perspectives. New information streams made this choice possible. As Walaszek argues, the United States was the most important, but by no means the only, emigration destination. Migrants were attracted by the high wages for low-skilled work. As soon as the U.S. economy slackened they went elsewhere, quite often migrating back to Europe. In other receiving societies of the Atlantic economy, the situation was markedly different. A majority of the Central Eastern Europeans who ended up in Argentina, for instance, settled there permanently. Walaszek also addresses the question of Jewish exceptionalism. Extending insights by Lloyd Gartner and several others, Walaszek links Jewish migration patterns to those of other groups in the Euro-Atlantic system, thus showing that Jews were not isolated from but were responding to broader social transformations. Following Jonathan Sarna, and contrary to a widely held conception, Walaszek notes that many Jews did return to their country of origin, which shows that economic factors often predominated over political and social adversities.

In "The 'Floating Homeland': The Ship As a 'Connectivity Space' in Greek Migrant and Public Discourse," Yannis Papadopoulos tells the story of Greek migration and its connection to shipping opportunities. The Greeks entered the shipping business late, and their enterprises were far from secure. Nevertheless, the first direct lines from Patras and Piraeus established in the first decade of the twentieth century added an important link between Greek immigrants and their nation of origin. The cultural aspects are also strong in the Greek story. The Greeks had a local orientation, and little love was lost for their authorities. However, during the passage they stayed close together with their kin and thus found out they were Greek after all, in comparison with other ethnic groups. Moreover, the shipping corporations became vehicles for national ties, and the authorities very much wanted to keep those ties in order to draw recruits for their military plans. The oceanic crossing was thus a rite of passage in Van Gennep's sense, which at once created and reinforced Greek identity. Papadopoulos also indicates the continued psychological importance of the shipping lines for those who had already become American citizens and their immigrant children who had never even been to their ancestral country. By citing from ethnic newspaper reports about Greek immigrants in New York going to look at Greek ships to satisfy their longing for home, Papadopoulos shows that those ships functioned as markers of what is, in Herbert Gans's famous phrase, "symbolic ethnicity" insofar as they allowed Greek-Americans to project an idealized image of their native country, and to preserve and recreate a sense of Greek identity inside of American society.

In his essay "A Lasting Transit in Antwerp: Eastern European Jewish Migrants On Their Way To the New World (1900-1925)," Frank Caestecker supports the tale of the migrants as active agents in his story about Jewish migrants who decided not to proceed to their transatlantic destinations but stay in the transit port of Antwerp. His essay shows how political decisions led to the increasing regulation of migration, both in Europe and North America. After the First World War, the American authorities perfected these procedures, completing the shift in immigrant control from companies to consulates. But even this measure did not deprive migrants from Eastern Europe of all agency. Caestecker claims that before 1924, America's restrictive measures were largely ineffective. Many migrants found destinations in Western Europe. This essay on Antwerp reveals how the transit authorities gradually became more involved in the migration process, since they had to cope with migrants who were stuck in transit or denied entrance into the United States. Though the passage became more difficult over time, most migrants eventually managed to reach their intended destination. Only migrants with mental problems had little prospects of moving on.

The final article in this section, Gur Alroey's "Shtetl on the High Seas: The Jewish Emigration from Eastern Europe and the Cross Ocean Experience," draws attention to the migration experience of the Jewish migrants at sea in the early twentieth century. Drawing on various sources, Alroey highlights the fears and insecurities which the ocean, and the colossal vessel harboring hundreds of passengers, instilled in many Eastern Jews. This unprecedented encounter, however, did not break old habits. On board, Jews were often physically separated by the crew from other ethnic groups. At the same time, the Jews set themselves apart from the other passengers through their ritualized behavior, their daily prayers, their dress code, and their food habits. In this way, they paradoxically reproduced the conditions of shtetl life from which many of them were trying to escape. Alroey's approach to some degree seems to confirm the established view of Jewish singularity, which has been nuanced and revised in recent historiographical literature. At the same time, through a close analysis of the passenger distribution of the Hapag flagship Imperator on its maiden voyage from Hamburg to New York in the summer of 1913, Alroey visualizes how the Jewish migrants made up a similar percentage on board the steamer as they did in Pale of Settlement: about thirteen percent. By no means all of them traveled in steerage, which testifies to the relative diversity of the Jewish passengers.

Off the Beaten Track

The closely interconnected concepts of travel and translation, spatial and linguistic mobility, are more complex than is usually supposed.[11] The concepts of "travel" and "translation" are often used metaphorically, causing the actual actors to remain out of sight. In addition, traditional binary models of identity and translation, of "home" and "abroad," sometimes blur the view. The essays collected in this second section avoid the pitfalls involved in these preconceptions. They focus on the specificities of historical protagonists who took up various roles in passing through different cultures. The essays try to get away from binary models of "here" versus "there," taking into account unusual and less studied areas of migration. Examples are the interaction between Germans, Swedes, Norwegians, and Russians with Brazil, Argentina, and Mexico which includes aspects such as return migration, serendipity, instability, and ambiguity. As Michael Cronin argues in *Translation and Identity*, it is important to provide a detailed analysis of intercultural contact and communication, paying attention to the actual translation issues involved in the travel experience. The four contributors to this section respond to this call in various ways.

Cecilia Alvstad's contribution, "The Transatlantic Transit as a Translational Process: What Migrant Letters Can Tell," explores the largely understudied ramifications of travel, transit, and translation in the letters of two early-twentieth-century Swedish migrants traveling to Argentina rather than the more common destination, the United States. The letters of these two migrants, Axel Lundberg and Eric Mellberg, are both linguistic and cultural translations. They contain many foreign words and phrases that are transliterated and explained in order to make sense of the foreign and negotiate the unfamiliar. Drawing on theories of Sakai, Malena, Gentzler, Cronin, and Pym, Alvstad interestingly argues that migrants already engage in a translational process during transit, even without a proper command of the foreign language or a deep knowledge of the discovered cultures. Already during transit, a transition is noticeable from one audience to the other, as the migrants move from translating others to themselves, to translating themselves to the home audience. Translational processes are thus closely related to the changing identities of migrants and their family and friends at home who become the new "others".

According to Gentzler, translating is both a means to conform to the new situation and a means to resist assimilation. Alvstad uses migrants' letters as a testing ground for a theoretical framework to approach textually negotiated linguistic and cultural translational processes. What she finds is equally applicable to travel books and migrant diaries, in which migrants negotiate between two audiences, the one at home and the one in the receiving culture. The source text does not exist prior to the translational practices but acquires its specific form through the letters in which the migrants mediate the source culture. Their letters thus function simultaneously as target texts as well, since the experiences take place in a foreign culture and are related in another language. Alvstad thus illustrates migrants' simultaneous crossing and drawing of borders. The essay shows how non-literary materials deserve scholarly attention from theorists in the field of translation studies. Multilingual letters in particular offer a challenge for scholars to take into account distance and familiarity, spoken and written language, ethnic stereotyping and changing identities.

In Elisabeth Vik's "Decisions in Transit: The Case of Scandinavian Immigrants to Argentina," the focus lies on fickle decision-making during transit. Here, coming to a decision on a destination is seen as a process, not a single act, and it takes place during the passage and not prior to departure. It can imply a journey through other countries, even traveling back and forth, and it can be influenced by the most unpredictable encounters. Using Thomas Faist's theory, Vik introduces a meso-level, taking into account interpersonal relations, social networks, collectives, and relationships between stayers and movers, and among migrants and the travelers they meet on the way. Just like Alvstad, Vik also focuses on Scandinavian immigrants traveling to Latin America and chooses a close reading of individual stories rather than a macro-focus on the overall reasons for migration. The letters, stories, and travel biography of Oscar, Otto, and Solveig show how serendipity and misfortune influence particular choices and actual itineraries. Most Norwegian migrants had not decided prior to departure to leave Norway for good and thus remained in transit for a long time, sometimes even decades. Others headed for a particular destination but never arrived due to all kinds of circumstances, acquaintances, and unexpected opportunities. These stories modify the grand narrative of economic migration and show that "migrant" is a multi-faceted category, taking people who were travelers, workers, adventurers, or tourists at first and making them actual immigrants at a later point in time. This transition was due to the contacts and ties that took shape during transit.

Apart from these individual stories, Vik draws attention to broader patterns in Nordic migration, investigating numbers of migrants, ports of departure, official registrations, common occupations, and business opportunities. In her contribution, Vik focuses on Norwegian networks and social relations formed during transit. Examples are churches, clubs, and associations. She notes how these Norwegian transit communities were quite different from those of, for instance, the more numerous Danish immigrants. A small case study of the Norwegian Seamen's Church in Buenos Aires, established in 1888, supplements the personal stories through an account of social networks and their impact on the decisions of the individuals to stay, move on, or return to Norway. Also in Norway itself, contacts were established and maintained between family members and return migrants, for instance in the Norwegian-Argentine Association based in Oslo. Vik's contribution thus modifies the conventional image of a one-way exodus by economic migrants looking for a better life. She brings us closer to an understanding of "what exactly happens in networks and collectives that induces people to stay, move and return."[12]

Ute Ritz-Deutch's "German Colonists in Southern Brazil: Navigating Multiple Identities on the Brazilian Frontier" illustrates how German migrants in Brazil remained permanently in transit. They did not follow the so-called beaten path, here conceived of as a more-or-less linear progression towards assimilation. Rather, they continued to negotiate between both worlds. To illustrate this being-in-transit, Ritz-Deutch focuses on the Protestant pastor Gustav Stutzer and his wife Therese, who lived in the German colony of Blumenau in Southern Brazil. Stutzer published his experiences in books made up of his stories and his wife's letters, such as *In Deutschland und Brasilien: Lebenserinnerungen* (1914) and *Meine Therese: Aus dem bewegten Leben einer deutschen Frau* (1916). Stutzer was thus not only an immigrant himself, he also functioned as a broker, promoting German emigration to Brazil. Stutzer's books actively promoted emigration to Brazil, while at the same time promoting German identity and the preservation of Germandom in Brazil. His writings proclaim the supposed superiority of the German culture and work ethic but simultaneously acknowledge the positive potential of living in Brazil, such as the country's greater equality and social mobility. His writings thus played a role in nation-building processes in both Brazil and Germany. Therese's letters testify to the problematic role of a transcultural actor, translating and constructing national differences and articulating a complex sense of traditional identity. The lack of education and intellectual stimuli was a recurrent theme, since in Brazil, the daily struggle for life was all that seemed to matter.

The Stutzers' tales of transit display a translational, circular, and continuing movement. Their reflections show a German-Brazilian ethnic identity in a transitional moment, constantly negotiating both worlds. The fact that they were traveling back and forth between Germany and Brazil is not only a literal illustration of this transitional state, it also illustrates that migration is multifaceted and that notions of "home" are complicated. As Ritz-Deutch writes, immigrant experiences in Brazil were situational, and ethnic identity among the German immigrants was hardly monolithic. German businessmen, government officials, and pastors or teachers generally thought of returning some day, while most immigrant farmers intended to stay. Still, among farmers, experiences also diverged, from immigrants working on coffee plantations in Sao Paulo to small-scale farmers in rural communities further south. The image of Brazil as a land of opportunities, but also an untamed wilderness and lawless place, is reminiscent of the way North America was portrayed for a European readership. The Brazilian government confirmed this image by heavily supporting German settlement in the south, to develop the region, "whiten" the nation, and create a buffer zone against the La Plata States to the South and West. Despite the hardships that farmers encountered in these areas, Blumenau and Joinville proved the most successful German colonies in Santa Catarina, and were sometimes even heralded as places where German language and culture could be better preserved than elsewhere. In some areas German private schools outnumbered Portuguese schools by ten to one, and German was retained as a mother tongue even after four or five generations. Not surprisingly, Luso-Brazilians were often suspicious of this German diaspora in Brazil. This suspicion also influenced the daily lives, ethnic identity, and standing of the German migrants.

An Van Hecke takes a more literary approach to migrants' testimonies, letters, and fictional travel biographies. In "Traveling Between Languages and Literatures: A Spatial Analysis of The Family Tree by Margo Glantz," she analyzes Margo Glantz's Las Genealogías (1981) and its multiple re-editions and translations. In this work, Glantz tells the story of her parents, Jacob Glantz and Elisabeth Shapiro, who migrated in 1925 from a Jewish enclave in Ukraine to Mexico. The book is a personal collection of interviews, childhood memories, and photographs but at the same time constitutes a collective history of the Jewish community in Mexico. Unlike other studies of The Family Tree, which tend to address the autobiographical dimension of the book, Van Hecke's essay focuses on the way the historical locations are represented in connection with language and translation. Thus, she examines various places related to the Jewish community in Mexico City, the many restaurants and cafés in which artists and writers used to congregate. These are the same as Pinsker's "essential spaces"[13] for immigrant writers and artists, or what Soja refers to as a "thirdspace."[14] Glantz also focuses on the streets the migrants lived in, thematizing their sense of disorientation, solitude, and the search for origins.

Van Hecke draws on Fernando Ortiz's notion of "transculturación" (a term also used by Mary Louise Pratt) to describe the competing cultural discourses in the process of transit. A first discourse discussed by Van Hecke is that of Jewish culture, which is contrasted with the many geographical locations the book refers to, and their links to fiction and literary locations. The intertextual layer, in which authors act as guides leading the Jewish-Mexican narrator in her search for her origin, is a second discourse. It is a layer in which multiple tales of transit collide and intersect. Hebrew, Yiddish, Russian, and Spanish are the languages involved in the collective history. Glantz's father went from a multilingual situation in which Hebrew, Yiddish, and Russian were involved, to a monolingual context in which Spanish was elemental. Margo herself makes the opposite move from a monolingual situation – she spoke only Spanish – to a multilingual one. The Spanish text contains foreign words like 'heder' or 'cholnt' for which narrator/

translator Glantz gives a short translation between brackets or an explanation, a strategy which Susan Bassnett reproduces in her English translation, thus preserving the multilingual nature of the story.

Van Hecke opts for a comparative perspective and links her case to similar ones in Mexican literature. The transit story is seen in the light of narratives of the discovery and conquest of America. Characters such as Columbus and Cortes are integrated into Glantz's story as the narrator's male doubles. Glantz, like other second-generation Mexican writers such as Juan Villoro, uses migration and displacement as basic building blocks of her work. She constantly creates a dialogue between literatures of Europe and Latin America. Van Hecke's essay, in which actual migration and storytelling are closely related, provides a bridge to the following section, where the concept of "liminality" forms the link between fictional or literary representations of migration on the one hand, and historical accounts of transatlantic travel on the other hand.

Liminal Spaces

In one important sense, migrant travelers can be said to possess liminal qualities. The experience of being a "passenger" may give rise to communal, ritualistic behavior, such as singing, cooking, storytelling, dancing, and praying on board Atlantic steamers or in transit communities on either side of the ocean. In tales of transit, migrants are frequently characterized as a rather homogeneous group displaying such features as invisibility, simplicity, speechlessness, and lack of structure. The process of mass transit can thus be compared to a *rite de passage* in Van Gennep's sense, since the migrant, like the neophyte in a life-crisis ritual, has to divest himself of his Old World garments, beliefs, and ideas in a series of what Mary Antin in *The Promised Land* described as "purifying operations."[15] In both cases, the "passenger" has to pass through a cultural realm "neither here nor there" in order to acquire a post-liminal identity. This sometimes takes the form of actual quarantine. However, Antin's account of the "purifying operations" at transit locations (involving among other things cross-questioning, disinfesting and pigeonholing) reveals the emigrants' suspicion that these "rituals" are merely performed to extort them. Therefore, the migration experience does not always readily conform to the Turnerian model of *communitas*.[16] In their capacity as quasi-liminars, migrants may choose to contradict their categorization as a homogeneous class by setting their personal experience off against that of their social group. They may openly fight over narrative power and contest the "official" account of their story, thus negating the expectation of submissiveness and silence. Or, they may refuse their eventual incorporation into the new social order by sticking to norms and behaviors associated with their pre-emigration, "pre-liminal" identity.

In his contribution "Steamships, Hospitals, and Funerals," Ron Geaves addresses the situation of the undocumented Lascars, the Muslim sailors from South Asia and Africa. His essay is set in the port city of Liverpool at the time of Britain's imperial expansion. It focuses on the mediating activities of William Henry Abdullah Quilliam, a Liverpool lawyer who converted to Islam after a life-changing journey to Morocco in the late 1880s. Quilliam championed the cause of the Lascars, performing funeral rites and marriages, visiting the sick, and also publishing a weekly newspaper *The Crescent*, which was circulated in more than eighty nations. Eventually, this turned him into the spokesperson of Muslim communities all over England. As Geaves convincingly argues, for the Lascar sailors the ship did not so much function as a bridge to or from their homeland, as was the case for many other migrants. Rather, for the Lascars it was a "territorialized" space where they constituted an identity in the first place. In this respect, the Lascar seamen were "threshold people" in Turner's sense. Given their itinerant lifestyle, the Lascars remained largely invisible as a social group, and this is often quite literally, since most Lascars worked at low-paying jobs below deck. Nevertheless, their fleeting presence accounted for the later establishment of the first permanent Muslim communities in Britain. Through his work for the Lascar sailors, "Shaikh" Quilliam provided them with a sense of community or even "communitas" and facilitated their "passage" to a more stable, visible identity.

Yet, as Geaves acknowledges, it is hard to conceive how the Lascars, in their precarious liminal existence, "could find a way out to a new stage of existence." It can be argued that, for these sailors (somewhat comparable to Asian workers in present-day Gulf states), liminality was a more or less permanent condition. This is much like the monastic and mendicant states analyzed by Turner in relation to the functional specialization characteristic of complex societies.[17] While some Lascars returned to a pre-liminal existence in their former homelands, others settled down in "dockland" society after marrying local girls and abandoning their former religious identity. One wonders whether there are no extant testimonies of the Muslim seamen themselves, and whether they were truly as silent and passive as the historical sources suggest. Why, as Geaves contends, should Islam have been the only "place of essential identity"? Taking issue with Edward Said's qualification of "Orientalism" as a unilateral instrument of cultural control, Geaves insists that Quilliam did not project romantic Western notions onto the Muslims in Liverpool. Rather, he overturned Orientalist stereotypes. However that may be, Quilliam was apparently perceived by the authorities as a subversive and eventually had to flee the country, only to return later under another name. Thus, Quilliam paid for his mediating activities with the loss of his own identity. Or, should we say that, by guiding the Lascars through their (incomplete?) rite of passage, he himself went through such a rite, breaking away from his former identity as a member of the English upper class and emerging as a leading representative of the British Muslim community.

In "Heavenly Sensations and Communal Celebrations: Experiences of Liminality in Transatlantic Journeys," Babs Boter focuses on the personal and collective experiences of (mostly) Dutch emigrants and travelers on board of transatlantic ships. As Boter states, these passengers were by no means "Turnerian pilgrims," since most of them were relatively well off and did not travel in steerage. Unlike liminars in Turner's sense, therefore, they did not enter a "limbo of statuslessness" where they were stripped of their pre-liminal identity. The transatlantic ships emerge from these historical accounts as highly stratified social worlds, with clear distinctions between travelers and emigrants, first- and third-class passengers, healthy and unhealthy ones, and between various national and ethnic groups. Among other things, Boter quotes from the diary of the Dutch emigrant Johannes Remeeus, which describes how an unmarried German couple is publicly put to shame for sleeping together, which squarely contradicts Turner's observation that sex distinctions fall away in the liminal stage. This is not to say that there are no traces of liminal experiences in these historical sources. But, as Boter astutely notes, most liminal moments take place in reference to the immensity of the ocean and the feelings of humility and ecstasy that it evokes. These moments often seem to presuppose a real or observed separation from other classes and groups on board. Thus, on several occasions in the writings of first-class tourists, spiritual reflections on the grandeur of the ocean occur in tandem with rather base observations about the exotic but somewhat repellent steerage passengers on the lower decks.

Interestingly, Boter suggests a break between fictional or literary representations of liminality on the one hand, such as that of Rebekka Vaark in Toni Morrison's A Mercy, and on the other hand the historical accounts of transatlantic travel in autobiographies, diaries, and travel narratives which she analyzes. In this way, Boter questions the "social basis" of the liminal experiences projected in fiction, which may not amount to an actual reflection of what actually went through the heads of travelers during their transatlantic journey. Boter shows how differences of class, gender, age, and social background were by no means erased on the transatlantic ships, as would be the case in Turner's liminal phase, but were sometimes even intensified, despite repeated efforts to reach out to the "mysterious" Other. Sporadic moments of communitas took place in defiance of the ship's authorities and mostly involved what can be called a licensed release on the part of first-class passengers who were fascinated by the "queer company" below. Such accounts of a descent to the lower decks are perhaps not unlike an anthropologist's journey into the heart of Africa. These descents appear more interesting in view of what they reveal about the prejudicial framework through which liminal moments are narrated than for their transgressive potential. To what degree, then, are such historical accounts a more privileged source of knowledge than novels or stories? After all, Mary Antin's description of solitary bliss on the wide ocean, which for Boter precludes a Turnerian interpretation of

Antin's sea voyage, was partly inspired by a literary model: "I would imagine myself all alone on the ocean, and Robinson Crusoe was very real to me."[18]

Massimo Zangari's "Competing Fictionalizations of the Lower East Side: Abraham Cahan's *The Rise of David Levinsky* and Michael Gold's *Jews Without Money*" offers an intriguing comparative analysis of two well-known Jewish-American immigrant novels, Abraham Cahan's *The Rise of David Levinsky* and Michael Gold's *Jews without Money*. Both of these novels are set in New York's Lower East Side during the first quarter of the twentieth century, then home to the garment industry. Zangari notes how, since the 1960s, at a crucial (liminal?) juncture in the nation's history, this crowded area of Manhattan underwent a significant symbolic development from slum to shrine in the collective imagination of the United States. The Jewish-American community, in particular, "rediscovered" the multiethnic Lower East Side as a site of remembrance onto which its ethnic identity was anchored to the exclusion of other, competing identity formations. Along with other means of symbolic inscription such as museums, festivities, Lower East Side walking tours, and so on, fiction played an important part in this process of transmitting and reconstructing the past. Zangari attests how the novels by Cahan and Gold, written in the 1910s and 1920s respectively, contributed to the creation of a national narrative that would eventually turn the Lower East Side into a founding site of American identity – next to, and apart from, other places of memory such as Plymouth or Jamestown. But, as Zangari argues, Cahan and Gold did more than just co-author this new national narrative of Jewish-American becoming. Each in his own way, these writers thematized the ideological limitations of that narrative.

Cahan does so by appropriating the traditional conversion narrative in his chronicle of David Levinsky's progression from poor Jewish immigrant to wealthy entrepreneur in the garment business. The tragedy of Levinsky is that, as he rises on the social ladder, he increasingly becomes alienated from the Lower East Side *communitas*. One could argue that Levinsky's transformation from "marginal" ethnic to prominent American remains incomplete. In Turner and Van Gennep's terminology, his reincorporation into the host society fails. While Cahan drew on the representational modes of literary realism and local color, Michael Gold was strongly influenced by the narrative experiments of modernism and tried to use its techniques to offer a "kaleidoscopic" or "cubist" picture of the ghetto. Contrary to Cahan's Levinsky, who manages to rise from the ghetto but does so at a price, most characters in *Jews without Money* are denied even this tragic fate. They remain stuck, so it seems, in the "limbo of statuslessness" which is the ghetto. As the novel's protagonist Mickey (Michael) puts it at the end, "I was nothing, bound for nowhere."[19] By drawing such a bleak, panoramic picture of the Lower East Side, with no apparent prospects of salvation – except for a universal workers' revolution – Gold thus counteracted the facile rags-to-riches scenario that figured prominently in ghetto sketches of the time, which makes *Jews without Money* a powerful indictment of American capitalism.

In the final essay of the volume, "Kishinev Redux: Pogrom, Purim, Patrimony," Nancy K. Miller tells the moving tale of her own search for her roots in the city of Kishinev (present-day Chisinau in Moldova), where her paternal grandparents would have lived before fleeing to America after the pogram of 1903. Miller's account of her personal "rites of return" can be read as an interesting commentary on the other essays collected in this volume. It highlights the self-defeating (but often compulsive) nature of all acts of remembrance and identification. Miller recounts her roots search as a frustrating and repetitive undertaking, mediated by technology and fictitious retellings of history. She attests how her interest in her past was awakened by quasi-accidental encounters combined with her reading of literary echoes of the Kishinev pogrom in the work of Bialik and others. Thus, the mention of a couple of dummies representing Orthodox Jews in Alexander Hemon's novel *The Lazarus Project* compelled her to retrace her steps to Kishinev and revisit the local museum. For Miller, the dummies or puppets dressed in Hasidic garb do not "represent" her secularized, middle-class grandparents. But they do signify both the impossibility of remembering and the necessity of going back to what has been irredeemably lost. An imperfect attempt to give life to the past for American tourists, the choreography of the puppets in the village museum at the same time reveal the insistent need to reenact the past, as in the annual Purim ritual or centenaries of the Kishinev pogrom.

Migration historians have repeatedly called for "an approach that sees through the eyes of the actual women and men who migrated, an approach from the bottom up, relying on letters, autobiographies, and other life writings."[20] Miller's return memoir, which is itself part of a flourishing genre of similar roots narratives, may stand as a warning that such bottom-up perspectives by "actual women and men" in the end prove to be dummies instead of the real thing. Through her own, highly personal retelling of her family history, which constitutes but a very small fraction of the larger history of the Eastern European Jewish diaspora and an even smaller fraction of the history of human migration and mobility as a whole, Miller draws attention to the fact that every form of identification involves not just an evidentiary but also an affective component. These components feed the search for authenticity at the same time as they lead us away from a truly authentic engagement with the past. Miller's second visit to Kishinev did not bring her much closer to the truth symbolized by the fact that the door to "House Number 13," an important memory site of the 1903 pogrom, remained closed to her. But the experience did underscore the importance of "going back," even if such a return leads one to places where one may never have been before.

As with any collaborative undertaking of this kind, the present volume inevitably contains some imbalances and lacunae in terms of the overall historical and geographical representativity of the cases treated in its pages. Important themes like seasonal or military migration, although they come up in the first section, are only dealt with tangentially. More could perhaps have been said about the specificity of and interactions among immigrant groups in Latin America discussed in the second section. And, while section three significantly broadens the historiographical debate by drawing on travel writings, fiction, and memoir literature by first-, second- and even third-generation immigrants, the significance of oral narratives is not considered. The reader may account for these shortcomings, if that is what they are, in terms of the sheer scope of the topic under consideration. The period between 1850 and 1950, when steam power revolutionized transatlantic travel, was one of unprecedented mobility on a global scale. Tales of Transit tells only part of that encompassing story, which continues to fascinate scholars working in a variety of disciplinary backgrounds. What sets the current volume apart from the continuing stream of publications on transatlantic migration is a concerted focus on the question of transit. The aim of Tales of Transit is not primarily to extend our knowledge on how migration has impacted particular receiving or sending societies, but rather to conceptualize what happens in between. One important finding cutting across all of the contributions in this volume is that, in spite of the directionality supposedly built into the very concept, migration is never a straightforward, linear process. So far, as Marjory Harper has argued, "little attempt has been made to explore rituals of disengagement" among migrants in a systematic comparative investigation.[21] While a lot of work remains to be done, Tales of Transit makes an important contribution to the study of such migration rituals by drawing attention to the role of transit places in the identity formation of migrants and travelers. Thus, the book shows that the process of ritual disengagement is never entirely complete and that it cannot be considered in separation from parallel processes of re-engagement. Far from being entirely value-free and uninvolved, this book, too, may be approached as such a form of re-engagement.

Notes

1. Melanie Perreault, "Waterways in the Atlantic World: Contact and Cultural Negotiation Across a Liquid Landscape," in New Perspectives in Transatlantic Studies, eds. Heidi Slettedahl Macpherson and Will Kaufman (Lanham, MD: University Press of America, 2002), 1-14. Mark Rennella, "Planned Serendipity: American Travelers and the Transatlantic Voyage in the Nineteenth and Twentieth Centuries," Journal of Social History 38 (2004): 365-383.

2. Dirk Hoerder, "Losing National Identity or Gaining Transcultural Competence: Changing Approaches in Migration History," in Comparative and Transnational History: Central European Approaches and New Perspectives, eds. Heinz-Gerhard Haupt and Jürgen Kocka (New York: Berghahn, 2010), 247-272.

3. Competition demanded the maintenance of regular departure schedules also during periods of low demand for passage. In 1908, the migration rate to the U.S. plummeted

to almost a third of the previous year. These kinds of drops increased the pressure on shipping companies to maintain their level of service and reliability. The brand name of the company became an important asset in the advertising campaigns targeting new or returning costumers. In addition, the company had to account for its standards and problems to an ever more critical press. Poor conditions and ill treatment could easily lead to coverage that damaged the ocean liner's reputation. Disclosure of the dismal steerage conditions in the 1880s led to significant improvements after 1900. So the passengers were not all or totally powerless.

4. Michael Cronin, *Translation and Identity* (London/New York: Routledge, 2006), 45. The twin themes of translation and migration are explored in two recent special issues of leading translation studies journals: Anna Malena (ed.), Traduction et (im)migration/ Translation and (Im)migration. TTR: *traduction, terminologie, rédaction* 16.2 (2003); Lordana Polezzi (ed.), Translation, Travel, Migration. *The Translator* 12.2 (2006).

5. For the concept of "thirdspace," see Homi K. Bhabha, *The Location of Culture* (London/ New York: Routledge, 1994); the concept of "contact zone" is taken from Mary Louise Pratt, *Imperial Eyes: Studies in Travel Writing* (London/New York: Routledge, 1992).

6. Anna Malena, "Presentation," TTR 16.2 (2003), 10.

7. Cronin, *Translation and Identity*, 4.

8. Arnold van Gennep, "Territorial Passage and the Classification of Rites," in *Readings in Ritual Studies*, ed. Ronald L. Grimes (Upper Saddle River, NJ: Prentice Hall, 1996), 531.

9. The concept of ritualization has been applied to non-religious domains by among others Ronald Grimes in his *Rite Out of Place: Ritual, Media, and the Arts* (Oxford/New York: Oxford University Press, 2006).

10. Dennis Conway and Robert B. Potter, "Caribbean Transnational Return Migrants as Agents of Change," *Geography Compass* 1 (2007): 25-45; Marjory Harper and Stephen Constantine, *Migration and Empire* (Oxford/New York: Oxford University Press, 2010), 306-337; Mark Wyman, "Emigrants Returning: The Evolution of a Tradition," in *Emigrant Homecomings: The Return Movement of Emigrants, 1600-2000*, ed. Marjory Harper (Manchester: Manchester University Press, 2005), 16-31.

11. Polezzi, "Translation, Travel, Migration,", 169-188.

12. Thomas Faist, "The Crucial Meso-Level," in *International Migration, Immobility and Development*, eds. T. Hammar et al. (Oxford and New York: Berg Publishers, 1997), 188.

13. Edward Soja, *Thirdspace: Journeys to Los Angeles and Other Real and Imagined Spaces* (Cambridge, MA: Blackwell, 1996).

14. Shachar Pinsker, "Spaces of Hebrew and Yiddish Modernism: The Urban Cafés of Berlin," in *Transit und Transformation: Osteuropäisch-jüdische Migranten in Berlin 1918-1939*, eds. Verena Dohrn et al. (Wallstein Verlag GmbH, 2010), 59-62.

15. Mary Antin, *The Promised Land* (New York: Penguin, 1997), 140.

16. Drawing on Van Gennep's characterization of rites of passage, the British cultural anthropologist Victor Turner defined ritual behavior by positing a dialectic between what he called "structure" and "communitas." While the former term refers to everything that keeps a tribal society from falling apart (distinctions of wealth, caste system, kinship rights, etc.), the latter term is defined by Turner quite simply as the absence of structural ties. As Turner stresses, the opposition between structure and anti-structure, or states and transitions, should not be conflated with that between

sacred and secular life, or between politics and religion. Rather, the Latin word "communitas" (as opposed to community) refers to an ambivalent phenomenon of transition, in which the sacred and the secular, as well as the high and the low, or power and weakness, are inextricably intertwined. In other words, communitas entails a "limbo of statuslessness" through which the ritual subject has to pass (for instance in an initiation or funeral ritual) in order to attain its new position in the structured social order. As Turner argues, without communitas there can be no structure, and vice versa. These two poles mutually reinforce each other. See Victor Turner, "Liminality and Communitas," in *A Reader in the Anthropology of Religion*, ed. Michael Lambek (Cambridge/Boston: Blackwell, 2008).

17. Turner, "Liminality and Communitas," 333.
18. Antin, *The Promised Land*, 142.
19. Michael Gold, *Jews without Money* (New York: Carroll & Graf, 1996), 308.
20. Dirk Hoerder, "Migration in the Atlantic Economies: Regional European Origins and Worldwide Expansion," in *European Migrants: Global and Local Perspectives*, eds. Dirk Hoerder and Leslie Page Moch (Boston: Northeastern University, 1996), 22.
21. Harper, "Introduction," 8.

Rethinking Atlantic Migration

Central Eastern Europeans in the Euro-Atlantic Migration System Before the First World War

Adam Walaszek

In the beginning of the twentieth century, the economist, sociologist, and historian Franciszek Bujak wrote that at that time, Polish peasants had "quite broad" contacts with the outside world. "Significant liveliness of labor migration after the emancipation proves that people living on the river in Ropczyce County [in Galicia, Austrian Poland] had known long distances and the roads leading to them."[1] Bujak's observation in Austrian Poland could refer to the whole area of Central Eastern Europe, the territory of both Austro-Hungarian and Russian multinational empires. After the abolition of serfdom, peasants' horizons and worldviews broadened. During fairs and other celebrations, one could hear about migrant adventures and the miracles of the distant world. Migration was a topic of conversations in village taverns. Wincenty Witos, a peasant politician noted, "Soldiers on leave ... would tell of marvels they had seen, and of things they usually did not understand ... They told about houses made of glass, golden churches, tenement houses as high as our Tatras [mountains], cows with stomachs ten times bigger than our cows, and with such an abundance of wine that people wash and bathe themselves in it" (author's translation).[2] And thus, peasants decided to seek new opportunities. "Migration, like any other social phenomenon with an economic background, is conditioned by a rise of new needs among people, and by a knowledge that these needs can be fulfilled," sociologist Florian Znaniecki wrote at the end of the nineteenth century (author's translation).[3]

Migrating peasants, agricultural workers, or petty craftsmen had a palette of options. Władysław Wiśniewski, a worker from the Kingdom of Poland, used these options well. He not only migrated short distances locally within the Kingdom of Poland (ruled by Russia) but also went to Mecklenburg, Westphalia, Hanover, Denmark, and Russia proper. Finally, he crossed the Atlantic to the U.S. and settled in Chicago.[4] Equally telling is the biography of Jan Bukowski from the Podhale region in Austrian Galicia. After having spent five years in Budapest, where his family worked in a brick factory, Bukowski migrated to the American "Promised Land" in 1899 and ended up in Pennsylvania, where he stayed for ten years before returning home.[5] Hermann Zeitlhofer writes that:

Some types of migration have been privileged over others in the study of migration history. For many decades the mainstream of historical migration research was dominated by research on two kinds of migration systems while others were more or less ignored. One focus of research was on atypical and extraordinary movements while most historical studies were closely linked with the longstanding persistence of the modernization paradigm ... migration was usually seen as a one-way movement: from rural areas to urban regions and from Europe to overseas or, to put it more generally: from "regions of out-migration" to "regions of in-migration."[6]

Likewise, Dirk Hoerder writes that migration was "a multi-directional process with manifold moves and possible return."[7] People could migrate internally, work seasonally within shorter distances, or travel to more distant labor markets to work in agriculture or in industry. Moreover, with time, they could choose between European and overseas destinations, where they could move temporarily or permanently. The expanding transnational and transatlantic economy modernized all regions. Migration to America, the biggest host country, should thus be seen in a broader context as one place among a variety of other destinations people could choose. All movements were interrelated and formed basically one migration system, linking the European periphery with the broader Atlantic world. Central Eastern Europe became part of a globalized economy mainly supplying a labor force to the industrial Euro-Atlantic world. The choice of destination and the decision about the length of stay depended on complex individual – usually family-related – decisions and on information networks existing where people lived. Thus, during the second half of the nineteenth century the history of human mobility in Central Eastern Europe (as in any other part of Europe) was a history of broadening possibilities. Although America was the most obvious destination, the choice to go there was often made only after many other options had been considered. It was a history of learning about the choices the late nineteenth-century economy offered. Markets, regions, and states competed to receive workers.

Reasons of Spatial Mobility

In the second half of the nineteenth century, the region of East Central Europe (inhabited by various nationalities: Poles, Ukrainians, Carpatho-Rusyns, Ruthenians, Lithuanians, Latvians, Byelorussians, Jews, Czechs, Slovaks, Magyars, Croats, Slovenes, Germans, and others) experienced an unusual demographic explosion, which peaked between 1860 and 1890. "Between 1860 and 1910, the average population growth in East Central Europe was over 75 percent."[8] The population of the Russian Empire rose from 74 million in 1879 to 161 million in 1910.[9] That of the Hungarian part of the Austro-Hungarian Monarchy (including

Croatia) rose from 16 to 21 million between 1869 and 1910, and that of the Austrian part from 20 to 29 million during the same period.[10]

The production of foodstuffs, raw materials, and agricultural products remained an important element of Central Europe's economy. The percentage of people associated with agriculture was higher than elsewhere: in Austro-Hungary it was sixty-five percent and in Russia seventy-eight percent. Eighty to eighty-five percent of the Hungarian population and sixty-five to eighty percent of the Lithuanian and Latvian populations worked in agriculture.[11] Post-emancipation villages were characterized by overpopulation and land hunger as well. Serfdom was abolished in Austria in 1848, in Russia proper in 1861, and in Russian Poland in 1864. In the Polish lands, seventy-two percent of peasant holdings were very small. Proto-industry in villages disappeared and rural handicraft disintegrated. The number of village proletarians rose everywhere. In the 1860s and 1870s, the mining industry in Slovakia faced deep crises. With their traditional agriculture, Croatia, Slovenia, and Serbia had a relatively small number of village proletarians, but they had to deal with poverty and economic stagnation. The traditional zadruga system, whereby people worked in the extended family framework, broke down.[12]

Money became a new reality and a new value in peasants' lives. But it was difficult to acquire money in the countryside. Everywhere, credit conditions were bad or nonexistent. For example, the debts of Galician villagers increased twelvefold between 1885 and 1905.[13] In Hungary, reports highlighted the misery of large groups of peasants in the eastern parts of the country. A few thousand families controlled more than fifty percent of the land. Seventy percent of peasants lived on very small lots and parcels, which were insufficient to feed them. In Slovakia, one percent of the population held 46.3 percent of all arable land, a fact that can explain the economic reasons for migration. In the 1890s, the agrarian proletariat increased from approximately 111,000 to 147,000. In practice, enfranchisement of the peasants meant the accelerated partitioning of holdings. Peasant holdings were divided into increasingly small sections. In the year 1902, forty-four percent of farms in Galicia consisted of two hectares (one hectare equals 2.471 acres), thirty-seven percent were between two and five hectares, eighteen percent between five and twenty, and only one percent more than twenty hectares. Not many of the farms were self-sufficient.

Those leaving their countries could be among the most dissatisfied and at the same time the most adventurous of people. Teenagers would emigrate illegally to avoid military service (in both empires this was often a reason young people sailed to America). Overall, political and national tensions were only marginal motives for emigration. To be sure, the first waves of Czechs arriving in the United States are associated with the revolutions of 1848-1849. Political and national suppression played a role in the decision to emigrate, predominantly among artisans, workers, and intellectuals. The post-revolution emigration of some activists from Hungary was equally attributed to political motivations. At the end of the century, the ruling Magyars in Hungary introduced a policy of Magyarization and implemented it in the compulsory educational system. Slovaks, Serbs, and Croats strongly opposed this policy, and demanded legal status for their languages, as well as political and cultural freedom.[14] While political oppression could be a motive for the migration of some, it should not be overstressed. The biggest centers of Slovak emigration were in regions where nationalist feelings were rather weak. Among Slovak immigrants in the U.S. and some other groups, there was a very high rate of return despite the fact that the political situation and the policy of Magyarization did not change before the First World War.[15]

Destinations

Agricultural migrations within some regions had long traditions. Unskilled workers were hired in the local labor market, skilled and qualified workers in more distant ones. Seasonally, Poles worked in agriculture in Saxony, Brandenburg, Mecklenburg, and even in the Hamburg region. According to some sources, 449,000 people from Galicia and the Kingdom of Poland worked in the eastern provinces of Germany during the season of 1912-1913. People circulated between Galicia and Saxony as early as the 1840s. The practice was called *obieżysastwo*.[16] The sugar beet fields of Denmark appeared as another destination for women at the end of the century. At that time, European destinations "competed" with the American ones. Migrations to different destinations were also correlated. During cyclical economic depressions in America (e.g. in the years 1885, 1894-1895, 1904, and 1907-1909), seasonal migration to Germany grew, providing an additional outlet for wage-seeking Austro-Hungarians. Thus, migrants functioned within one interrelated migration system.

Germany was a popular destination because, although the standard of living for most migrants was problematic, the country offered important advantages. Seasonal work in spring and summer paid better than in Russian Poland and allowed easy and cheap return with one's savings. The emotional cost of separation from relatives was smaller than was the case of migration to overseas countries.[17] Migration regions were not evenly distributed. In the diocese of Tarnów in Galicia, the heaviest migration to Germany was from the northern part. From the other regions, people sought employment in Austrian, German, and Hungarian agriculture and industry. A large Polish migration stream was associated with the industrialization of the Ruhr district. Industrialized territories of Austro-Hungary became another destination for Poles, Czechs, Croats, Slovenes, and Jews. Slovaks, particularly people from Šariš (Hungarian Sáros) and the northern mountainous regions, had worked seasonally in Hungary and Transylvania since the eighteenth century. In 1845 crop failure and hunger pushed them again to seek work in the Great Hungarian Plain (Nagy Magyar Alföld), and each year harvesters from eastern Slovakia traveled to the Alföld. In 1910, approximately half a million people from Croatia-Slavonia, Bukovina, Transylvania, and Slovakia worked in Hungary. Another destination could be Austria proper.

In addition to the main "push" factors mentioned above, some efforts at modernization also facilitated spatial mobility in Central and Eastern Europe. In the second half of the nineteenth century, the construction of railway systems made travel easier. Cost barriers fell when prices did. Travel became faster, safer, and cheaper. In isolated eastern regions (e.g. Polesie, or Horodło county in Podolia in Russia), long distances to the railway line resulted in weak migration. Steamships made transatlantic travel cheaper and faster as well.[18] This change was important for the growth of local or regional migrations but above all explains why America rose in prominence as a destination. Without railway lines, labor migrations most likely would have remained regional in character. Without steamships, easy returns to Europe or back-and-forth movements would not have been possible either.

America[19]

The United States was but one destination among others. Why did it become such a strong magnet for so many decades? For potential migrants, the U.S. had a couple of advantages. First, it offered many, mostly unskilled jobs with higher earnings than in Europe. Second, the move to America, in contradistinction to other destinations, was usually not considered to be a permanent one; people went back and forth across the ocean. Until the Great War they could choose between staying in America or returning to their own country in Europe.

After the 1880s, the inhabitants of East Central Europe discovered distant destinations, and migration streams started to flow almost without interruption. The United States became the main and the most popular destination for migrants from this part of Europe. Franciszek Bujak, describing emigration from the Galician village of Maszkienice, has shown how transatlantic movement simply added to the existing repertoire of historical migration patterns.[20] Information networks made overseas travel easier. Migrants from Galicia usually crossed the Austrian-German frontier at the border station in the city of Myslowitz. From the Hungarian part of the Monarchy, Slovaks, Jews, and Magyars could transfer to trains in Budapest or Vienna destined mostly for German ports. Southern Slavs also used this route, but of course Slovenes, Croats, Dalmatians, and others could also choose the ports of Trieste or Fiume (Rijeka).[21]

Migrants from Russian Poland or Lithuania had to obtain official permits in order to cross the Prussian border and travel to harbors. To avoid this requirement, people from northern Russian Poland pretended that they were going to the nearest German town or market. Walking or riding in carts, they sometimes bribed the gendarmes or soldiers. Usually, they had connections on the Prussian side of the border and were well informed by letters from their relatives or acquaintances about what to do and how to behave. In taverns near the border there was always someone providing assistance, or smuggling people across the border. This was a well-developed business.[22] Tavern keepers who read German newspapers supported migration movements as well. Here and there travel agents appeared. In the 1880s, agents were blamed for the rising waves of migration everywhere in Central Eastern Europe. Some contemporary commentators, among them journalists, politicians, and nationalists, were of the opinion that eliminating the agents' posts and offices would successfully stop migration hysteria. The agents' activity was not the main cause of migration, but the presence of representatives of ship companies and other intermediaries did facilitate departure.[23] Travel company agents distributed literature propagating overseas destinations. Brochures, posters, and leaflets portrayed big ships on calm waters, taking people safely and quickly to America. Shipping companies and travel agencies advertised widely in newspapers.[24]

Ukrainians or Jews from Russian Ukraine usually traveled to Brody, which was the closest town next to the Austria-Russian border and a center for emigrants or Jewish refugees. From there, they continued to travel west in Austrian trains. It is very difficult to establish why some "pioneers" decided to take a long and risky journey to America. Microstudies suggest that the first to emigrate to America were most likely those who were only loosely associated with village communities, those who had settled in a village recently, usually marginalized agricultural laborers. "Emigration attacked the village from its periphery," wrote the sociologist Krystyna Duda-Dziewierz, describing the situation in the village of Babica in the Rzeszów County, between Kraków and Lwów (Lviv, Lemberg) in western Galicia.[25] The first emigrants from the village were not village natives. They had married "into" the village and were agrarian proletarians or small owners only loosely connected with the rest of Babica. After the first Maszkieniczaner (from Bujak's study) left for Pennsylvania, the floodgates opened in earnest. In 1911, the number of migrants headed for the U.S. grew fourteen times. Twenty percent of the migrants from this village in Brzesko County worked on the other side of the ocean.

People were drawn not only by the need for a better life but also by the desire for social improvement. The notion of advancement – a better future, prestige – was of course understood in the context of their own culture. For better or worse, work in the fields afforded a living. Using cash obtained from outside the village, migrants could build a house, achieve greater authority, or buy more land. The expansive economy in the United States at the end of the nineteenth century offered peasants an opportunity to fulfill "their aspiration for social rise defined by their own hierarchy of values."[26] They worked and saved money in order to buy land at home. In two weeks, one could earn as much in America as during a whole season in German or Hungarian agriculture. Knowledge of potential opportunities was essential to the popularity of America as a migrants' destination.

ADAM WALASZEK

For a majority of migrants, the movement to America was to be temporary in nature. Indeed, for many it was. Before the First World War, return migration and transatlantic circulation of migrants were common phenomena. Nineteen percent of Slovaks and eleven percent of Magyars who migrated to the U.S. between 1899 and 1910 had been there previously. Research conducted earlier in Hungary in the years 1895-1896 established that twenty-three percent of emigrants had visited the U.S. before. In their intention to return, Poles were not different from many other groups migrating to America from Southeastern Europe towards the end of the nineteenth century. In the U.S., these people were labeled "birds of passage." If we place them in the context of the Atlantic economy, it would be more appropriate to call them "migrant workers." In the case of Austria-Hungary, on average seventeen to twenty-seven percent of migrants returned. For some ethnic groups estimates are higher – for Croats between thirty-three and forty percent, for Magyars 46.5 (but between 1899 and 1913, on average 24.3 percent returned), for Lithuanians the number is twenty percent, for Slovaks between twenty and thirty-six percent. Polish returnees amounted to nearly thirty percent of the total migrant population.[27]

Chain migration

Regional variations in migration trends were also associated with the ethnic composition of the peripheries of the empires. This aspect seems particularly important in the case of transatlantic migration. Mass migration to America started in areas that were ethnically diverse and in the borderlands. In Hungary, Germans and Jews were the first movers (probably following German and Czech examples); Magyars and Slovaks followed. Poles followed the German experience in the Oppeln Silesia. Migration waves later spread to Prussian Poland, East Prussia, and northern Russian Poland. Lithuanian mass emigration began in the western Suwałki district and moved northward and eastward.[28] The western part of Slovakia belonging to Hungary was economically the most developed region. Migration to the U.S. started in the 1860s and was the highest from the northeastern counties (Šariš, Spiš, and Zemplín). The region had poor agriculture and some mining industry. The predominantly Slovak ethnic population, as mentioned above, had long traditions of seasonal migration to agricultural work in Alföld. Between 1899 and 1913, thirty-one percent of the people leaving the Hungarian part of the dual monarchy originated from there. Between 1881 and 1910, half of the population of Šariš county left. Ninety percent of Slovak migrants traveling to America came from the eastern counties. Magyars left the same region and neighboring counties. In Transylvania, the movement of Saxons caused Romanians to migrate; in Croatia-Slavonia, Slovenes transmitted the emigration fever to Croats and Serbs.[29] In Austrian Galicia, gorączka emigracyjna [emigration fever] had started in the middle of western Galicia, soon spreading to the east and west, but the inspiration probably came from Slovakia. Migration waves coming from the west and south encouraged the movement of various national and cultural groups (Poles, Lemkos, Ukrainians, Jews, and Germans). Poles, Jews, and Germans traveled at the same time. During the first phase of migration to America, people originating from a particular region formed their own districts. Cleveland attracted Slovenes from the Karlovac, Gorski Kotar, and Lower Carniola regions which bordered on a Slovenian area. From there, Slovenes traveled to America. And Slovenes, in turn, informed Croats about American possibilities.[30]

Once it gained momentum, migration was typically organized by families, relatives, and friends. Recent migrants to America invited others to follow in their footsteps. Close ties existed between those who left for America and those who remained in European villages. Letters constantly crossed the ocean. Everyday communication was conducted at a very great distance with the help of those able to write letters. The migrants not only sent money and steamship tickets to the old country, they also gave advice and persuaded their friends that they, too, should leave. Possibilities and dangers were considered in these "conversations."

Volume of Overseas Migration

It is estimated that 450,000 people from Prussian Poland, 900,000 from Austrian Poland, and 950,000 from Russian Poland left for the United States (when we consider the high return migration, the number would be smaller: 1.3 to 1.5 million).[31] Until the First World War, approximately 1.8 million Jews, 300,000 Lithuanians, 250,000 Ukrainians, and 100,000 to 150,000 Ruthenians left for America. Ukrainians (who could call themselves Galicians, Bukovynians, or Carpatho-Rusyns, depending on the region from which they originated) were also distinguished by their religion – some from Eastern Galicia were predominantly Unites or Ukrainian Greek Catholics, while minorities from Volhynia and Bukovina belonged to various Orthodox churches. In the United States and Canada, they formed the Ukrainian Greek Orthodox church.

According to careful estimates by Juliana Puskás for the period between 1861 and 1924, 4,116,988 people left the Austro-Hungarian Monarchy for the U.S., including approximately 684,000 to 728,000 Slovaks, 381,000 to 390,000 Jews, 568,000 to 544,000 Croatians-Slovenes, 549,000 to 526,000 Magyars, 442,000 to 434,000 Germans, 169,000 to 175,000 Bohemians-Moravians, 261,000 to 267,000 Ruthenians, 98,000 to 93,000 other South Slavic groups, and 153,000 to 154,000 Romanians. These groups can also be differentiated according to religion: Catholics, Protestants, Orthodox, and Unites. Religious affiliation remained an important element in the process of (re)constructing groups abroad.[32]

In contrast to destinations in the U.S., most other destinations were planned to be permanent. This was the case for settlements of Poles and Ukrainians on farms in the Argentinean province of Misiones, southern Brazil, or in Canada.

Settlers chose the western peripheries of the industrial Atlantic world. Between 1860 and 1910, Argentina, with a population of half a million people, transformed into a modern and important nation. It systematically tried to populate the country according to the slogan *gobernar es poblar* (to govern is to populate).[33] Among the immigrants who went there were people from Austro-Hungary, about 31,000 Ruthenians and Poles, although they did not necessarily identify themselves as such. The distinction between *polacos* and *rutenos* appeared later. They formed agricultural settlements in the Misiones province (Apóstoles, Azara, San José, and Corpus) and smaller enclaves of workers in Buenos Aires, Rosario, Tucumán, and the province of Corrientes.[34]

Among the four million immigrants who reached Brazil between 1888 and 1939, Poles constituted only 4.7 percent. In the late nineteenth century, Brazilian authorities tried to form farms and attract newcomers to the valleys of Iguaçu and Paraná. This policy, together with legends circulating about the country's wealth, attracted approximately one hundred thousand Poles, peasants from Oppeln Silesia (in Prussia), the Kingdom of Poland, and Galicia before the First World War.[35] Immigrants arrived during the so-called "Brazilian fevers" – a first wave from Russian Poland in 1890 and 1891, a second from Galicia in 1895 and 1896, and the third one between 1907 and 1908. The emigration was planned as permanent and peasants settled on farms in Parana, Santa Catarina, and Rio Grande do Sul, where people received land for cultivation. The task proved very difficult, as Polish agricultural practices were irrelevant in the new surrounding. Settlements remained peripheral and isolated. Ukrainians and Rusyns from East Galicia and Bukovyna caught the "Brazilian fever" as well. Approximately 70,000 people from these regions settled in South America (half of them in Parana).[36]

Until 1914, Polish emigration to Canada was neither large nor significant. In 1858, Kasubians (an ethnolinguistic group living in Pomerania, in the northern region of Prussia close to the Baltic Sea) started to emigrate to Canada and soon numbered around 20,000 people. In the 1880s, they were joined by Poles from Greater Poland (Prussian Poland) and Galicia. In Canada, the newcomers either worked as agricultural laborers, railway workers, or independent farmers.[37] Far stronger was the Ukrainian presence in Canada: after 1895, approximately 180,000 Ukrainians and Carpatho-Rusyns arrived as farmers in Manitoba, Alberta, and Saskatchewan.[38]

Jewish Exceptionalism?

In the case of Jews, compulsion and freely taken decisions to migrate could mix. After the partitions of Poland, the largest number of Ashkenazi Jews lived in the so-called Pale of Jewish Settlement comprising parts of Lithuania, Belarus, Ukraine, and the Kingdom of Poland, in the Russian Empire. In the nineteenth century, five out of seven million East European Jews lived in Russia. The group also experienced a remarkable population explosion. In 1816, Jews composed 8.7 percent of the entire population in Congress Poland; by 1865, they constituted 13.5 percent. Jews were concentrated in big cities, small towns, and countryside villages, the *shtetls*. Social and economic changes, urbanization, and pauperization hurt them to the same degree as the non-Jewish peasantry. Furthermore, in the Russian Empire their legal status was restricted. After 1835, their presence was limited to the Pale. Pushed towards the west, Jews created a large group of urban proletarians, craftsmen, and petty merchants. Their internal mobility within the Kingdom of Poland was very high, much higher than that of Gentiles.[39] Poverty (in 1898, one-fifth of Jewish families depended on charity), discrimination, and finally a wave of pogroms and persecutions created a climate conducive to emigration. The anti-semitic atmosphere and evident persecutions have often been stressed in the argument that the Jewish migration experience was different from that of other migrants.[40] After the assassination of Czar Alexander II on 1 March 1881, Jews were accused of conspiracy. In Russia they were the target of violent attacks in the years 1881-1884. The May Laws of 1882 established Jewish quotas in particular professions. The Minister of Internal Affairs, Count Nikolai Pavlovich Ignatiev, promulgated laws to forbid Jewish rural settlement and to outlaw work on Sundays and during Christian holidays.[41] Eastern European Jews left their countries afraid to lose their positions but also attracted by the ideology of freedom.[42]

At least since 1960, with Lloyd Gartner's publication *The Jewish Immigrant in England*,[43] (supported later by the works of Simon Kuznetz,[44] John D. Klier[45] and others[46]), the exceptionalism of Jewish emigration and the role of the pogroms have been questioned. According to recent literature, Jewish emigration until the year 1903 should be explained from the perspective of economic transformations, urbanization, and social changes, which regionally coincided with the pogroms in Russia. Jewish emigration started before the first wave of pogroms. When the anti-Semitic incidents occurred (e.g. in 1883 in Yekaterinburg or Nizhny Novogrod), Jewish emigration to America actually diminished. Also, emigrants were recruited from the northwestern part of the Empire, which until the twentieth century was not plagued by anti-Jewish riots. Thus, one of the arguments goes, it was rather the crises in agriculture, the pauperization of the peasant clients of Jewish merchants and craftsmen, crop failures, and the famines of the years 1869-1870 and 1891-1892 that explain the exodus. Most recently, Gur Alroey has summarized his archival research as follows: "It has, further, been demonstrated that the Great Emigration from Eastern Europe that became the Great Immigration to overseas destinations was not an outcome of pogrom panic and flight."[47] Of the few new social movements which appeared among Jews (the Haskalah, Zionism, and socialism), mass migration was by far the greatest and most popular answer to distress.[48] Finally, the argument of voluntary of Jewish emigration was supported by Jonathan Sarna's discovery that before the year 1903 twenty-two percent of Jewish migrants returned home, while in the 1890s the percentage was even higher: twenty-six percent. The level of returns for Jews was not much smaller than among groups that are usually considered examples of classic labor migrations.[49]

Between 1800 and 1880, 250,000 Jews left Eastern Europe; between 1881 and 1900, this number rose to one million, and between 1901 and 1914, it further increased to approximately two million. Two-thirds originated in the Russian Empire, where their situation was the worst. Jews had better conditions in the Austro-Hungarian Monarchy, where they enjoyed legal protection according to the Act of 1867. But Jewish emigrants were also leaving Galicia, northern Hungary (Slovakia), Hungary, and Romania. In those countries, expectations associated with the American *goldene medine* were more realistic, based on hopes of finding work in the textile industry. There was anti-Semitism in Hungary, visible in the 1870s. The infamous trial about ritual murder in 1882, however, did not provoke a social reaction and did not lead to mass migration.

The United States of America was the main destination of Jewish overseas migrants. There were some others as well. Before the First World War, a few thousand reached Canadian towns (Montreal, Toronto, and Winnipeg). Larger and more significant were the Jewish colonies in Argentina (Russian Jews predominated in the group of one hundred thousand European Jewish immigrants there). More than forty thousand Jews, mostly Lithuanian, settled in South Africa. A smaller number went to Australia.[50] London's East End, the *Pletzl* tailoring businesses in Paris, and other French and English towns attracted Jewish migrants as well.[51] The Zionist idea pushed some settlers towards Palestine in the first of three *aliyahs* – Jewish migration waves to Palestine.[52]

Conclusion

Searching for work, migrants from Central Eastern Europe could select from a range of destinations. They moved within established migration systems and extended them when globalization trends formed the Euro-Atlantic world economy. As Herman Zeitlhofer remarked, "... different migration streams often operated simultaneously and ... in-migration and out-migration were often nearly evenly balanced."[53] His observations about Bohemia can be applied to the rest of Central Europe as well. People from the two Central Eastern European empires moved easily and comfortably within the western world during the latter half of the nineteenth century. Decisions about their destinations – made in the context of family economies – were rational. The technical improvements and dynamism of U.S. economic development made it the strongest magnet. The U.S. was not the only destination, however. In times of economic depression or social upheaval, potential migrants could and did choose European destinations. During the long and dramatic American coal miners' strike of 1902, for example, return migration to

Austro-Hungary reached fifty percent. Poles, Slovaks, and Hungarians who depended heavily on work in the Pennsylvania coalmines had to seek new possibilities either elsewhere in the U.S. or – more likely – back in Europe.

During the decades before the Great War, people were circulating within one extensive migration system. As Władysław Wiśniewski and Jan Bukowski mentioned above, most migrants from Central Eastern Europe were constantly searching for better opportunities – be it within the region's known social spaces or within the Atlantic world. Whether they really succeeded and fulfilled their plans is another question. Many failed. Successful transit, in terms of material gains but also cultural change from the post-feudal world of Central Eastern European empires to the new realities, required time. Millions of people tried, and without the migration phenomenon, the region would have lagged behind. The migrants acted within existing structures of the global world, and they changed them at the same time.

Notes

1. Franciszek Bujak, "Kilka przyczynków i sprostowań do pracy dra St. Hupki o rozwoju stosunków włościańskich nad Górną Wielopolką w Galicji zachodniej (pow. Ropczyce)," *Ekonomista* 4 (1913): 222-223. Author's translation.
2. Ludwik Stomma, *Antropologia kultury wsi polskiej XIX wieku* (Warszawa: PAX, 1986), 86, also 142, 45, 78.
3. Florian Znaniecki, "Wychodźstwo a położenie ludności wiejskiej zarobkującej w Królestwie Polskim," quoted by Zygmunt Dulczewski, *Florian Znaniecki redaktor Wychodźcy Polskiego* (Warszawa: LSW, 1982), 125.
4. William I. Thomas and Florian Znaniecki, *The Polish Peasant in Europe and America* (Chicago: University of Chicago Press, 1918).
5. Jan Bukowski, Życiorys tułacza syna Podhala, manuscript in *Pamiętniki wiejskich działaczy społecznych*, Vol. 1 (Warsaw: Instytut Gospodarstwa Społecznego), 1-6.
6. Hermann Zeitlhofer, "Bohemian Migrants: Internal, Continental, and Transatlantic Migrations in Bohemia at the Beginning of the Twentieth Century," in *European Mobility. Internal, International, and Transatlantic Moves in the 19th and Early 20th Century*, eds. Annemarie Steidl, Josef Ehmer, Stan Nadel, and Hermann Zeitlhofer (Göttingen: V & R Unipress, 2009), 189.
7. Dirk Hoerder, "Individuals and Systems: Agency in Nineteenth and Twentieth Century Labour Migrations," in *European Mobility*, 53; also Dirk Hoerder, "Migration and the International Labor Markets in the Atlantic Economies," in *Overseas Migration from East-Central and Southeastern Europe, 1880-1914*, ed. Julianna Puskás (Budapest: Akadémiai Kiadó, 1990), 21-42. Hoerder's interpretation is elaborated in his opus magnum, *Cultures in Contact. World Migrations in the Second Millenium* (Durham-London: Duke University Press, 2002).
8. Ewa Morawska, *For Bread with Butter: The Life-Worlds of East Central Europeans in Johnstown, Pennsylvania, 1890-1940* (New York-Cambridge: Cambridge University Press, 1985), 25.

ADAM WALASZEK

9. Walter Nugent, *Crossings. The Great Transatlantic Migrations, 1870-1914* (Bloomington: Indiana University Press, 1992), 20-25.

10. Heinz Fassmann, "Emigration, Immigration, and Internal Migration in the Austro-Hungarian Monarchy. 1910," in *Roots of Transplanted*, eds. Dirk Hoerder and Inge Blank, Vol. 1 (Boulder-New York: Columbia University Press, 1994), 256-257; Morawska, *For Bread with Butter*, 314.

11. Ewa Morawska, "Labor Migrations of Poles in the Atlantic World Economy, 1880-1914," *Comparative Studies in Society and History* 31.2 (April 1989): 241; Ildikó Kríza, "Ethnic Identity and National Consciousness of the Hungarian Peasantry During the Age of Dualism," in *Roots of Transplanted*, 175-76.

12. Ivan Čizmič, "Emigration from Croatia, 1880-1914," *Overseas Migration*, 143-154; Olga Supek, Jasna Čapo, "Effects of Emigration on a Rural Society: Demography, Family Structure and Gender Relations in Croatia," in *Roots of Transplanted*, 316-18.

13. Morawska, *For Bread and Butter*, 22-62; Władysław Bronikowski, *Drogi postępu chłopa polskiego* (Warszawa: Państwowy Instytut Gospodarstwa Wiejskiego, 1934), 156-58.

14. Julianna Puskás, "Overseas Emigration from Hungary and the National Minorities, 1880-1914," in *Ethnicity and Society in Hungary*, ed. Ferenc Glaz (Budapest: MTA, 1990), 285, 289-291; Ladislav Tajták, "Slovak Emigration: Its Causes and Consequences," in *Overseas Migration*, 83.

15. Julianna Puskás, *Ties That Bind, Ties That Divide: 100 Years of Hungarian Experience in the United States* (New York: Holmes and Meier, 2000), 33-34; Hoerder, "Individuals and Systems," 54, 57-58.

16. Kazimierz Wajda, „Wymiana siły roboczej między ziemiami polskimi a Niemcami w drugiej połowie XIX i na początku XX wieku," in *Mechanizmy polskich migracji zarobkowych*, ed. Celina Bobińska (Warszawa: Książka i Wiedza, 1976), 65; Lothar Elsner, "Foreign Workers and Forced Labor in Germany During the First World War," in *Labor Migration in the Atlantic Economies. The European and North American Working Classes During the Period of Industrialization*, ed. Dirk Hoerder (Westport: Greenwood Press, 1985), 189-222. Some estimations talk about 600,000; see Morawska, "Labor Migrations of Poles," 251; Lars Olsson, "Labor Migration as a Prelude to World War I," *International Migration Review* 30 (1996): 876; Karl Kaerger, *Die Sachsengängerei; Auf Grund persönlicher Ermittelungen und statistischer Erhebungen* (Berlin: Perey Paul, 1890); Klaus Bade, "'Kulturkampf' auf dem Arbeitsmarkt: Bismarcks 'Polenpolitik' 1885-1890," in *Innenpolitische Probleme des Bismarckreichs*, ed. O. Pflanze (München: Oldenburg Verlag, 1983), 121-142.

17. Fassmann, "Emigration," 253-308.

18. Morawska, "Labor Migrations of Poles," 240; Hoerder, "Individuals and Systems," 59; David Turnock, "Railway Development in Eastern Europe as a Context for Migration Study," in *Patterns of Migration, 1850-1914*, eds. Aubrey Newman and Stephen W. Massil (London: Jewish Historical Society, 1996), 293-312; Horst Rössler, "'The Time has Come, We are Going to America.' The Main Travel Routes and Emigrant Ports," in *Leaving Home. Migration Yesterday and Today*, eds. Diethelm Knauf and Barry Moreno (Bremen: Temmen, 2010), 94-98.

19. This section draws on Adam Walaszek, "Do Ameryki za chlebem: Central-Eastern Europeans Cross the Atlantic," in *Leaving Home. Migration Yesterday and Today*, eds. Diethelm Knauf and Barry Moreno (Bremen: Temmen, 2010), 63-77.

20. Morawska, "Labor Migrations of Poles," 261-2; Morawska, *For Bread and Butter*, 25-29.

21. Dirk Hoerder, "The Traffic of Emigration via Bremen/Bremerhaven: Merchants' Interests, Protective Legislation, and Migrants' Experiences," *Journal of American Ethnic History* 13.1 (1993): 68-101.

22. Witold Kula, Nina Assorodobraj Kula, and Marcin Kula, *Writing Home: Immigrants in Brazil and the United States, 1890-1891* (Boulder-New York: Columbia University Press, 1986), 264, 355, 365.

23. Bukowski, *Życiorys*, 4.

24. Winston Chrislock, "Cleveland Czechs," in *Identity, Conflict, and Cooperation. Central Europeans in Cleveland, 1850-1930*, eds. David Hammack, Diane Grabowski, and John Grabowski (Cleveland: Western Reserve Historical Society, 2002), 78-80; Frank Vlchek, *The Story of My Life*, ed. Winston Chrislock (Kent: Kent State University Press, 2004).

25. Krystyna Duda-Dziewierz, *Wieś małopolska a emigracja amerykańska. Studium wsi Babica powiatu rzeszowskiego* (Warszawa-Poznań: Polski Instytut Socjologiczny, 1938), 29.

26. Morawska, *For Bread and Butter*, 63-64.

27. Adam Walaszek, "Preserving or Transforming Role? Migrants and Polish Territories in the Era of Mass Migrations," in: *People in Transit. German Migrations in Comparative Perspective, 1820-1920*, eds. Dirk Hoerder and Jörg Nagler (Cambridge: Cambridge University Press, 1995), 106.

28. Puskás, *Ties That Bind*, 25; Andrzej A. Zięba, "Procesy migracji zamorskich z Galicji," in *Mechanizmy zamorskich migracji łańcuchowych w XIX wieku: Polacy, Niemcy, Rusini, Żydzi*, eds. Dorota Praszałowicz, Krzysztof A. Makowski and Andrzej A. Zięba, (Kraków: Księgarnia Akademicka, 2004), 121-146.

29. Puskás, "Overseas Migration," 286-8.

30. Matjaž Klemenčić, "Slovenes in Cleveland," in *Identity, Conflict, and Cooperation*, 308.

31. Ewa Morawska, „Motyw awansu w systemie wartości polskich imigrantów w Stanach Zjednoczonych na przełomie wieku: O potrzebie relatywizmu kulturowego w badaniach historycznych," *Przegląd Polonijny* 4.1 (1978): 61-67; Kazimiera Zawistowicz-Adamska, *Społeczność wiejska. Wspomnienia i materiały z badań terenowych. Zaborów 1938-1939* (Warszawa: LSW, 1958).

32. Julianna Puskás, "Some Results of my Research on the Transatlantic Emigration from Hungary on the Basis of Macro- and Micro-Analysis," in *Overseas Migration*, 48-49; Puskás, "Overseas Migration," 284-5; Hoerder, "Individuals and Systems," 59; Zięba, "Procesy migracji," 123-125.

33. Diethelm Knauf, "To Govern is to Populate! Migration to Latin America," in *Leaving Home*, 142-148.

34. Ryszard Stemplowski, "Liczebność i rozmieszczenie słowiańskich osadników rolnych w Misiones (1897-1947)," in *Słowianie w argentyńskim Misiones 1897-1977*, eds. L. J. Bartolomé, Danuta Łukasz and Ryszard Stemplowski, (Warszawa: PWN, 1991), 43-89; Krzysztof Smolana, "Polska diaspora w Ameryce Południowej, Środkowej i Meksyku," in *Polska diaspora*, ed. Adam Walaszek (Kraków: WL, 2001), 130-148; Krzysztof Smola-

na, "Za Ocean po lepsze życie," in *Dzieje Polonii w Ameryce Łacińskiej*, ed. Marcin Kula (Warszawa: Ossolineum, 1983), 39-64.

35. Stomma, *Antropologia*, 79.

36. Krzysztof Groniowski, *Polska emigracja zarobkowa w Brazylii 1871-1914* (Wrocław-Warszawa: Ossolineum, 1972); Marcin Kula, *Polonia brazylijska* (Warszawa: LSW, 1981).

37. Anna Reczyńska, "Polska diaspora w Kanadzie," in *Polska diaspora*, 32-35.

38. Valerie Knowles, "'In Search of Fame, Fortune and Sweet Liberty': European Emigration to Canada, 1830 to the Present," in *Leaving Home*, 131-135; Andrzej A. Zięba, "Ukraińcy i karpaccy Rusini," in *Polska diaspora*, 447-452.

39. Artur Eisenbach, *Z dziejów ludności żydowskiej w Polsce w XVIII i XIX wieku* (Warszawa: PIW, 1983) 11-16.

40. Jonathan D. Frankel, "The Crises of 1881-82 as a Turning Point in Modern Jewish History," in *The Legacy of Jewish Migration: 1881 and Its Impact*, ed. David Berger (New York: Social Science Monographs, Brooklyn College Press, 1983), 9; Colin Holmes' article from 1995 underlines pogroms as the first cause of Jewish emigration: "Jewish Economic and Refugee Migrations, 1880-1950," in *The Cambridge Survey of World Migrations*, ed. Robin Cohen (Cambridge: Cambridge University Press 1995), 148.

41. Inge Blank, "A Vast Migratory Experience: Eastern Europe in the Pre- and Post-Emancipation Era (1780-1914)," in *Roots of the Transplanted*, Vol. 1, 203-208; Lloyd P. Gartner, *History of the Jews of Cleveland* (Cleveland: Western Reserve Historical Society, 1978), 102; Ewa Morawska, *Insecure Prosperity. Small-Town Jews in Industrial America*, 1890-1940 (Princeton: Princeton University Press, 1996), 6; Ewa Morawska, "A Replica of the 'Old Country' Relationship in the Ethnic Niche: East European Jews and Gentiles in Small-Town Western Pennsylvania, 1880s-1930s," *American Jewish History* 77 (1987): 36; Nugent, *Crossings*, 93.

42. Naomi Cohen, *Encounter with Emancipation: The German Jews in the United States, 1830-1914* (Philadelphia: Jewish Publication Society of America, 1984), 4.

43. Lloyd Gartner, *The Jewish Immigrant in England, 1870-1914* (Detroit: Wayne Stet University Press, 1960), 41, 45-46, 48-49. He repeated his observations later: "The largest voluntary international migration of Jews in history took place between 1881 and the coming into force of the Johnson Act"; see Gartner, *History of the Jews*, 102.

44. Simon Kuznetz, "Immigration of Russian Jews to the United States: Background and Structure," *Perspectives in American History* 9 (1975).

45. John Klier, "Emigration Mania in Late-Imperial Russia: Legend and Reality," in *Patterns of Migration*, 21-29.

46. Ralph Mahler, "The Economic Background of Jewish Emigration from Galicia to the United States," *YIVO Annual of Jewish Social Science* 12 (1952): 255-267; Morawska, *Insecure Prosperity*, 5; Tobias Brinkmann, "Jewish Mass Migrations between Empire and Nation-State," *Przegląd Polonijny* 31.1 (2005); Charlotte Erickson, *Jewish People in the Atlantic Migration 1850-1914*, in *Patterns of Migration*, 1-9; David Weinberg, *East European Jews in the Context of the Development of French Immigration Policy, 1881-1939*, in *Patterns of Migration*, xx; Klaus Hödl, "Galician Jewish Migration to Vienna," *Polin* 12 (1999), 147-163; Kuznetz, "Immigration of Russian Jews," 88-93.

47. Gur Alroey, "Patterns of Jewish Emigration from the Russian Empire from the 1870s to 1914," *Jews in Russia and Eastern Europe*, 57.2 (2006): 46.

48. Morawska, *Insecure Prosperity*, 17, 26; Sydney S. Weinberg, *The World of Our Mothers. The Lives of Jewish Immigrant Women* (New York: Schocken Books, 1988), 44, 54-56.

49. Jonathan Sarna, "The Myth of No Return: Jewish Return Migration to Eastern Europe, 1881-1914," *American Jewish History* 71 (1981-82): 256-268; also Nugent, *Crossings*, 92-94.

50. Mahler, "The Economic Background," 266-267; Richard Mendelsohn, "Between Boer and Brit: Jewish Immigrants in the Transvaal in the Late Nineteenth Century," in *Patterns of Migration*, 199-200; Anthony P. Joseph, "Patterns of Migration 1850-1914," in Newman, *Patterns of Migration*, 336.

51. Nancy L. Green, *The Pletzl of Paris. Jewish Immigrant Workers in the Belle Epoque* (New York-London: Holmes and Meier, 1986), 34-41; Nancy L. Green, *Ready-to-Wear and Ready-to-Work. A Century of Industry and Immigrants in Paris and New York* (Durham-London: Duke University Press, 1997), 35-39; Nancy L. Green, "A Tale of Three Cities: Immigrant Jews in New York, London and Paris, 1870-1914," in *Patterns of Migration*, 81-98; Nancy L. Green, Laura Levine Frader, Pierre Milza, "Paris: City of Light and Shadow," in *Distant Magnets: Expectations and Realities in the Immigrant Experience*, eds. Dirk Hoerder and Horst Rössler (New York: Holmes & Meier, 1993), 43-47.

52. Andrzej A. Zięba, „W drodze z Warszawy do Syjonu: przypadek rodziny Sokołowów," in *Nahum Sokołów, życie i legenda*, ed. Florian Sokołów and Andrzej A. Zięba (Kraków: Księgarnia Akademicka, 2006), XXVIII- LVII; also Steve J. Gold, *The Israeli Diaspora* (Seattle: University of Washington Press, 2002), 3.

53. Zeitlhofer, "Bohemian Migrants," 189, 204; Hoerder, "Individuals and Systems," 53.

ADAM WALASZEK

The "Floating Homeland": The Ship as a "Connectivity Space" in Greek Migrant and Public Discourse

Yannis G.S. Papadopoulos

To what extent does the experience of travel and the encounters in connecting spaces influence self-perceptions and collective identifications? By drawing upon the experience of immigrants from Greece to the United States of America, this essay explores travel not as simply a bridge that connects two countries – the homeland and the host country – but rather as a transformative space and time.

Travel in this sense contributes to framing public discourse and it shapes collective attitudes in both cosmoi: in the national and in the idealized, prospective host country. This essay focuses on travel as connectivity rather than as transit space. Although many scholars have approached travel as a "dead time," travel is perhaps the first real migration phenomenon. It is the place where passengers interact, where they shape and re-shape expectations and views on the country, and see anew the self's position in it.[1] I perceive the transatlantic crossing as a "rite of passage" for most migrants.[2] Migrants' identifications were modified through their encounters with people from other regions of their own countries, and with other ethnic groups. And all this took place in the liminal space of the ship and during their stay in Ellis Island. In this respect, travel provides a useful heuristic device for analyzing emigrants' developing relationship with their country of origin and with their host country.

Sea Routes of the Greek Transatlantic Migration

The massive wave of Greek Orthodox immigrants to the United States started during the last decade of the nineteenth century as part of the "new immigration," a term introduced in the 1880s to describe the wave of immigrants from Eastern and Southern Europe.[3] The majority came from the provinces of the Greek kingdom although, at the beginning of the twentieth century, large numbers of Greek Orthodox Ottoman subjects started to settle in America as well.[4] By 1924, 397,987 Greek subjects and 102,476 Greek Orthodox Ottoman subjects had migrated to the United States.[5] The main push factor for the majority of emigrants from the Greek kingdom was an economic crisis that hit the agricultural sector during this period and the subsequent indebtedness of the farmers. The prospect of a better life should not be underestimated.[6] The most important reason for emigration of Greek Orthodox Ottoman subjects was the imposition of compulsory military service for Christian subjects of the Ottoman Empire after the Revolution of Young Turks in 1908.[7] An equally important factor for both Greeks and Greek Orthodox Ottoman subjects was the role played by shipping agents. Roaming the provinces of both the Greek Kingdom and the Ottoman Empire, these agents, as contemporary sources so vividly described, propagated the "bright" prospects awaiting migrants in the United States.

From about 1890, when the major Greek transatlantic migration movement started, until 1905, when Patras became a port of call for transatlantic steamers, migrants from Greece traveled by ship and train to major European ports in the United Kingdom, France, and Germany. After varying lengths of stay in these ports, they embarked for the United States. The terminals of Cunard and White Star lines were in Liverpool and Southampton, those of Nord-deutscher Lloyd and Hamburg-America were in Bremen and Hamburg, and those of Compagnie Generale Transatlantique were in Le Havre and Cherbourg.[8] Over time, this scene changed. Due to the growing number of immigrants from the Mediterranean basin, steamship companies organized regular lines from the ports of Marseille, Genoa, Naples, and Trieste to New York, initiating what has been characterized as the "Mediterranean migratory route."[9] French and Italian steamship companies were leading the race for numbers of passengers on transatlantic journeys. By 1905, ten steamship companies from seven European countries had agencies in Greece,[10] while the Austrian steamship company Austroamericana offered a direct trip to the United States from the port of Patras in western Peloponnese.[11]

Greek steamship companies soon realized they could profit from the transatlantic migration. Since shipping was one of the major activities of Greeks both in the Greek kingdom and the diaspora, Greek shipping firms understood that emigration gave them the chance to expand their activities in a new and promising domain.[12] The first Greek shipowner to initiate transatlantic trips from the port of Piraeus in 1907 was Dimitrios Moraitis. He had a steamship the *Moraitis*, built especially for transatlantic journeys.[13] It sailed from Piraeus and stopped in Calamata and Patras before sailing towards the Atlantic.[14] In 1907, the year when the number of immigrants from the Kingdom of Greece doubled, the ships of Austroamericana, the Prince Line, the Fabre Line, the Messageries Maritimes, and Moraitis's Line had regular trips from Patras.[15] In 1908, Moraitis's company was declared bankrupt, a result of accumulated debts from the economic crisis of 1907-1908.[16] Nevertheless, Moraitis's lenders founded the Greek Transocean Steamship Line (Υπερωκεάνειος Ελληνική Ατμοπλοΐα) that continued carrying immigrants to the United States with Moraitis's ships, the Athenai and the Themistocles. In 1909, the Embeirikos brothers founded the National Greek Line, and in 1912, after the bankruptcy of the Greek Transocean Steamship Line, they acquired that company too. Until the end of the transatlantic migration flow from Greece in 1924, the National Greek Line remained the only Greek transatlantic shipping company, in spite of the sinking of three of its ships during the First World War. As Nicolas Manitakis has pointed out, "despite their late entrance into the market, their lack of experience and their relative financial weakness, the Greek maritime carriers managed finally to prevail over most of their powerful northern European rivals."[17] The ease of direct travel from Greece to the United States was not the only reason for this success. As I will discuss in more detail below, Greek ships symbolized for immigrants a part of the familiar space of "homeland" and thus psychologically made the transition to the coveted and yet feared America that much easier.

The Role of Travel Agents in Stimulating Emigration and the Greek State's Efforts to Control Shipping Companies

Steamship companies and especially their local agents soon acquired notorious fame. By the end of the nineteenth century, steamship company agents roamed through the provinces to illustrate the rich and multi-faceted possibilities the United States had to offer to immigrants. The competition for a share in the transport market resulted in an inflation of promises of secure jobs with high salaries awaiting those who dared abandon the microcosm of their village. The testimony of a migrant woman illustrates the role of these agencies:

> ... at that time the steamship companies were carrying on a great deal of competition to bring immigrants to the United States because there was a great need for them in building the railroads out toward the west and our factories, shoe factories, textile factories, steel factories ... and so the companies, the steamship companies, proceeded to entice the young men particularly from southern and central Europe to come to the United States.[18]

Prospective immigrants thus compared a society that suffered from mass unemployment where both agricultural and industrial workers received low salaries and worked long hours under poor conditions to a society of abundance offering not only a choice of employment but also a good working environment. Travel agents used every means to fire villagers' imaginations in order to convince them to emigrate. One immigrant remembered that agents presented the labour movement's demands, such as the eight-hour day, as a reality in the United States. As an immigrant recalled in his later years: "I hear over here there's plenty of jobs and they make good money ... I hear you work only eight hours here ... the whole Europe knew about it, and everybody wants to come here."[19]

A visible marker of this promotional activity on the part of shipping companies was "the pictures of ships and advertisements for transatlantic migration that constituted the main, if not the only, decoration of small coffeehouses, taverns and grocery stores of every Greek village."[20] The ships in the pictures were links to an idealized America. "[They] signified the possibility of mastering distance and dominating geography and culture."[21] Thus ships rather than mere means of transport were hints of a promised land in the here and now.

Both the promotional activities of the shipping agents and the letters of those who had already settled in the United States cultivated the prevalent idea that "streets in America were paved with gold."[22] The reality the immigrants encountered when they arrived in the United States did not, of course, match the promises of the travel agents. The majority of immigrants were exploited by *padrones* (labor contractors) and worked under appalling conditions in factories, mines, and in the construction of railways. They lived in salubrious tenement houses and often faced unemployment. Often the travel agents that promised them a rosy life were the very *padrones* who exploited the migrants in the United States. Nevertheless, in order to enhance their social status in their village of origin, few had the courage to admit the truth in their letters about the working and living conditions. The Greek diplomatic authorities in the United States, who often had to deal with migrants who were unemployed and had no means of returning to Greece, wanted to make it mandatory that those who asked for a ticket home write a public letter explaining that the employment possibilities in the United States were not as ideal as travel agents and many migrants described. As early as 1888 the consul general of Greece in New York noted that, "Mediterranean steamship companies pay commissions to those who procure for them emigrants bound for the United States ...Those agents tour the villages and the cities of Italy promising villagers work and a comfortable life in the United States and thus push them to emigrate."[23] He estimated that, since steamship companies paid a commission of five Italian lire for every immigrant, the total profit for the average annual number of 80,000 immigrants amounted to 240,000 lire.[24] Prospective migrants often mortgaged their land in order to collect the necessary money for the transatlantic journey.[25] The steamship companies acted as creditors so that they would acquire the migrants' lands if they failed to pay the mortgage. Furthermore, steamship companies ignored state regulations restricting emigration to certain categories of prospective emigrants. For example, although the Ottoman government in 1890 issued an official note to the Greek government demanding that the Greek steamship companies not furnish tickets to prospective emigrants without a valid passport,[26] prospective emigrants procured travel documents reserved for journeys inside the Empire (*mürur tezkeresi*), which they used as passports once they were sure that it did not contain the seal: "reserved for the interior" (*dahiliyeye mahsustur*).[27]

Another charge that state authorities directed against the shipping companies was that they swindled emigrants, abandoning them in Mediterranean transit ports without the means to survive. This practice forced Greek consular authorities to take them into their care.[28] Other agents collaborated with labor contractors in order to furnish them with child workers. These agents also instructed underage migrants how to bypass the age control at Ellis Island.[29] Already in 1888, the Greek consul in New York informed the Greek foreign minister that, "Poor immigrants are victims of the agents of sailing companies in the United States, who contribute to their hardships since their main aim is to profit from them."[30]

Such incidents compelled authorities of the sending states to control the "migration industry," which was mainly interested in maximizing profits from increasing the flow of emigrants.[31] In 1906, following the German and Italian examples, a Greek parliamentary committee proposed a bill for regulating emigration. Though it never became law, its aim was to protect prospective emigrants against "emigration contractors and shipping agents."[32] The committee in charge of the law recognized that the experience of the transatlantic crossing "not only has an impact on the life and the health of the emigrant but also may exert a critical influence on his future life."[33] Henceforth, it would be obligatory for every steamship company to deposit in advance a sum that would cover any "breach of its obligations towards emigrants."[34] Among other things, the law was intended to control the activities of middlemen, who took advantage of the ignorance of prospective emigrants and cultivated false impressions about the prospects in the United States.[35] It would have become illegal for "any emigration contractor and its agents to stir emigration through advertising."[36] Moreover, the project suggested that the Greek government should "take all the necessary measures to support Greek shipping companies" in order to secure that "emigrants would sail from a Greek port for their transatlantic journey," so that the state could have better control over whether the law protecting the rights of emigrants was respected or not.[37] We may deduce from the provisions of the above-mentioned proposal that the Greek administration was initially interested only in protecting prospective emigrants from exploitation by shipping agents rather than in formulating a broader policy towards the Greek transatlantic diaspora. Emigration was considered a safety valve against the socioeconomic problems facing Greek society. They worried that the high rates of unemployment and the indebtedness of agricultural households, along with contempt for the incompetent administration, constituted fertile ground for the spread of revolutionary ideas.

During the following years, the Greek state started to show a greater interest in strengthening links with Greek immigrants in the United States. After 1909, a military pronunciamento imposed a change of policy on the king, and the country started to reorganize. Military leaders wished to prepare the country for a war with the Ottoman Empire in the hope of accomplishing the "manifest destiny" of Greece: the restoration of the Byzantine Empire. At that point, several scholars and politicians pointed out the disastrous consequences of the demographic losses caused by transatlantic emigration, and some proposed putting an end to emigration. However, due to the Greek state's failure to discourage prospective emigrants, reform efforts focused on strengthening migrants' ties with their country of origin. Additionally the Greek state wished to convince the emigrants to make systematic financial contributions in the form of a migrants' tax and to draft them into the Greek army in the event of a possible Greco-Ottoman war. At that time, the strengthening of the links with citizens abroad became an important aspect of state policy for many European countries.[38]

Ships As Links To the Homeland

By the beginning of the second decade of the twentieth century, the Greek administration realized the need to strengthen migrants' bonds with Greece. Therefore, Greek authorities supported Greek steamship companies "as a way to cultivate closer relations between the nation and its migrants in the United States."[39] The introduction of direct shipping lines connecting Greece with the United States facilitated the communication of migrants with their homeland. At the same time, Greek ships in the New York harbor were a continuous visual reminder of Greece. The Greek-American newspaper *Atlantis* reports on the Greek immigrants' enthusiasm for the first arrival of Greek Transocean Steamship Line's ship, the *Athenai* in New York.[40] Solon Vlastos, the editor of the *Atlantis* and one of the leaders of the emerging Greek-American community, addressed the assembled immigrants on this occasion, underscoring the national importance of the existence of Greek steamship companies. In his speech, Vlastos expressed his enthusiasm for the inauguration of a direct link that shortened the real, but also the psychological, distance with Greece. At this point, the interests of the Greek state coincided with those of Greek shipowners.

Within this framework, the presence of Greek transatlantic steamship companies that could guarantee a direct link between Greece and the United States was essential. A shorter maritime route diminished the distance between the two countries. It facilitated the contacts and might convince migrants occupied in seasonal jobs to return to Greece during the winter. Until the passage of the Temporary Quota Act in 1921, a considerable part of the migrants did not settle permanently in the United States. Many returned for shorter or longer periods to Greece due to a variety of reasons, such as the wish to retain a traditional way of life instead of assimilating into American society, nostalgia, health problems, unemployment, or a desire to use the profits accumulated in the U.S. to enhance their social status in the home country. About forty percent of the Greeks that migrated to the United States during the first quarter of the twentieth century returned to Greece, one of the highest return rates of all ethnic groups.[41] During the Balkan Wars of 1912-13 and, to a lesser extent, during the First World War and the Greco-Turkish War of 1919-1922, many immigrants returned to volunteer in the Greek army.

YANNIS G.S. PAPADOPOULOS

The direct maritime link to Greece was thus necessary to facilitate Greek emigration policy goals. In this context, the Greek government was interested in enhancing the idea of the ship as a "Greek microcosm," a space reminding people of their bonds to the Greek Kingdom. In Greek public discourse, the ship acquired importance as a marker of the ability of Greece to minimize the (physical and psychological) distance that separated the migrants from their country of origin. As the newspaper Independent of Athens pointed out in 1909:

> The boat is a bridge that connects the foreign land with the homeland; it is the link that binds the migrants to the idea of homeland. When they board the boat at Piraeus ... our migrants have the impression that they are not separated from their native land ... they feel that they stand on Greek territory not in the abstract sense of international law, but in reality.[42]

The Greek state that had proved incapable of safeguarding employment and good working conditions for its citizens now tried to take advantage of the emotions stirred by the presence of a "Greek floating space." It aimed to reverse immigrants' previous perceptions and juxtaposed an idealized homeland to the harsh reality of life in the United States. In order to appeal to the Greek citizens in the United States, the Greek administration had to overcome the contempt that most migrants felt for their native country's political establishment. The nationalistic fervor of the majority of emigrants was combined with contempt for King George I of Greece and the country's political and military elites. These forces were considered corrupt and were held responsible for Greece's defeat by the Ottomans in 1897 as well as for the economic crisis that had forced many to emigrate. For Greek migrants who left their village for the United States, strong religious sentiments as well as close family and local ties were key elements of identification. In America, mutual help associations uniting migrants from the same village or county (ethnotopika somateia) constituted the most powerful hub of social life and group identity. Greek immigrants tended to settle in cities where people from their village or province had settled previously (chains of migration). Localism played an important role in social networks. Attachment to Greek state institutions and solidarity with Greeks from other provinces of Greece and the Ottoman Empire were not self-evident. In order to fight localism among immigrants and ensure that both those from Greece and the Ottoman Empire became or remained supporters of the Greek nationalist project, the Greek state transformed the Pan-hellenic Union – a loose federation of local Greek societies in the United States – into a society with a director appointed by the Greek government.[43]

The strength of localism was evident in the fact that most migrants on the ships clustered in groups with people from their village or district of origin, reproducing the familiar space that they had left behind.[44] During the journey, however, they had the chance to realize the similarities that tied them to other members of the broader Greek nation as envisaged by the Greek state ideology. On board, emigrants were exposed to an experience similar to that of those drafted into the national army. For the duration of the journey they coexisted and socialized in a secluded space with Greeks from other provinces and with Greek Orthodox migrants from the Ottoman Empire, thus realizing the cultural bonds that united them. Common rituals played an important role in impressing upon migrants a feeling of community. Constantine Papamichalopoulos, the appointed director of the Panhellenic Union, underlined the importance of these experiences for shaping migrants' collective perceptions. He described the celebration of Greek Easter aboard ship as evidence of the fact that in this transitional space, migrants from various regions realized they shared common customs, irrespective of the local variations.[45] The emotions stirred by lighted candles during a midnight mass celebrated on the deck of the steamer conveyed the image of the ship as a "floating homeland." Further, as other scholars have pointed out, these rituals contributed to assuaging migrants' stress during the transatlantic journey.[46]

On a second level, Greek emigrants' national identification aboard the ship was strengthened since it was there that they encountered for the first time people belonging to various ethno-linguistic groups from other countries of Southeastern Europe. This was due to the fact that by 1909, Patras had become a major port of embarkation for the United States not only for Greeks but also for others from the Ottoman Empire. Turks, Jews, Albanians, Greek Orthodox, and Slav Macedonian migrants left from Patras for New York.[47] The multiethnic reality aboard the Greek ships was not different from that aboard ships sailing from western European ports. But one has to take into account the tense relations between states and nationalist movements in Southeastern Europe. Therefore immigrants' comments reflect the shock they felt upon encountering the "other" on board...others who were also members of groups portrayed by Greek state propaganda as enemies. Various migrants mention in their testimonies, preserved in the Ellis Island archive, how they realized a distinction between a collective Greek identity and the identity of other ethnic groups. These realizations emerged on board the ship and during their stay at Ellis Island, the transit space of entrance to the multi-ethnic reality of the United States. As Anastasia Kalogarados Argianas recalled, "The boat stops in Syria, it stopped in Italy, to pick up more people. It was all different languages in there. I couldn't talk to everybody. I was going to talk but nobody talks to me."[48] Even the inability to communicate with members of other linguistic groups, under these circumstances, could strengthen the image of strangers as "enemies." Without therefore suggesting that the transatlantic crossing erased migrants' localism, it is nevertheless important to stress the role the voyage played in broadening migrants' perceptions of their familiar frame of reference. The journey hinted to people who were to a great extent illiterate and had not done their military service that they belonged to the same "imagined community."[49]

On the one hand, the transatlantic journey strengthened bonds that existed in the homeland and enhanced immigrants' nationness. On the other hand, it gave them the chance to imagine themselves as members of groups that used different criteria from those they were accustomed to or to which they were consigned by state authorities both in the sending country and in the host country.[50] For example, members of different ethnic groups realized affinities existed with those belonging to the same linguistic community. A Jewish immigrant from Salonica recalled from his stay at Ellis Island: "There was Turks and Chinese and Hawaiians. In fact my father met somebody from Hawaii, and they started talking Spanish."[51]

Moreover, the Ellis Island testimonies reveal that immigrants were strongly impressed by the visible social stratification projected in the different travel conditions existing in third and first class.[52] Some mentioned with pride that, when they later returned for short stays to their country of origin, they traveled first class.[53] This marked the realization of the dream of social ascendancy, which had convinced them to emigrate in the first place. The return trip served as a time capsule reminding them of the hardships they endured, but also highlighting their financial success.

After their arrival in the United States, the majority of immigrants realized that equal opportunities were guaranteed only on paper and that the American dream covered a harsh reality of inequality and labor exploitation. According to a saying that circulated among immigrants and which squarely contradicted the idealized image created by travel agents, "the streets were not paved with gold and we were supposed to pave them." Subsequently many, besides belonging to local, religious or ethnic networks, chose to participate in the labor movement. Thus they could claim through collective struggle the realization of the hopes visualized in the Statue of Liberty, the first image of the New World that they encountered.

The transatlantic crossing, the "rite of passage" that transformed the inhabitants of the "Old World" into ethnic Americans, often had consequences that neither the states of origin nor the host society could predict or influence. The encounters with people from other regions or ethnic groups in the "connectivity space" of the ship were an introduction to the diverse identifications the immigrants would develop in multiethnic American society.

In this respect, the testimonies of immigrants from Southeastern Europe exemplify a pattern common to all immigrants: the hope for a better life, the hardships of the journey, the encounter of people from other regions or ethnic groups, the disappointments upon arrival in the host country, and the subsequent idealization of their country of origin. The testimonies contribute to a better understanding of both the transatlantic immigration movement and the often tense relationship between diasporas and homelands.

Concluding Remarks

The high rate of return migration until 1921 and the subsequent yearly pilgrimages to the ancestral homeland organized by major ethnic associations could explain the viability of at least one Greek transatlantic shipping company during the first half of the twentieth century. After 1920, a considerable part of the first wave of immigrants settled for good in the United States, and fears became prevalent that the second generation would be fully assimilated and lose any interest in the culture of their parents' country of origin. Going to the port to see Greek ships became a ritual for subsequent generations of immigrant families who wanted to impress on their children, who had never seen Greece, the importance of their ancestral homeland. As the pictures of transatlantic steamships showcased the promise of a new life for prospective immigrants, for immigrants in the United States the ships with the Greek flag became a symbol of their origins, but also of their life trajectory. Through the ship, Greece became for their children a tangible place that acquired the attributes that immigrants had projected onto it. In an interview conducted eighty years after her transatlantic crossing, Anastasia Kalogarados Argianas lingered on the name of the National Greek Line steamer that had brought her to America: Patris: "You know what it means? Patris means what we call in the United States, Patris. Patris, like from one nation where you come from."[54]

Although the period after the Second World War marked the decline of the ethnic enclaves and the suburbanization of the ethnic communities, this residential shift did not result in the dissolution of ethnic identity. White ethnics gradually abandoned external ethnic characteristics but retained a form of "symbolic ethnicity," a collection of patterns that "must be visible and clear in meaning to large numbers of third generation ethnics, and must be easily expressed and felt, without requiring undue interference in other aspects of life."[55] Therefore, although the successive Greek governments did not succeed in retaining their control over the immigrants, the Greek ship became one of the elements of Greek-American "symbolic ethnicity," an identifier that kept a link with the country of origin.

Notes

1. Considering how people interact within "mobility socioscapes," Sven Kesselring argues that "[t]ransit spaces are characterized by directionality and linearity; places, meetings and interactions are just transitory situations of goal attainment." By contrast, for some people these spaces constitute "spaces of interaction, optionality and contact. Travelling time is experience time and not 'dead time' between starting point and destination... People moving through connectivity spaces live in intense relation to others, are less structured and more open to contingency." Sven Kesselring, "New

mobilities management, Mobility Pioneers between first and second modernity," *Zeitschrift für Familienforschung* 17.2 (2005): 141.

2. For the notion of "rites of passage," see Arnold van Gennep, *Rites de Passage* (Paris: Picard, 1992).

3. On 'New Immigration' see John Higham, *Strangers in the Land, Patterns of American Nativism 1860-1925* (New York: Atheneum, 1967), 65. North American scholars during the first quarter of the twentieth century, based upon eugenics, divided the "older" immigrants from Germany, Ireland, and Scandinavia from the "new immigrants" from Eastern and Southern Europe, since "the former were assumed to have consisted of pioneer settlers, and the latter of unskilled proletarians". Modern scholarship, however, tends to distinguish an earlier immigration wave of "surplus labor" from the "Core countries" of Western Europe: the German Lands; France, and the United Kingdom and a latter wave from the "Periphery" that includes, apart from Southern and Eastern Europe, Scandinavia. Dirk Hoerder, *Cultures in Contact; World Migrations in the Second Millennium* (Durhan & London: Duke University Press, 2011), 336, 339-342.

4. For methodological reasons, I will use in my analysis the term "Greek Orthodox" for the members of the "Rum Milleti" the ethno-religious community under the head of the Patriarch of Constantinople, and "Greek" for the subjects of the Greek kingdom.

5. 61st Congress, Third Session, 1910-1911, Senate Document No 747, v. 1, "Emigration Conditions in Greece," Abstracts of Reports of the Immigration Commission with Conclusions, Recommendations and Views of the Minority, Dillingham Commission Reports, (Washington, 1911), 408. Thirteen Census Population – 1910, τ. 3: 216-7. Cited in Triandafyllia N. Kourtoumi-Hadji, "Η Ελληνική Μετανάστευση προς τις Ηνωμένες Πολιτείες και η Πολιτική της Ελλάδας (1890-1924)" (Ph.D. thesis, Aristotle Universtiy of Thessaloniki, 1999), 53.

6. Papastergiadis Nikos, *The Turbulence of Migration; Globalization, Deterritorialization and Hybridity* (Cambridge: Polity Press, 2000), 36-37, 47-48.

7. The "Committee of Union and Progress" that was in charge of the movement imposed on the Sultan Abdul-Hamid II the restoration of the constitution of 1876 and proclaimed the equality of all subjects of the Ottoman Empire, irrespective of their religion. The new government announced that henceforth Christians would be drafted into the army. Subsequently many Greek Orthodox who did not believe in the sincerity of the proclamations for equal treatment and were unwilling to serve in the Ottoman Army for fear of facing discrimination by Muslim officers decided to leave their homeland. IAYE (Historical Archive of the Greek Foreign Ministry), F. B53, Greek consul in Trebizond (Trabzon) to the Greek Foreign Ministry, 2412, December 10, 1911. Leland James Gordon, *American Relations with Turkey 1830-1930, An Economic Interpretation* (Philadelphia: University of Pennsylvania Press, 1932), 306.

8. Cf. Gunter Moltmann, "Steamship Transport of Emigrants from Europe to the United States, 1850-1914: Social, Commercial and Legislative Aspects," in *Maritime Aspects of Migration*, ed. Klaus Friedland (Köln: Böhlau, 1989), 313-314. Cited in Nicolas Manitakis, "Transatlantic Emigration and Maritime Transport from Greece to the US, 1900-1924: A Major Area of European Steamship Company Competition for Migrant Traffic," in *Maritime Transport and Migration: The Connections Between Maritime and Migration*

Networks, Research in Maritime History, Vol. 33, eds. Torsten Feys et al. (International Maritime Economic History Association, 2007), 64.

9. Ibid. 65.

10. Ibid. 66.

11. Ibid. 73.

12. On the history of Greek shipping, see Gelina Harlaftis, *A History of Greek-Owned Shipping: The Making of an International Tramp Fleet, 1830 to the Present Day* (London: Routledge, 1996).

13. Gelina Harlaftis, "Η Εμπορική Ναυτιλία. Η Μετάβαση από τα Ιστιοφόρα στα Ατμόπλοια," in Ιστορία του Νέου Ελληνισμού, 1770-2000, v. 5 (Athens: Ellinika Gramata, 2003), 98. see also Αλέξανδρος Κιτροέφ, "Η Νέα Διασπορά, η Μετανάστευση στις ΗΠΑ 1909-1922," in Ιστορία του Νέου Ελληνισμού, 1770-2000, v. 5 (Athens: Ellinika Gramata, 2003), 368.

14. Theodore Saloutos, *The Greeks in the United States* (Cambridge Massachussets: Harvard University Press, 1964), 35.

15. Ibid. 35.

16. Harlaftis, "Η Εμπορική Ναυτιλία," 98; Manitakis, "Transatlantic Emigration," 70.

17. Manitakis, "Transatlantic Emigration," 73.

18. Ellis Island Project, AKRF-91, Euterpe Boukis Doukakis testimony, born in 1903 in Larissa, immigrated to the United States in 1920. I thank the film director Maria Iliou for providing me the transcripts of the immigrants' interviews I used in this paper from her research at the Ellis Island Project archive.

19. Ellis Island Project, EI-378, Angelus Cotsidas testimony, born in 1900 in Pleasani, Epirus, immigrated to the United States in 1913.

20. Emmanouil Repoulis, Μελέτη Σχεδίου Νόμου περί Μεταναστεύσεως (Athens: Ypsilantis, 1912), 57.

21. Laliotou, *Transatlantic Subjects*, 61-2.

22. IAYE, F. B12/1907, Greek consul in New York Dimitrios Botassis to Greek Foreign Ministry, 16572, 23 October 1907.

23. IAYE, F. B12.1/1902, Greek consul in New York Dimitrios Botassis to Greek Foreign Minister Stephanos Dragoumis, 07945, June 28/July 10 1888, "Αι ατμοπλοϊκαί εταιρείαι της Μεσογείου πληρώνουσι προμηθείας εις τους προμηθεύοντας μετανάστας δι'Αμερικήν ... Οι μεσίται ούτοι έχουσι πράκτορας διατρέχοντας τα χωρία και πόλεις της Ιταλίας και υποσχόμενοι εργασίαν και άνετον βίον εις Αμερικήν, ωθούσι προς μετανάστευσιν".

24. Ibid.

25. Repoulis, Μελέτη Σχεδίου Νόμου, 154-5.

26. IAYE, F. A.12.1/1890, Note Verbale by the Ottoman Foreign Ministry, 97809, 24 July 1890 transmitted by the Greek ambassador in Constantinople, Nicolas Mavrokordatos, to the Greek Foreign Minister Stephanos Dragoumis, 08651, 17 July 1890.

27. Ibid: "Les autorités Ottomans refusant de délivrer aux individus ne pouvant justifier de leurs moyens de subsistance des passeports pour l'etranger, le strategème auquel ils recourent pour tromper leur vigilance consiste à obténir une feuille de route pour une autre localité de l'Empire et à se faire donner par les compagnies de navigation les

YANNIS G.S. PAPADOPOULOS

billets soit pour l'Amérique, soit pour l'Europe d'où ils poursuivent leur voyage vers le Nouveau Monde".

28. IAYE, F. B12.1/1902, Greek consul general in Marseille to Greek Foreign Minister Alexandros Zaimis, 07567, 29 May 1902.

29. IAYE, F. B12.1/1903, Greek consul in New York Dimitrios Botassis to Greek Foreign Ministry, 08142, 26 May/ 8 June 1903.

30. IAYE, F. A12.1/1888, Greek consul in New York Dimitrios Botassis to Greek Foreign Minister Stephanos Dragoumis, 07945, 13 July 1888. "Οι δυστυχείς μετανάσται έρμαια γενόμενοι των πρακτόρων των ενταύθα ατμοπλοϊκών εταιρειών και των εδώ οδηγών, οίτινες έτι μάλλον συντελλούσιν εις την ταλαιπωρίαν των χάριν ιδίας κερδοσκοπίας". IAYE, F. B12.1/1902, Greek consul in Marseille to Greek Foreign Minister Alexander Zaimis, 07567, 29 May 1902. See also Ellis Island Archive, mss. AKRF-91, Euterpe Bouki-Doukakis testimony.

31. On migration industry see IAYE, F. B12.1/1902, Greek consul in New York Dimitrios Botassis to Greek Foreign Minister Stephanos Dragoumis, 07945, 28 June/10 July 1888.

32. Η εξ Ελλάδος Μετανάστευσις. Η Έκθεσις της Επιτροπής της Βουλής και η Σχετική Πρότασις Νόμου (Athens: Royal Printing House Raftani-Papageorgiou, 1906), 22. The same clauses were included in the project of law on immigration proposed in 1911. See Repoulis, Μελέτη Σχεδίου Νόμου, 18.

33. Ibid. 21.

34. Ibid. 22.

35. Ibid. 23.

36. The proposal prohibited "εις πάντα εργολάβον μεταναστεύσεως και τους αντιπροσώπους και υπαλλήλους αυτού να διεγείρωσιν την μετανάστευσιν διά δημοσιεύσεων", Ibid. 37. The same provision exists in the immigration law project of 1911, "Απαγορεύεται εις πάντα πράκτορα μεταναστεύσεως και εις αντιπροσώπους ή υπαλλήλους αυτού να διεγείρωσι τους πολίτας προς μετανάστευσιν, είτε διά δημοσιευμάτων, είτε δι'εγκυκλίων ή οδηγιών αφοροσών την μετανάστευσιν, δημοσιεύοντες εν γνώσει ψευδείς ειδήσεις ή οδηγίας ή θέττοντες εις κυκλοφορίαν εντός του Κράτους ειδήσεις ή οδηγίας τοιούτου είδους τυπωθείσας εν τη αλλοδαπή", Repoulis, Μελέτη Σχεδίου Νόμου, 171.

37. Ibid. 24.

38. Nancy L. Green – François Weil, "Citoyenneté et Emigration", Les politiques du départ (Paris: Éditions de l'École des hautes études en sciences sociales, 2006), 11.

39. Laliotou Ioanna, Transatlantic Subjects: Acts of Migration and Cultures of Transnationalism between Greece and America (Chicago and London: University of Chicago Press, 2004), 61.

40. "Μια ωραία υποδοχή επί του ατμοπλοίου "Αθήναι," Atlantis Newspaper, 7 June 1909, 3.

41. On return migration see John Bodnar, The Transplanted: A History of Immigrants in Urban America (Bloomington and Indianapolis: Indiana University Press, 1985), 53-4. Hoerder, Cultures in Contact, 344.

42. Anexartitos newspaper, 4 February 1911, cited in Laliotou, Transatlantic Subjects, 62.

43. Yannis G. S. Papadopoulos, "The Role of Nationalism, Ethnicity, and Class in Shaping Greek American Identity, 1890–1927, A Historical Analysis," in Identity and Participation in Culturally Diverse Societies – A Multidisciplinary Perspective, eds. Assaad Azzi, Xenia

Chryssochoou, Bert Klandermans and Bernd Simon (London: Blackwell/Wiley, 2010), 17. Especially during the Balkan Wars, the Panhellenic Union served as the unofficial recruiting office for the Greek army and organized the return of volunteers to Greece.

44. Ellis Island Project, EI-173, James Apanomith testimony, born in 1895 in Afetes near Volos, immigrated to the United States in 1911.

45. "Κορομηλάς και Παπαμιχαλόπουλος," Atlantis newspaper, 6 September 1913, 4.

46. Hans Krabbendam, "Rituals of Travel in the Transition from Sail to Steam," cited in Babs Boter, "Heavenly Sensations and Collective Celebrations: Communal and Private Experiences of Dutch Transatlantic Journeys" in this volume. The experience of religious rituals had a different connotation aboard a Dutch ship. Boter remarks that the celebration of Christmas aboard constituted a unifying experience for travelers from various ethnic groups.

47. Saloutos, The Greeks, 35.

48. Ellis Island Project, AKRF-106, Tessi (Anastasia) Kalogarados Argianas testimony, born in 1903 in Cephalonia, immigrated to the United States in 1914.

49. For the term 'imagined communities,' see Benedict Anderson, Imagined Communities: Reflections on the Origin and Spread of Nationalism (London and New York: Verso, 2006). Ellis Island Project, AKRF-106, Tessi (Anastasia) Kalogarados Argianas testimony, born in 1903 in Cephalonia, immigrated to the United States in 1914.

50. I use the term 'taxonomies' following Michel Foucault's analysis of the classification mechanisms used by modern states. See Michel Foucault, The Archeology of Knowledge (London and New York: Routledge, 2002).

51. Ellis Island Project, EI-368, Charles Milos's testimony, born in 1902 in Douviani-Albania, immigrated to the United States in 1920.

52. This experience of social distinctions aboard the ship and the exploitation of immigrants by labor contractors is showcased in the recent film Brides by Pantelis Voulgaris, which tried to represent the experience of picture brides from various parts of Eastern Europe that cross the Atlantic in a Greek ship. Pantelis Voulgaris, Brides (Νύφες) (Odeon SA 2004).

53. Ellis Island Project, AKRF-86, Marianthe Dimitri Chletsos testimony, born in 1895 in Lemnos, immigrated to the United States in 1910.

54. Ibid.

55. The notion of symbolic ethnicity was introduced by Herbert Gans. "Symbolic Ethnicity: The Future of Ethnic Groups and Cultures in America," Ethnic and Racial Studies 2.1 (1979): 1-20. It was further developed by Mary C. Waters, Ethnic Options, Chosing Identities in America (Berkeley-Los Angeles-Oxford: University of California Press, 1990). For a recent critique, see Yiorgos Anagnostou. "A critique of symbolic ethnicity, The ideology of choice?" Ethnicities 9 (2009).

A Lasting Transit in Antwerp: Eastern European Jewish Migrants On Their Way To the New World, 1900-1925

Frank Caestecker

Migrants are often depicted as pawns in the hands of transport and state agencies. The most notorious example of migrants being denied any agency is the story of the Russian Jews whom an English shipping captain duped by making them believe that the Irish port Cork was the port of New York. As the story goes, Jewish emigrants from Lithuania arrived in the port of Cork on a ship from Hamburg and were instructed to disembark on the pretext that they had arrived in America.[1] These gullible Russian Jews thought they indeed had arrived at their destination and started life in the New World in Dublin. The founding myth of the Jewish community in Dublin as an "accidental" community has an alternative story in which the Jewish migrants are depicted as even more ignorant. According to this story, the calls of "Cork, Cork" were mistaken for "New York," prompting the befuddled Jews from Russia – lost in the great world – to disembark in Ireland.[2]

In scholarly studies, migrants are often perceived as passive victims as well. Thus, in a study of Jewish migration from German ports, Tobias Brinkmann is impressed by the mechanisms put into place at the end of the nineteenth century to control transit migration throughout the German Empire. He writes that "most European migrants were deprived of agency."[3] Indeed, the decisions of migrants were constrained by other, more powerful actors. It seems, however, that denying most of them agency is an overstatement of the power of the state and economic interest groups.

This article aims to point out the means by which migrants overcame the obstacles erected by powerful actors to stop them from arriving at their planned destination in the New World. Outlining first the policy directed towards Jewish migrants from Eastern Europe passing through the port of Antwerp, it will consider the Jewish migrants' responses to constraints imposed upon them. The focus is on the first quarter of the twentieth century, as this was a period in which international migration slowly but steadily became a focus of state intervention. By the second quarter of the twentieth century, the era of experimentation was over. In 1924, the American Congress passed a draconian quota law, and the U.S.

authorities found the means to limit transatlantic migration in an efficient manner for the next four decades. Before 1925 a very small number of Jewish migrants was sent back at Ellis Island while quite a few who had planned to migrate overseas were forced to stay in Belgium. It turns out, however, that most of these Jewish migrants, by dint of sheer grit and determination, did succeed in executing their original migration project.

Jewish Transit Migration Through the Port of Antwerp

The number of Jewish transatlantic migrants originating in imperial Russia and Austria-Hungary and moving through Antwerp remained small until the very end of the nineteenth century, when the numbers exploded. The peak years were 1906 and 1907. Nearly 80,000 people from the Russian and Austro-Hungarian Empires, mainly Jews, left the continent through Antwerp. After a dip in 1908, the upward trend resumed, and in 1913, almost 90,000 people from these countries left through the Belgian port for the New World.[4]

The mass migration to the U.S. was no stampede or unselective flight. Transatlantic migration was structured and selective. Most migrants did not leave for the unknown. Mostly pioneers left their place of birth and if they found they were on economic solid ground, they called upon their relatives and friends to join them, which established a pattern of chain migration. Although separated by wide oceans, emigrants stayed in close contact with the home region. As Adam Walaszek shows in this volume, emigrants seldom left their homelands without knowing exactly where to go, how to get there, and even what kind of work they would do. The head of the Belgian emigration service mentions this as early as 1895: "Out of 1000 emigrants, 950 know in which state, city or village they will settle."[5]

John Bodnar has pointed out that Jewish migration, in contrast to other migration flows to America, had a gender balance.[6] This does not mean that Jewish emigrants moved in family units. As Gur Alroey has shown, the migration pattern of these families was characterized by two stages. In the first stage, male heads of household went in advance to the U.S. where they prepared everything for the arrival of their dependents. When they became financially able to support their family members and to fund the journey for those left behind, they sent remittances or the steamship tickets themselves, the so-called pre-paid tickets.[7]

By the early twentieth century, more than thirty percent of the tickets for passage to the U.S. were sold by agents residing in the U.S. These travel agents did business with a relative of the travelers, a relative already in the U.S. who paid for the crossing.[8] This follow-on migration was abruptly stopped due to the First World War. Thousands of fathers, brothers, and husbands were separated for four years from their family members. Shortly after the end of the war, in 1920, European Jewish aid organizations, investigating the emigration potential in Eastern Europe, concluded that 65,000 Jews would be emigrating in the very near future. According to these estimates, 86 percent of these 65,000 emigrants would join a close relative.[9] Thirty-nine percent would be wives and children of U.S inhabitants who had left Eastern Europe before the war. They were immediately proven correct. Of the estimated 75,000 Jewish immigrants to the United States in 1920, 92 percent came to join immediate family or other close relatives. Women and children made up three-fourths of these migrants.[10]

Between July 1920 and December 1921, a total of one hundred thousand transit migrants passed through the port of Antwerp.[11] Of these, the Jewish aid organization had registered 11,281 by December 1921, 55 percent of whom were Polish citizens, 25 percent Romanian, and 12 percent Russian. This was largely a follow-on migration, confirmed by the large share of female migrants (34 percent) and children under the age of eleven (17 percent) among those registered by the Jewish aid organization.[12] The quick recovery of the transatlantic traffic in Antwerp can be explained by the fact that the ports of Hamburg and Bremen were closed for overseas traffic until the end of 1921. In addition, this quick recovery was connected to the policy of English shipping companies like the Cunard Line, the White Star Line, and the Canadian Pacific Railway Company, which had selected the port of Antwerp to bring all their East European passengers through to reach England. About 20 percent of the transit migrants who left Antwerp for overseas destinations in 1920 and 1921 sailed from ports in Liverpool and Glasgow to America.[13] The mass migration was hampered considerably by the end of 1921 – a prelude to the virtual closing of the border by 1925.[14]

The Policy Towards Jewish Migrants Passing Through Antwerp

From the 1860s onwards, there was a consensus among political elites in Western Europe and North America that immigration should not be regulated. This was the heyday of liberalism and the belief in the beneficial effect of the free interplay of market forces. At worst, European states refused destitute immigrants and criminals access to their territory. Law-abiding, able-bodied immigrants could migrate through the North Atlantic space without hindrance.

When the legal authorities in the U.S. decided that migration was a federal domain, Congress quickly synchronized its legislation with that of Europe. In 1882, Congress enacted the first immigration law and charged border control officers with the power to refuse admittance to "any convict, lunatic, idiot, or any person unable to take care of himself or herself without becoming a public charge." In the same year, immigration policy was racialized by largely excluding immigrants from China.[15] The legislation was an expression of the changing American attitudes towards immigration. The rise of anti-immigration feeling was shaped by the then-emerging economic crisis. In the 1890s, the U.S. became the trendsetter of a restrictive immigration policy and developed an administrative capacity to control immigration. But since the U.S. was a liberal regime in need of an unrestricted inflow of labor to meet the enormous demand of its booming industrial economy, this new American state capacity was used in a restrained manner. Only after the First World War would the American authorities decide to use the administrative capacities developed since the 1880s to call mass immigration to a halt.

The economic crisis of the last quarter of the nineteenth century, combined with the cholera epidemic of 1892, offered nativist forces leverage to push through broader exclusionary practices. These nativist forces considered mass immigration as a threat to the integrity of the American nation. Organized labor wanted immigration to be curtailed not only for nation-building considerations but also because newcomers offered economic competition in the labor market. Immigration control stations were set up. The most important was Ellis Island, opened in 1892. A medical check became part of immigration control. Those who were considered unfit for industrial America were debarred. Not only people carrying diseases but anyone who, in the opinion of the Ellis Island medical staff, could not meet the productivity requirements of the industrial world was to be rejected. The insane as well as deaf and feeble-minded immigrants could be barred from entering U.S. territory.[16]

Early twentieth-century American immigration policy became a public-private mix in which transport companies were lured by financial incentives. Expenses incurred for the return of "unfit" passengers had to be paid by the transportation companies. In these ways, the American authorities wanted to make the transport companies accountable for unwanted immigration even as the authorities tried to involve them heavily in their immigration policy. The main shipping line sailing from Antwerp to New York, the Red Star Line (RSL), became a subcontractor for American immigration policy from 1898 onwards. The Red Star Line organized its own team of medical examiners in the port of Antwerp to exclude those immigrants who they could foresee might be turned back upon arrival at Ellis Island. In this manner, those migrants deemed medically unfit by American standards were barred from ever leaving Antwerp.[17]

The medical check-up in Antwerp was rigorous to ensure that no immigrant liable to deportation was able to board the carrier. The Red Star Line had done its arithmetic; this policy of prevention cost less than the maintenance and repatriation of passengers who would be turned back in New York. For example, RSL physicians rejected any migrant with an eye infection, which they diagnosed as trachoma.[18] In contrast, the Belgian government's medical inspectors who also inspected the transit migrants allowed those migrants to pass through and complained that Red Star Line doctors made no distinction between trachoma and other infections. Diagnosing trachoma at an early stage was not a simple matter in this period, and the Red Star Line physicians did not want to take any risks. It was better to refuse too many than too few.[19] The general exclusion rate of the American authorities at Ellis Island when it started was 1 percent. There was a slight rise to 1.5 percent by 1914.[20] Given the low numbers of immigrants being refused entry to the United States by American immigration policy, it appears to have been little more than symbolic. Economic interests and the wish of political parties not to antagonize their ethnic constituents explain this lenient policy on the East Coast. Those interests were also used by ethnic lobbyists advocating a liberal, non-discriminatory policy and representing themselves as spokespersons of immigrant voters.[21] Thus, more migrants were kept from entering U.S. territory by the control subcontracted to the transportation companies than by immigration services in the harbor of New York.

After the First World War, new grounds for refusal were added to immigration legislation. The Immigration Act of 1917 included a literacy test. With the passage of that act, immigrants over the age of sixteen years would have to show that they could read a recognized language. This became the first general restriction that applied to all immigrants, but if the head of a household was literate, his female dependent was free to enter the country regardless of whether she was literate or not. There was a strong belief in the U.S. that the country was about to receive an unprecedented flood of immigrants from war-torn Europe. This belief appeared to be confirmed by rising immigration rates in 1921, the first year that civilian shipping resumed its full capacity. In fact, in the first decade of the twentieth century, immigration averaged almost 900,000 a year, while in 1921 only 650,000 immigrants were admitted. The movement to restrict immigration gained momentum. The severe post-war depression started in the summer of 1920 and lasted until the spring of 1922. It also fueled the movement that advocated immigration restrictions. In 1921, these restrictionists secured approval for a numerical cap on immigration – namely, a percentage of the number of foreign-born from each country listed in the 1910 population census. The result was ethnic discrimination, a policy that established national quotas on the basis of one's country of origin. Between 1922 and 1924, a maximum number of 350,000 persons were admitted to the U.S. Within each country's quota, allocations were on a monthly basis and worked on the basis of first come, first served. Once the limits were reached, immigrants were refused entry even if they had a visa.[22]

In addition to these broad grounds for exclusion, the visa became an innovative tool used in the selection of immigrants. Wartime security concerns in Europe had imposed passport requirements for all travelers going abroad. The passport obligation enabled the American authorities to impose a statutory counterpart after 1918: the U.S. visa. This was the way to control immigration at its source, since entry permits were now granted before departure.[23] Consuls were instructed to refuse visas in the country they were assigned once the quota of that country was filled. The new system required a more efficient administration that was only attained by the middle of the decade. From then onwards, the consular officers sought to fill their quota with only the most desirable immigrants. To that end, in 1926, the U.S. authorities in Antwerp opened a medical inspection station.

By 1930 this was generalized to the whole of Europe. About 5 percent of the applicants were rejected in these stations. Remote control was now firmly in public hands, and the transport companies lost their pivotal role in American immigration policy.[24]

In the meantime the 1924 Act further reduced the number of immigrants admitted. A ratio of only two percent of the American population would be admitted. This diminished the annual quota to about 180,000 immigrants. More importantly, the baseline of the quota system was pushed back to the census of 1890, a time when the heaviest immigration from Eastern Europe still had not started.[25]

In the wake of America's restrictionist policy, British and Canadian immigration authorities stepped up their control. Remote control would remain the most important migration control mechanism of these countries. The visa system and border control gave public authorities the power to manage migration efficiently. The continental European countries had a harder time slowing or halting immigration due to their land (or green) borders with the East and South European emigration regions. Moreover, the political elites in continental Europe still considered a largely uncontrolled immigration flow beneficial.

It is unclear whether American restrictionist policy in the first quarter of the twentieth century influenced the volume of migration from Eastern Europe, but it definitely influenced the direction. Shortly after the First World War, the intervention of the American authorities in migration caused a fundamental shift in the destinations of Jewish migrants from Eastern Europe. Continental Western Europe became the final stop for the Jewish mass migrations of the 1920s.

How Transit Migrants Got into Trouble

Different kinds of obstacles confronted migrants on their voyage to the New World. Being short of funds could impede a quick transit through Europe. Spending too much on travel to the port or while waiting for the ship, or being robbed could prove devastating for migrants.[26] The migration pattern of Jewish migrants – the male head of household leaving first, and his dependents following later – created special problems. Once the men were settled in America with a minimum of security, they contacted a travel agency to bring their wives and children over. The trip was usually paid in two installments – one when the contract was signed, and the second due before the family boarded the ship at the port city. During the economic crisis of 1907-1908, many East European Jews in the United States were not able to come up with the second installment. As a consequence, wives and children arriving in Antwerp were stranded there. These women and children became an important clientele for the local Jewish charity organizations.[27]

Other transit migrants successfully arrived at Ellis Island only to find they couldn't enter the country because they were considered paupers. David Hershik was such a case. He arrived at Ellis Island to join his uncle and told the authorities he had left a pregnant wife and a child behind but that his uncle would provide for him. When, in response to an inquiry, his uncle said that he himself was a poor man with six children, the authorities refused to accept him as a guarantor. They considered David Hershik likely to become a public charge, and therefore he was denied entrance and sent back to Antwerp.[28]

Most of the transit migrants debarred at Ellis Island but also in Antwerp itself were stranded because of reasons associated with their medical examination. As noted, about three percent of passengers were denied passage by the Red Star Line in Antwerp or entry at Ellis Island due to a diagnosis of trachoma.[29] Another reason for refusal at either end of the line was mental illness. These cases are well documented because those migrants usually required the help of others to sort out the situation for them. Marie Dutka from Galicia came to Antwerp with her husband and three children in August 1904 to emigrate to Canada. While the four other members of her family left Antwerp for Canada, she was debarred from the ship and sent to an asylum close to Antwerp, in Duffel. On 19 October 1904, she planned to board a vessel bound for Canada again, but she was overtaken by such a deep fear on the day of departure that she could not leave the asylum.[30]

Other mentally ill emigrants were refused entry to the U.S. at Ellis Island. Seventeen-year-old Chaja Grodsky from Lithuania in Czarist Russia is a case in point. In the summer of 1904 she had received a prepaid ticket for the Red Star Line from her uncle who was living in New York. On arrival at Ellis Island, the medical staff considered her feeble-minded and she was returned to Europe. Back in Antwerp, Chaja was transferred to the insane asylum in Duffel.[31] Joseph Helmans, a fifty-seven-year-old Rumanian worker embarked in the port of Antwerp in the summer of 1905 and passed successfully through Ellis Island. He started a new life in New York City, but after a few months he was struck by madness. The 1891 Immigration Act authorized the deportation of anyone who was likely to become a public charge within one year after arrival. Under the provisions of this act, Joseph Helmans was sent back to Antwerp and interned in an insane asylum.[32]

After the First World War, mentally ill immigrants continued to be debarred in Antwerp or at Ellis Island. Etta Gorka Nudelman, born in Warsaw in 1913, was set to sail from Antwerp to New York with her mother and brother in September 1921 to join her grandfather in the U.S. The shipping line refused to board the eight-year-old girl because she was considered retarded. She was left in Antwerp on her own.[33] Rachel Zylbergeld was thirteen years old when she arrived at Ellis Island on October 1921 with her brother and mother. She was diagnosed as feeble-minded and returned to Antwerp. Both Rachel and Etta were placed in a Jewish orphanage.[34] David Hirschfeld suffered a similar experience. In 1921, at age twenty-three, he left Poland together with his mother and two sisters for Antwerp where they boarded a ship for New York. The rest of his family was already in

Chicago. Suffering from schizophrenia, David was not permitted to disembark at Ellis Island and was sent back to Antwerp. He was sent to the same mental institution where Joseph Helmans had stayed before the war.[35]

Stories like those of David and Rachel, two fragile individuals separated from their families at Ellis Island, became the subject matter of Sholom Asch's novel, *America*, in which a son is separated from his family because of a bodily defect. Asch describes the anger of the father:

> His heart was burning with an indignant sense of outrage, and his lips tight shut. He dramatized inwardly a long remonstrance before "Americas evil-doers." To tear a father from his children – who even heard the like? An outcry rose from his inwards: verily, this exceeds the wickedness of Sodom! What was he expected to do? Throw this child into the water? Do they mean to deport the lad?[36]

These cases show the determination of the American immigration authorities to impose a selection process on newcomers to America. Though few were stopped at the border, for those who were considered unwanted, even if they were children, there were no mitigating circumstances.

In addition, after the First World War, the grounds for refusal multiplied. In 1922, Hinda Chane Grosbard arrived in Antwerp at the age of fifty-seven. She was a Polish Jew and a widow who wanted to join her four children living in the U.S. Nevertheless she was not permitted to leave for the U.S. when authorities determined she was illiterate.[37] Other migrants were refused because they did not have the right papers. After the First World War, passports were necessary for international travel and East European Jews also needed a visa for the U.S. and for each transit country, which clearly formed a new hindrance to international travel. In the early 1920s, most migrants who were stranded in Antwerp could not leave for the U.S. – not because of personal defects but because the U.S. had filled the national quota for their country. In January 1924, for example, there were about 5,000 Russians in Western Europe waiting to leave for the United States, of whom about 250 were in Antwerp. The quota for Russia had been met, and these migrants would be able to depart in June at the earliest. Because the new quota allocated to Russia was limited to 1,792 people annually, the departure of all 5,000 Russians would take years.[38]

The Belgian Authorities and Stranded Jewish Migrants

By the early twentieth century, there was growing hostility towards the Red Star Line in Belgian official circles, as the authorities were forced to foot the bill of the U.S. admission policy. An earlier law passed on 14 December 1876 stipulated that transport companies had to abide by the laws of the country of departure and arrival. When a ticket was sold to a migrant who was not allowed to disembark, not only did the price of the ticket have to be reimbursed, the stranded migrant could also charge the transport companies for the costs of food and lodging while in Antwerp. When delays were caused by the shipping agency itself, the Belgian authorities required the transport company to reimburse the living expenses of their passengers at two francs a day. But passengers stranded in Antwerp due to the American immigration policy seem to have been considered *force majeure*.[39] By threatening to withdraw the license of the companies, the Belgian authorities could have exerted additional pressure to reimburse the costs, but it seems that before the First World War the Belgian authorities hardly did so. It was, however, put on the political agenda a few times.[40]

By 1893, Belgian authorities tried to address the problem of stranded migrants by granting entry into Belgium only to those who had the means to pay for their own repatriation. In part, this was due to a cholera epidemic in some regions of Russia and a very strong American reaction, if not overreaction, to the inflow of Jewish migrants from the Russian Empire. At that time, the Red Star Line and other shipping companies lobbied the Belgian authorities strongly and successfully for an inhibited flow of transit migrants. The shipping agencies had promised they would assume the cost of repatriating all stranded migrants. However, when the Belgian authorities tried to make this oral concession into a contractual obligation, the shipping agencies refused to do so.[41] The urgency of the problem waned when the cholera epidemic ended, and the Belgian authorities did not insist any further.

In 1903, the Red Star Line adamantly refused to pay for the repatriation and living expenses of migrants stranded in Antwerp if they had been refused by RSL's own doctors on medical grounds.[42] In 1906, at the peak of the transit movement, Eugène Venesoen, the Belgian Emigration Commissioner, called upon the authorities to stop the invasion: "(Just) As America, we have to protect ourselves against the invasion of undesirable people, suffering from defects and who cannot render any service to our population."[43] Venesoen attributed the rise of the Jewish community in Antwerp to the stranded transit migrants. In September 1906, in an alarmist report, he estimated the number of Russians stranded in Antwerp since 1905 to be at least 1,500.[44] His figure is difficult to verify, and given that it was used as part of a political strategy to restrict immigration, this estimate should not be considered reliable.

The number of stranded migrants considered a nuisance seems to have remained manageable for the Belgian authorities, since no drastic public action was taken against this inflow or against the shipping companies, the magnet attracting these migrants. Until the First World War, transit migration flow remained largely uncontrolled. Free mobility was a corollary of free trade and was in these liberal times considered a benefit to all. The business interests in the growing popularity of tourism as well as the transatlantic migrants' trade were powerful economic motives that favored unrestricted international mobility.

The only migrants stranded in Antwerp for whom the Red Star Line was willing to pay repatriation were those who could not continue travel to the New World due to mental illness. When it took several months before they were considered fit enough to be repatriated, their stay in a mental asylum was paid for by the Belgian authorities. In June 1905, the asylum director in Duffel claimed that Chaja Grodsky's mental situation had improved – "she was slowly coming back to her senses and anyway she was very meek" (author's translation). He determined that, if she were accompanied, she could go home. Her father Chaïm Grodsky, who was still in Russia, had kept in touch with his daughter. He was completely willing to have his daughter back, but he was not able to pay for her stay in the asylum nor for her trip home. The Red Star Line agreed to pay for Chaja's trip. On 31 July 1905, one year after she had left Lithuania in Czarist Russia, she returned home. During this trip, she was accompanied by a Belgian military officer. The Red Star Line also paid for the round trip of this officer.[45] The mental patients mentioned above were also repatriated at the expense of the Red Star Line. Respectively after eleven and seven months in an insane asylum, Marie Dutka and Joseph Helmans were considered in sufficient health to be repatriated.[46] Handling their repatriation was largely a symbolic gesture by the Red Star Line in order to appease the Belgian (and American) authorities and to prevent having obligations imposed on them by law.[47]

Repatriation was the preferred solution of the Belgian authorities to the problem of stranded migrants. Aid organizations also tried to convince the stranded to return "home." But repatriation represented the total failure of the migration project and was not an option for most of the migrants.[48] Using force to return stranded migrants was not straightforward. Many were a long way from home and, in order to return, they had to pass through the German Empire. In the 1880s, Germany resented the Russian and Austro-Hungarian subjects who had been forced to leave the Netherlands, France, and Belgium but who were unable to return home directly due to their lack of adequate financing. Some ended up stranded in Germany, thereby increasing its population of poor but also ethnically unwanted individuals, given the German authorities' interest in an ethnically homogenous German population. In 1884, the German authorities imposed a national logic upon deportation procedures. Destitute aliens who had been expelled to the German Reich by the police force of neighboring countries were rejected at the Prussian border. Only if these migrants could prove they needed to pass through the German Empire to return home and only if they could show sufficient funding for their fare would the Prussian border guards allow them to cross the border.[49] Nevertheless, the German authorities found that, even if these returnees had funding, the selective border control was not very effective. In some cases, the Russian or Galician Jews whose return was subsidized by the Belgian authorities or by the transport agencies, saw arrival at the Cologne train station in Germany as an opportunity to sell their return ticket.[50] The small capital they accrued from this sale gave them an opportunity to either settle in Germany or attempt departure overseas on another occasion.

In the early 1920s in Antwerp, when migrants were denied entrance to the U.S. at Ellis Island because their national quota had been filled, they lodged complaints with the Belgian migration department. In this they were helped by the Jewish aid organization, Ezrah. The Belgian authorities argued that the transport lines knew of the quotas and that they had enough advance time to prevent these returns. Furthermore, they insisted that the shippers were financially responsible for all costs caused by America's restrictive immigration policy.[51] The White Star Line, which had started massive operations in Antwerp in 1920, refused to pay and even questioned the authority of the Belgian state in this matter. "As the passengers are not of Belgian nationality, we fail to see what jurisdiction the Authorities at Antwerp have in this matter."[52] This refusal to even consider compensation was not well received by the Belgian authorities, but the outcome of these disputes is unknown.

How Jewish Transit Migrants Coped with their Forced Stay in Antwerp

Migrants who were short of funds tried to get to the New World the cheapest way possible. At the end of 1906, between eight and ten Russian stowaways were discovered every time the ships of the Canadian Pacific were set to sail.[53] Those debarred at Ellis Island because of the likelihood of becoming a "public charge" were a bit more cunning on their second trip to the U.S. [54] Those who were stranded in Antwerp due to lack of money did odd jobs or had relatives send them money. Other migrants tried alternative routes to reach America. Canada was a much-used backdoor and other American ports aside from New York were known for greater leniency in controlling the influx of migrants. In 1904, a transatlantic steamship line run by the Canadian Pacific Railroad company opened in Antwerp. Antwerp turned into a nodal point for illegal migration to the U.S. through Canada.[55]

Some migrants took years to execute their migration project. An example is the story of sixty-year-old Jacob Leschinsky who arrived in Brussels in 1907 with his wife, Baelia Hoerevitsch. He listed his occupation as Hebrew teacher. The couple only had the meager funds sent to them by their children in the U.S. Leschinsky and his wife survived by begging and from the limited support they received from the local Jewish community. Although they were born in Russia, they had come to Brussels from London. When asked how long they would stay in Brussels, they answered they had not the faintest idea. A few months later they moved on to Bremen. In October 1909, they returned to Belgium and took up residence in Antwerp. Finally in 1910, after having tried to depart from British, Belgian, and German ports, they sailed from Antwerp to the United States to join their children.[56] Fifteen years later, Hinda Chane Grosbard, who had been refused passage at Antwerp in 1922 because she was illiterate, had to stay in Belgium for more than two years before she could join her children in the U.S. She received about 300 dollars annually from her children to cover her living expenses.[57]

Hinda Chane Crosbard, Jacob Leschinsky, and his wife were all supported by their children and by the local Jewish aid committee. Just before the war, only about eight percent of the transit migrants contacted the Jewish aid organization in Antwerp in any given year, and only one percent received some kind of financial aid. This increased to 12 percent and nine percent respectively by 1921.[58] Before the war, most of the financial aid given by Jewish charity organizations was spent on shipping tickets, while immediately after the war nearly half of their budget went to food and lodging. Such aid had been limited before the war to, at most, twenty-four days in order to encourage the migrants to communicate with friends and relatives. After the war, this timeframe was no longer upheld.[59]

Even if transit life became much more difficult, most of the migrants arrived at their intended destinations. Their determination to execute their original plan sustained them, and relatives and the local Jewish community gave them practical support. Ezrah contacted relatives of the migrants for financial support. It also directly subsidized the departure of these transit migrants by providing tickets, and gave them pocket money and better clothes. According to the Russian-Jewish journal of the Jewish Colonization Association, Der Yidisher Emigrant, emigrants' dress was important. The American immigration officers took appearance into serious consideration. Being clean and clothed in a respectable manner prevented a transit migrant from being treated as a pauper.[60] And because the American authorities had imposed a head tax on all arriving immigrants from 1882 onwards, small sums were given to needy emigrants so they would not arrive in America penniless. After the First World War, administrative formalities such as passports and visas became even more important. The Jewish aid organization in Belgium spent five percent of its budget in 1920-1921 on the necessary papers for East European Jews. Before 1914, proper papers had hardly been an issue.[61]

After the First World War, because illiteracy was grounds for refusing a migrant entry to the U.S., the Jewish aid organization set up a school in Antwerp to remedy the problem. Medical treatment also helped stranded migrants to qualify for the transatlantic journey by curing them of simple ailments.[62]

Others who did not qualify for migration to the United States moved on to Great Britain, usually not considered an end station. For many poor Jews, Great Britain was just another stage in their transatlantic journey.[63] From 1905 onwards, Britain erected its own immigration barriers: each emigrant had to carry five pounds. But this did not impede the flow from Belgium to Britain. It only increased the price for crossing the English Channel. Russian and Galician Jews stranded in Belgium had to buy second-class tickets, as the Belgian shipping lines abolished all third-class tickets to Britain. This, however, had the added benefit of relieving all patrons from examination. Only vessels with more than twenty steerage passengers were classified as migrant ships and subject to inspection.[64]

America's restrictive immigration policy in the end only delayed the original migration project. It did not cause many to abandon plans. When they had acquired basic reading skills, were cured of disease, or when they were finally included in the quota, these transit migrants were keen to move on and execute their original plan.[65] Even in the early 1920s, very few who were stranded in Belgium settled there permanently, nor did they return to Poland or Russia. Nevertheless, the transit in Belgium could take years. Even those transit migrants who found work in Belgium moved on as soon as it was possible.[66] In 1923, the cobbler Leib Moszek Lesz arrived in Antwerp from Warsaw. He was twenty-seven years old. He had married Eva Sapirsztein about a year and a half before, and his wife was already in New York. He wanted to join her. Two years later, he was still in Belgium asking for a permanent residence permit there, "as he had abandoned all hope of being able to leave for America." Records show that he finally left Belgium in 1926 for an unknown destination, never to return.[67]

Among those who stayed in Belgium, the mentally ill were clearly overrepresented. None of the seven Jewish emigrants who were stranded in Antwerp after the war due to mental illness were repatriated. They all stayed in Belgium. The best-documented case is David Hirschfeld who was sent back from Ellis Island because of schizophrenia. From 1925 onwards, he stayed in the psychiatric hospital of Geel, which worked on the basis of de-institutionalized care. Patients were placed with a host family. David Hirschfeld was a resident in two families, first for fifteen years with the Loots family and then from 1945 onwards with the Mols family. His brothers in Chicago paid for the costs of his stay in Belgium through a Jewish organization. It appears the organization kept in regular contact with him. When, in 1959, David was transferred to hospital because of a lung disease, he informed his brother in Chicago. His brother wrote the director of the asylum saying that David "wanted to move back to the family of 'Mols,' where he had been quite happy for a very long time when he resided with them."[68] Shortly afterwards, David returned to the Mols family and stayed there until his death in 1967.[69] Eight-year-old Etta Gorka Nudelman, who could not board ship with her mother and brother in 1922 because of mental retardation, was placed in a Jewish orphanage in Antwerp. In 1940, at age twenty-seven, she was also transferred to Geel and remained there until she died in 1965.[70] The feeble-minded Rachel Zylbergeld, who had been sent back from Ellis Island at age thirteen, was put in the Antwerp Jewish orphancy. She was financially supported by her mother who resided in the U.S. until Rachel was eighteen. After 1927, all contact (and financial transfers) with her mother stopped. Rachel Zylbergeld remained in Belgium for the rest of her life.[71]

In contrast to similar cases before the war, these mentally ill Jewish migrants were not repatriated. Their very different fate is probably due to the fact that they were the last of their families to leave for the U.S. When misfortune struck and all other family members went on to the U.S., there was little to return to in Eastern Europe. Therefore these stranded migrants stayed in Belgium, stuck between their Old World in Eastern Europe and the New World. For them, the door to the U.S. remained closed. For many other Jews who wanted to leave Eastern Europe in the 1920s, the American door remained equally closed.

East European Jews who arrived in Antwerp from the mid-1920s onwards had already given up the hope of leaving for overseas. Their destinations now were Belgium and France. France, and in particular Paris, had already attracted East European Jews in ever greater numbers by the beginning of the twentieth century.[72] Belgium gained mass appeal in the 1920s. Until 1914, Jewish settlement migration to Antwerp from Eastern Europe had been a very selective immigration flow. Antwerp as a port attracted Russian Jewish grain traders who underpinned the intensive traffic between Russian ports and Antwerp.[73] At the end of the eighteenth century, Antwerp had gained prominence as a diamond center and could attract jewelers from Russia, mainly from Odessa and Bialystock, but mostly diamond traders from Galicia and in particular from Krakow. These two economic sectors which were increasingly dominated by East European entrepreneurs also seem to have exercised a pull on less wealthy Jews in Eastern Europe. While Antwerp had a few thousand people active in the diamond sector at the end of the nineteenth century, the number of diamond workers alone had risen to 14,000 by 1914.[74] Those people were a selective lot, by region of origin as well as by professional qualifications.[75] Only in the 1920s would the pull of Belgium on Eastern European Jews be less selective.

Conclusion

Different Jewish migration flows to Antwerp should be distinguished, each with its own logic. Analysis shows a very limited overlap between them. The migration flow through Antwerp from Eastern Europe to the U.S. is different from highly selective migration in which Belgium was the final destination. Emigration to the Antwerp diamond industry and the grain trade had little to do with the Jewish mass migration to the U.S. Only when the U.S. started to close its borders did Jewish emigrants from East Europe, a very heterogeneous lot, start to look for a new destination, and only then did Belgium gain mass appeal among Jews.

Before 1925, the barriers erected by the U.S. were not solid enough for the Jewish migrants to change their plans. The presence of stranded Jewish transit migrants in Antwerp was ephemeral, and only a few of them finally settled in Belgium. Jewish migrants were not solitary individuals moving to America. They were whole families, some of whom had started a new life in the New World already and had firmly turned their backs on the Old World by the early 1920s. In the light of this migration dynamic, the determination of the follow-on migrants to arrive in America is comprehensible. Most migrants stranded in Antwerp had relatives in America who took care of them and the migrants' aid organizations offered a hand in getting them back on track. Before 1924, the authorities could at most postpone the plans of these migrants but not cancel them. Transit life became more difficult after the First World War. While the mentally ill at the beginning of the twentieth century could return to the old home when some family members were still there, this was no longer the case after the war. Whole families were transplanted. There was no way back to the Old World. Only from the mid-1920s onwards, when the American authorities closed the door to the New World for new immigrants, did stranded migrants stay put. Only then did Antwerp come to the fore as a new destination for the East European migrants.

Notes

1. Gerald Y. Goldberg, "'Ireland is the only country,' Joyce and the Jewish dimension," in *The Crane Bag Book of Irish Studies*, eds. M. P. Hederman and R. Kearney (Dublin: Blackwater Press, 1977-1984), 5-12; Nick Harris, *Dublin's Little Jerusalem* (Dublin: A. & A. Famar, 2001). We thank Rosa Reicher for bringing this story and its bibliography to our attention.

2. Ó Gráda Cormac, "Notes on the Early History of Cork Jewry," in *Gerald Goldberg: A tribute*, eds. Dermot Keogh and Diarmud Whelan (Blackrock: Mercier Press, 2008), 73-100.

3. Tobias Brinkmann, "Travelling with Ballin: The impact of American Immigration Policies on Jewish Transmigration within Central Europe, 1880-1914," *International Review of Social History* 53 (2008): 480.

4. These figures are based on the annual reports of the Emigration Commissioner. Archive Ministry of Foreign Affairs Brussels, Emigration, 2020, VIII, 2951, I-IV and 2953 I-II and Provincial Archive Antwerp [henceforth, PAA], Landverhuizing- Emigratie, 45, 54, 67.

5. Annual report of the Emigration Commissioner 1895. PAA, Scheepvaart, 83.

6. John Bodnar, *The Transplanted: A History of Immigrants in Urban America* (Bloomington: University of Indiana Press, 1987), 20.

7. Gur Alroey, "And I Remained Alone in a Vast Land: Women in the Jewish Migration from Eastern Europe," *Jewish Social Studies: History, Culture, Society* 12.3 (2006): 50-51.

8. Torsten Feys, "Prepaid tickets to ride to the New World: the New York Continental Conference and transatlantic steerage fares 1885-1895," *Revista de Historia Economica – Journal of Iberian and Latin American Economic History* 26.2 (2008): 173-204; Dillingham Commission Reports (Washington: Government Printing Office, 1911), vol. 3: 359-363.

9. Conférence de Bruxelles, 7.8.1921. Yiddisher Visns Haftelekher Institut, New York [henceforth, YIVO], folder 131/5960-6071 (MKM 1.5).

10. Lloyd P. Gartner, "Women in the great Jewish migration," *Jewish Historical Studies* 40 (2008): 133.

11. Walter Willcox, *International Migrations* (New York: Gordon and Breach, 1969), 617.

12. Interview with Emigration Commissioner in *Le Matin*, 18.6.1921. City archive Antwerp, 27.816; Ezrah, Report for the period 1.7.1920-31.12.1921 (in total 23.636 emigrants would have called upon the aid organization, but only 11.278 registered). At the Conférence de Bruxelles, 7.8.1921 (YIVO, folder 131/5960-6071 (MKM 1.5)), the representative of Erza mentions that between June 1920 and the first months of 1921 40,000 transit migrants had passed through the port of Antwerp and that 17,000 emigrants had called upon the Jewish aid organization for assistance.

13. PAA, Landverhuizing 1912-1993, 99, quoted by De Coster, *Eindverslag research in Provinciaal Archief*. In 1913, there had been 114,000 emigrants, of whom 14,000 went indirectly overseas, passing through England. Tobias Brinkmann, "Ort des Ubergangs-Berlin als Schnittstelle der jüdischen Migration aus Osteuropa nach 1918," in *Transit und Transformation. Osteuropäisch-jüdische Migranten in Berlin 1918-1939*, ed. Verena Dohrn and Gertrud Pickhan (Göttingen: Wallstein, 2010), 33; Willcox, *International Migration* (New York: Gordon and Breach, 1969), 617.

14. On the Canadian restrictive policy in the wake of the policy of the United States, see N. Kelley and M. Trebilcock, *The Making of the Mosaic: History of the Canadian Immigration Policy* (Toronto: University of Toronto Press, 1998).

15. In 1891, the phrase "persons who were unable to take care of themselves" was transmuted into "paupers or persons likely to become a public charge" or the "LPC clause" and would later be used to bar also able-bodied immigrants. Roger Daniels, *Guarding the Golden Door: American Immigration Policy and Immigrants Since 1882* (New York: Hill and Wang, 2004).

16. Amy L. Fairchild, *Science at the Borders: Immigration Medical Inspection and the Shaping of the Modern Industrial Labor Force* (Baltimore: John Hopkins UP, 2003); Vincent J. Cannato, *American Passage: The History of Ellis Island* (New York: HarperCollins, 2009), 127-260; Aristide Zolberg, *A Nation by Design: Immigration Policy in the Fashioning of America* (Harvard: Harvard University Press, 2006), 199-242.

17. Emigration Commissioner to Governor, 6.4.1898. PAA, Scheepvaart, 98. We presume 1898 is the year when the Red Star Line started to medically check the transit migrants before departure and thus not only to assure that they were fit for the voyage, but also to stop those from boarding the vessel who would be debarred in Ellis Island. However, the Belgian authorities (the only source on the Red Star Line, as there are no archives on the company) explicitly mentioned this broader objective no sooner than 1902. Emigration Commissioner to Governor, 25.4.1903. PAA, Scheepvaart, 98.

18. Trachoma is an eye disease that can lead to blindness if left untreated and, in the 1890s, was regarded at Ellis Island as a dangerous infectious disease; it was often a reason to deny entry to the U.S. Barbara Lüthi, *Invading bodies. Medizin und Immigration in den USA 1880-1920* (Frankfurt: Campus, 2009), 248-290; Krista Maglen, "Importing Trachoma. The Introduction into Britain of American Ideas of an 'Immigrant Disease,'" 1892-1906," *Immigrants and Minorities* 23 (2005): 87-99.

19. Annual report of the Emigration Commissioner, 1903, PAA, Scheepvaart, 67; Head of emigration inspection to governor, 6 April 1898, PAA, Scheepvaart, 98.

20. Frank Caestecker and Torsten Feys, "East European Jewish Migrants and Settlers in Belgium, 1880-1914: A Transatlantic Perspective," *East European Jewish Affairs* 40.3 (2010): 266-271.
21. Zolberg, *A Nation by Design*, 220-232.
22. Cannato, *American Passage*, 330-331.
23. Zolberg, *A Nation by Design*, 241; John Torpey, *The invention of the Passport, Surveillance, citizenship and the state* (Cambridge: Cambridge University Press, 2000).
24. Fairchild, *Science at the Borders*, 259ff.; Zolberg, *A Nation by Design*, 254.
25. Zolberg, *A Nation by Design*, 244.
26. Jean-Philippe Schreiber, *L'immigration juive en Belgique du moyen-âge à la première guerre mondiale* (Bruxelles: Editions de l'université de Bruxelles, 1996), 200. Schreiber refers to 418 Jews stranded in Antwerp in 1906 due to the bankruptcy of the travel agent who would have provided them with shipping tickets upon arrival in Antwerp.
27. Ezrah, *Société philanthropique pour la protection des émigrants*, Anvers Rapport 1907, Anvers, 1908, AAD, 1029; Gur Alroey, "Out of the Shtetl. On the trail of the Eastern Jewish emigrants to America," 1900-1914. *Leidschrift*, 22.1 (2007): 96; Lloyd P. Gartner, *The Jewish Immigrant in England, 1870-1914* (London: Simon Publications, 1973), 170-171.
28. David Toback, *The Journey of David Toback (As Retold by his Granddaughter Carole Malkin)* (New York: Schocken Books, 1992).
29. In September 1906, three percent of the passengers (n=1830) were not permitted to board a ship in Antwerp bound for the U.S. due to medical reasons: "Report on the conditions existing in Europe and Mexico affecting Emigration and Immigration being a compilation in digested form of reports submitted," 114. National Archives Washington, Records of Immigration and Naturalization Service [henceforth, NAW, RINS], 54411/1. Thanks to Torsten Feys for sharing this document with me. The Emigration Commissioner gave a similar figure but only for trachoma. He estimated that the Red Star Line's medical control rejected each week about fifteen to thirty Russian emigrants in 1906. Emigration Commissioner to Minister of Justice, 22 December 1906, General Belgian archives, Archives Aliens Department [henceforth, AAD], 265-268. See also AAD, individual alien's file, 1.422.625 and 1.489.597.
30. AAD, individual alien's file, 764.787.
31. AAD, individual alien's file, 772505; www.ellisisland.org, Chaja Grodsky (20.8.2010) (refers to list of alien passengers from the U.S. immigration officer at port of arrival).
32. AAD, individual alien's file, 782.563.
33. AAD, individual alien's file, 1.5222.408; www.ellisisland.org, Etla Nudelman (10.4.2011).
34. AAD, individual alien's file, A 126.787; www.ellisisland.org, Rachel Silberg...ld (10.4.2011) .
35. AAD, individual alien's file, 1.212.950. On the passenger list of Ellis Island, the file David Hirszfeld is marked as deported. www.ellisisland.org (10.4.2011).
36. Sholem Asch, *Amerika* (Warsaw/New York: 1911), 71-72. The novel was translated into English as *America* (New York: Alpha Omega Publishing Group, 1918), 93. Thanks to Michael Boyden for providing me with the original version.
37. AAD, individual alien's file, 1.368.768; See also AAD, 1029.

38. Red Star Line to Governemental Commissaire, 6.6.1924. PAA, Landverhuizing – Emigratie, 66 quoted by De Coster, *Eindverslag research in Provinciaal Archief*; AAD, 1029.

39. Torsten Feys, *De regeringspolitiek met betrekking tot de Belgische emigratie naar de Verenigde Staten via de haven van Antwerpen* (Gent: Universiteit Gent, unpublished Master's thesis, 2003), 179.

40. Another manner to force the transport companies to pay the bill is through private litigation. We are, however, unaware of court cases in which stranded transit migrants accused the shipping lines of breach of contract.

41. E. Spelkens, "Antwerp as a port of Emigration, 1843-1913," in *Two Studies on Emigration through Antwerp to the New World*, eds. G. Kurgan and E. Spelkens (Brussels: Center for American Studies, 1976), 73.

42. Emigration Commissioner to Governor, 25.4.1903. PAA, Scheepvaart, nr.76, quoted by De Coster, *Eindverslag research in Provinciaal Archief*.

43. Emigration Commissioner to Governor, 28 September 1906, AAD, 265-268; document quoted at length in Ronin, *Antwerpen en zijn 'Russen' Onderdanen van de tsaar, 1814-1948* (Gent: Stichting Mens en Kultuur, 1993), 229-231. Author's translation; Spelkens, "Antwerp as a Port of Emigration," 72-73.

44. Emigration Commissioner to Governor, 28.9.1906. AAD, 265-268.

45. AAD, individual alien's file, 772505.

46. AAD, individual alien's file, 764.787 and 782.563.

47. Letter of Minister of Justice to Minister of Foreign Affairs, 12 May 1905, PAA, Scheepvaart, 104 quoted by De Coster, *Eindverslag research in Provinciaal Archief*.

48. Schreiber, *L'immigration juive en Belgique*, 11; Toback, *The Journey of David Toback*, 11, 12.

49. Frank Caestecker "The Transformation of Nineteenth-Century West European Expulsion Policy, 1880-1914," in *Migration Control in the North Atlantic World. The Evolution of State Practices in Europe and the United States from the French Revolution to the Inter-War Period*, eds. A. Fahrmeier, O. Faron and P. Weil (New York/Oxford: Berghahn, 2003), 126-128.

50. Report of special immigrant inspector Marcus Braun in Report of the Commissioner General on immigration, 1903, 94, NAW, RINS, 52320/47; Brinkmann, "Travelling with Ballin," 479.

51. In January 1924, the Emigration Commissioner was still in negotiation with the Red Star Line about paying the living expenses of the migrants stranded in Antwerp. City archive Antwerp, Modern Archive, 27.816 quoted by De Coster, *Eindverslag research in Provinciaal Archief*.

52. Correspondence between F. Van den Abeele, agent of the White Star Line and Emigration Commissioner, 1921-1922. PAA, Toezichtscommissie van de dienst voor Landverhuizing 1912-1993, 94. General State Archive Beveren Waas, Archief van de Dienst voor Emigratie, 118.

53. Maritime commissaire to Minister of Justice, 22.12.1906. AAD, 265-268.

54. See Toback, *The Journey of David Toback*.

55. NAW, RINS, 52320/47, Marcus Braun, European investigation, 1903-1904, report 23 August 1903.

56. AAD, individual files, 855063. These were the only Russian transit migrants we came across in a random sample of about 1,000 immigrants registered by the Belgian authorities in 1904 (842) and 1906 (150). In this sample we counted 31 immigrants

from Russia. The sample is skewed in favor of arrivals in the fall. This caused an over-representation of students who arrived at the start of the academic year: 17 of these 31 migrants from Russia were coming to Belgium to follow higher education. Most Russians who were not students declared immediately upon arrival that they would be active in the diamond and grain trade. In these files there is hardly any reference to the ethnic or religious orientation of these migrants. For the registration of aliens in Belgium, see Frank Caestecker, Filip Strubbe and Pierre-Alain Tallier, *Individual files on foreigners opened by the Sûreté publique (Police des étrangers) (1835-1943)* (Brussel: Algemeen Rijksarchief, 2009); Frank Caestecker and Lieselotte Luyckx, "Het individuele vreem-delingendossier, een unieke bron over migratie en migranten?" in *Grensgevallen. De vreemdelingenadministratie in België*, ed. Pierre-Alain Tallier (Brussel: Rijksarchief, 2010), 15-28.

57. AAD, individual files, 1.368.768.

58. Conférence de Bruxelles, 7.8.1921. YIVO, folder 131/5960-6071 (MKM 1.5); Caestecker and Feys, *East European Jewish Migrants and Settlers*, 275. On Ezrah, see Vladimir Ronin, *Antwerpen en zijn 'Russen'*, 248-250 and Schreiber, *L'immigration juive en Belgique*, 338.

59. Alexander Harkavy, "Diary of a Visit to Europe in the Interests of Jewish Emigration," 1906-1907, 24. *American Jewish Historical Society*, Harkavy Papers, 5. Archival document generously put at our disposal by Gur Alroey [henceforth, Harkavy Diary]. The financial reports of Ezrah point out that in 1913, 70 percent of its expenses were spent on tickets. In the period 1.7.1920-31.12.1921, only 14 percent of the expenses went to tickets and five percent to travel documents, but 41 percent to food and lodging, expenses which only amounted to 24 percent of the budget in 1908. Caestecker and Feys, "East European Jewish Migrants and Settlers," 281; Ezrah, *Verslag voor de periode 1.7.1920-31.12.1921*.

60. The Jewish transit travelers in Belgium in *Der yidisher emigrant*, 14.12.1912 (24). An archival document generously put at our disposal by Gur Alroey and translated by the care of the team of the future migration museum in Antwerp, RSL People on the Move.

61. Ezrah, *Verslag voor de periode 1.7.1920-31.12.1921*; Hatikwah, organe bimensuel de la Fédération des Sionistes de Belgique, XV, 1922, 5, 59.

62. For example, medical treatment for trachoma could take a considerable time, and it seems that the public authorities in Antwerp rather than the Jewish aid organization paid the expenses due to this treatment. Governor to Minister of Foreign Affairs, 31.5.1894. PAA, Scheepvaart, 60; City archive Antwerp, MA 27816 quoted in De Coster, *Eindverslag research in Provinciaal Archief*. Immediately after the war, 11 percent of the expenses of Jewish charity went to medical assistance, while in 1908 this was only 3 percent of the budget. Ezrah, *Verslag voor de periode 1.7.1920-31.12.1921*. Sholem Aleichem wrote a novel on the transit migrants in which he evoked the lot of the Jewish girl Goldele who had to stay in Antwerp due to trachoma while her family left for the U.S. She was not yet cured after a treatment of one year. Sholem Aleichem, *Adventures of Mottel, the Cantor's Son* (New York: Henry Schuman, 1953).

63. According to an American official, Marcus Braun, rumors had it that it would be easier for diseased passengers to get to the U.S. from London. Report of special immigrant inspector Marcus Braun in Report of the Commissioner General on immigration,

1903, 88, NAW, RINS, 52320/47. The trip over the Channel from Belgium was inexpensive: in the 1890s, a one-way trip cost 14,70 francs. AAD, individual files, 467.272.

64. Maritime commissioner to Minister of Justice, 22 December 1906, AAD, 265; Report of agents sent to Europe, 1907, NAW, RINS, 54411/01; Karin Hofmeester, *Jewish Workers and the Labour Movement: A Comparative Study of Amsterdam, London and Paris (1870-1914)* (Ashgate: Imprint, 2004), 156-174.

65. Annual report of head of emigration inspection for 1898, PAA, Scheepvaart, 98.

66. Note 12.1.1924. Antwerp city archive, Modern Archive, 27.816. Correspondence between Emigration Commissioner and Ministry of Foreign Affairs, 7.1924. PAA, Landverhuizing-Emigratie, 66. On a sample of fifty Jewish transit migrants who were stranded in Belgium in the first half of the 1920s and most of whom were supported by Ezrah, Lars Vancompernolle found positive information that nearly half of them (22) finally arrived in the United States. Sometimes this took years to realize. On eighteen others, we have no conclusive data on their whereabouts, but as the alien police did not add any information on them, it is highly likely that they left Belgium but their destination is unknown. Eight of the fifty stayed in Belgium, seven of them due to mental illness. Lars Vancompernolle, *Oost-Europese Joden in België. Casestudies over Amerikareizigers in de Jaren 1920* (Gent: Universiteit Gent, unpublished Master's thesis), 100-154.

67. AAD, individual alien's file, 1.295.991. Author's translation.

68. James Hirschfield to Raedemaeckers, director of Geel, 11.12.1959. Patient file David Herschfeldt, mental institution Geel (documentation Dr. Carl Henrik Carlsson).

69. AAD, individual alien's file, 1.212.950; *Nieuwsblad van Geel*, 22 September 1995, 4; Interview Bernard Levatin (David's nephew) and other relatives by Carl Henrik Carlsson. Dr. Carl Henrik Carlsson (Göteburg) put his documentation generously at my disposal.

70. AAD, individual alien's file, 1.5222.408.

71. AAD, individual alien's file, A 126.787.

72. Of the 50 debarred transmigrants of the first half of the 1920s whose trajectory Lars van Compernolle analyzed, two moved on to France. Vancompernolle, *Oost-Europese Joden*, 100-154. Just before the First World War, the Belgian Jewish committee in Brussels insisted that destitute stranded migrants move to Paris, as assistance was more likely to be available for them, given that the Jewish community in the French capital was wealthier than in Brussels. Schreiber, *L'immigration juive en Belgique*, 180-181. In France by 1914, 44,000 East European Jews settled down, mostly after 1905. Nancy Green, "A Tale of Three Cities: Immigrant Jews in New York, London and Paris, 1870-1914," in *Patterns of Emigration, 1850-1914*, eds. Aubrey Newman and Stephen W. Massil, (London: Jewish Historical Society of England and the Institute of Jewish Studies, University College, 1996), 201-206.

73. Ronin, *Antwerpen en zijn 'Russen,'* 275-279.

74. These, at least, are the figures given by De Coster of the emigration service. Heertje, as quoted by Schreiber in *L'immigration juive en Belgique*, mentions 7,200 diamond workers in 1913. De Coster to the Governor, 31.5.1919; PAA, Landverhuizing-Emigratie, 102; Ronin, *Antwerpen en zijn 'Russen,'* 265-275 and 289-292.

75. The Austro-Hungarian emigrants who settled in Antwerp originated mostly from Krakow. In a sample of 150 Galician Jews settling in Antwerp prior to the First World War and who obtained a leave to remain after the First World War, the professional and geographic homogeneity is outspoken. Eighty of them were born in Krakow itself. Frank Caestecker and Antoon Vrints, Project Belgian Germans, unpublished paper "Galician Jews"; Sylvie Renneboog, "De Antwerpse diamantsector en 'de Groote Oorlog,'" *Bijdragen tot de Eigentijdse Herinnering* 9 (2010): 13-32. *Der yidisher emigrant*, 14.12.1912 (24) stressed that it was very difficult for a transit migrant without experience in this trade to settle in the diamond trade.

Shtetl on the High Seas: The Jewish Emigration from Eastern Europe and the Cross-Oceanic Experience

Gur Alroey

Introduction

The mass migration from Europe to America at the end of the nineteenth and the beginning of the twentieth century has been accorded extensive historiographical discussion. This was an exodus that changed the face of human society and led to far-reaching social changes both in the countries of origin and in the countries of immigrant absorption. Many books and articles have traced the causes for this migration and tried to understand the character traits of the migrants and their demographic composition, examining the ways in which the migrants were accepted by the surrounding society and their integration into the country of destination. On the other hand, the process of transference to the new country and the difficulties involved have been given less attention in historiography and has been perceived as a marginal stage of no special importance. As compared with the pangs of absorption in the new country and the attempts of the immigrants to integrate with the surrounding society, decision-making and realization have hardly been seen as significant. All that was required from the migrant was to reach the port of exit and to sail to the country of his destination. His transitional stage and his arrival in that country have been shunted aside in the research and was hardly dealt with in the historiography.[1]

Any attempt to trace the difficulties that befell a migrant, from the moment he came to a decision until he arrived at his desired destination, shows that the transitional stage was indeed complex and involved hardships, many of which were beyond the abilities of the migrant to bear. Migrants had to cope with numerous bureaucratic obstacles, steering their way from towns in which they had spent lives towards the port of exit and, from there, leaving for their desired destinations. In his book *On the Trail of the Immigrants* (1906), Edward Steiner compared the ship to a floating state. "The ship is just like Russia, Austria, Poland or Italy. The cabin passengers are the lords and ladies, the sailors and officers are the police and the army, while the captain is the king or czar."[2] For Jewish migrants in particular, the ship was a town that floated on the Atlantic Ocean. Demographic segregation between Jewish and non-Jewish travelers in steerage, the needs of each migrant population, the disputes that arose among the travelers as a result of the intense daily friction, and even the mutual help that emerged at critical moments all created elements characteristic of town life during the twelve days at sea. This article examines the contribution of the shipping companies to the scale of migration from Europe to America at the beginning of the twentieth century. I attempt to trace the sailing routine, life within the ship's hold, the difficulties of the voyage, and how migrants solved problems themselves during their journey westward.

Shipping Companies and Migration from Europe at the Turn of the Twentieth Century

The shipping companies had an enormous influence on the scope of migration from Europe to the American continent. On 28 March 1838, the steamship Sirius set out from London to New York. At the beginning of April it arrived in the industrial city of Cork in Ireland to take on coal. On April 4th it set sail to New York harbor. A few days after it had sailed, another steamship set out – the Great Western, which was stronger and faster than the Sirius. The two ships began a dramatic competition. Which one would be the first to cross the ocean by the power of steam? On April 22nd, eighteen days and ten hours after its departure, the Sirius arrived. On the next day the Great Western arrived after a voyage of just fifteen days and five hours.

Crossing the ocean by steam power opened a new period in the history of sea transport. From that moment on, the total replacement of sailing ships with steamships was only a matter of time. The Sirius and the Great Western were still wooden ships with sails in which a steam engine had been installed. They were relatively small; the quantity of coal they carried was limited, and the number of passengers they carried could not exceed a few score. But the ships built afterwards sailed on steam power alone, and they were made of steel. Instead of a voyage of forty days, the steamships crossed the ocean in twelve days. For the migrants, the transition to steamships saved sailing time. Even the conditions of sailing underwent radical changes. Until the middle of the nineteenth century the migrants shared their quarters with animals and merchandise. In the spring of 1849, one of these ships carried in its hold 280 passengers, 240 head of cattle, 206 pigs, nineteen sheep, and four horses.[3] And though steamships led to a significant improvement in the quality of the voyage, they were still accompanied by a considerable number of difficulties, as I shall show further on.

Shipbuilding, like the development of trains and railway lines, was an inseparable part of industrialization. The efficient exploitation of raw materials – iron and coal – was one of the main factors that led to the construction of the ships. From the second half of the nineteenth century, ships made of iron gradually replaced those of wood. By 1876, more ships were built of steel than of wood in the shipyards of Europe and America.[4] There were also social implications in the transition from wooden ships to those cast in iron and steel. Slowly dockworkers, sailors, and seafarers who were familiar with the complicated system of ropes, masts, and sails began to disappear. Their places were filled with scores of stokers who were experts in operating steam engines and those whose sole function was to maintain their constant combustion. The rate of change in shipbuilding was a rapid one. In 1848, the average tonnage of a steamship was 717 tons, and the average dimension was ten meters wide and 65 meters long. At the beginning of the twentieth century, ships were being built weighing 16,500 tons with a width of 20 meters and a length of 202 meters.

Two factors accelerated the process of building steamships. The first was the need among warring nations for steamships made of iron and steel during the Crimean War (1853-1856) and the Civil War in the United States (1861-1865). The second was the opening of the Suez Canal in 1869. Sailing ships were unable to pass through the canal on their own power, and their inability to adjust to the changing times made them irrelevant. Navigation from Europe to India and the Far East through the Suez Canal saved so much time and money that even the most conservative of shipowners who harbored doubts about the utility of steel ships understood that a new era had dawned.

The ability to cross oceans swiftly and securely was an economic advantage. Trade routes widened and their range increased. From the second half of the nineteenth century, the shipping fleets of European countries expanded. Now they constituted not only warships of steel but also heavily laden cargo ships containing hundreds of tons of industrial products. Many shipping companies understood the economic significance implicit in trans-Atlantic trade and began to adapt themselves to the new market conditions. There was not a single industrialized state in Europe that did not have its own reputable merchant fleet. In Germany there were two large shipping companies: Nord-deutscher Lloyd based in Bremen, and HAPAG (*Hamburg Amerikanische Packetfahrt Actien Gesellschaft*) based in Hamburg.[5] In Belgium, the largest shipping company was the Red Star Line; in France, it was the Frances Messageries Maritimes; in Holland, the Royal Netherlands Steamship Company,[6] and in England, the Cunard Steam Ship Company owned by Samuel Cunard.[7]

The first ships of these companies were cargo ships carrying merchandise and mail. From the middle of the nineteenth century, with the increased migration to the American continent, the shipping companies began to recognize the economic value of human cargo. They geared up to meet the desire of thousands of people wanting to leave the European continent for the New World. Unlike the Sirius and the Great Western on the decks of which were only a few score of migrants, the cargo companies converted the ships so that they could carry hundreds of migrants. This idea originated with the shipping magnate and director of HAP-

AG, the German Jew Albert Ballin. He eliminated separate bedrooms and created spacious sleeping halls between the upper and lower decks that could contain many hundreds of migrants. The maximum utilization of the ship's structure for accommodations made it possible for HAPAG to significantly reduce the cost of sailing.[8] The company began to compete for the migrant's money. This led to a reduction in travel fares and the opening of new and direct routes to main ports in New York, Boston, Buenos Aires, Rio De Janeiro, and others.

The number of migrants departing from European ports increased from year to year. For example, graph 1 indicates the increase in the number of migrants who left the port of Hamburg between 1886 and 1906. From the official records of HAPAG, it appears that in 1891 the company transported more than 144,000 migrants across the Atlantic Ocean. Between 1892 and 1894, there was a significant reduction in the number of migrants leaving the port of Hamburg due to the cholera epidemic that had broken out in the city, which had led to the closing of the German-Polish border. From the beginning of the twentieth century, however, there was a dramatic rise in the number of migrants leaving from that port. In 1897, the company transported about 73,000 migrants across the Atlantic Ocean. In 1899, it transported more than 100,000 migrants, and two years later its ships carried 211,000 migrants. In 1906, 430,000 migrants used the services of the company.

Graph 1: Number of Passengers Departing from the Port of Hamburg, 1886-1906

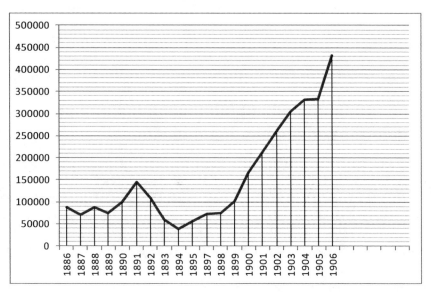

Source: Kurt Himer, Die Hamburg-Amerika Linie, 1897-1907, (Hamburg 1907), 52; Kurt Himer, Geschichte Der Hamburg Amerika Linie, (Hamburg 1914), 39.

Ballin was a gifted and energetic businessman who understood the economic potential in migration. In the 1880s the company he owned was the first to initiate regular sailing routes from the port of Hamburg to ports throughout the world. The first regular route was the route between Hamburg and New York. It proved to be the most profitable of all the routes for the company. The opening of this route created a regular schedule and allowed migrants to plan their migration and carry it out. The profits of the shipping companies in general, and of HAPAG in particular, were very high by any standard. Graph 2 indicates the rise in profits for Ballin's German shipping company during the period of mass migration.

Graph 2: The Profits of HAPAG during the years 1886-1913 (in millions)

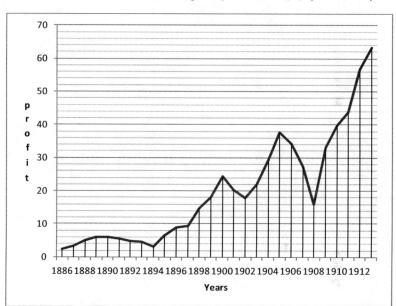

Source: Kurt Himer, Geschichte der Hamburg-Amerika Linie, 2. Teil, (Hamburg 1913), 11; 35; 39; 59; 81; 105; 127.

Once the shipping companies understood the money that could be made from migrants, they began to compete among themselves for the highest number of migrants. Jewish migrants were among tens of thousands of potential customers for the European steamship lines, and companies vigorously courted them.

Jewish migration came from two main countries: Czarist Russia and Galicia in the Austro-Hungarian Empire. The Jews who lived in the northwestern part of the Pale of Settlement usually crossed the Polish-German border and from there traveled by train to Hamburg and Bremen. Migrants who lived in the south and southwest of the Pale of Settlement crossed the Russian-Galician border and usually reached ports in Belgium and Holland. Naturally, there were cases in which the accepted pattern was not followed and people found themselves on a different route from the one typical for Jewish migrants. Table 1 below shows that more than half of the Jews traveled to their countries of destination by means of the German steamship companies. The company that had the most Jewish travelers was HAPAG, followed by the East Asia Company owned by HAPAG, and the Nord-deutscher Lloyd in third place.

Table 1: Distribution of the Jewish Emigrants According to Steamship Companies, 1906-1914

Steamship Companies	Country	Percentage of Jewish Emigrants
HAPAG	Germany	24.5
Russian East Asian	Germany	18.5
Nord-deutscher Lloyd	Germany	9.5
Red Star Line	Belgium	6.5
American Line	U.S.A.	5.5
Cunard Line	England	4.3
Karlsberg	England	4.2
Others[9]		27
		100

Source: Applications of 6,000 Jewish emigrants who applied to Information Bureaus in the Russian Empire.[10]

Since the Russian East Asian Company was also owned by Ballin, this means that 43 percent of the Jewish migrants sailed to the Americas by HAPAG and 52.5 percent sailed by means of a German steamship company. Thus the table above not only gives us information about the popular routes for the migrant population, it also shows the economic implications of the migration for Germany. Because the majority of the migrants passed through Hamburg and Bremen, a huge amount of money entered Germany. It is enough to multiply the fifteen million migrants – Jews and non-Jews – who passed through ports in Germany by the price of one ticket, and add port taxes and the expenses of the journey while in German territory to realize what a substantial sum was paid into state koffers. The outbreak of the First World War and the closing of the gates in the countries of destination from the 1920s onwards led to an almost complete halt in migration. The economic prosperity of thousands of residents in the exit ports who had profited from the stream of migrants did not continue after the First World War. Germany sank into harsh economic privation, the outcome of the First World War, the Versailles Treaty, and the payment of reparations. To this gloomy reality, the cessation of the flow of migrants through its ports must be added.

The majority of the ships in which the migrants sailed to their destination were the most advanced of that period, and the flag that waved above them embodied the potency and might of the state. The ability of the ships to cross seas and oceans was an expression of the imperialistic aspirations of the world powers and proof of their reach in outlying areas of the globe. The slogan of Ballin – *Mein Feld ist die Welt* [The world is my playground] – was an expression of globalization at the beginning of the twentieth century. A study of the advertisements from that time illustrate that besides the transport of migrants to their desired destinations, voyages were also a form of leisure for wealthy Europeans and Americans.[11] Each steamship company had its own flagship. HAPAG had three main passenger ships that crossed the Atlantic – the *Amerika*, the *Deutschland*, and the *President Lincoln*. In 1913, Ballin launched the flagship *Imperator*, which was the largest and fastest of all the ships in the world. The Russian East Asian Company in Libau had Russian, Lithuanian, Estonian, and Korean ships.[12] The Nord-deutscher Lloyd had a fleet of 84 ships, the four largest being the *Kaiser Wilhelm der Grosse*, the *Kaiser Wilhelm II*, the *Kronprinz Wilhelm*, and the *Kronprinzessin Cecilie*.[13]

The Migrant Experience

Two factors influenced the daily routine of the migrants on board ship. The first was the ethnic composition of the migrant population and the cultural differences between groups. The second was the life led on the ship and the level of services supplied to them. To understand the ethnic mix of migrants in steerage with all its levels and variations, let us look at a cross-section of the population aboard the *Imperator* on its maiden voyage from Hamburg to New York at the beginning of the twentieth century.[14]

The building of the *Imperator* began in 1910 and ended in 1913. Its construction was the result of precision planning by engineers and architects, and it expressed the control HAPAG held over sea transportation routes. It was 268 meters long, 30 meters wide, with a depth of 19 meters, and a weight of 50,000 tons. There was place for 706 passengers in first class, 611 passengers in second class, and 2,732 passengers in third class and steerage. There were about 1,178 professional crew members with various functions. At full capacity, the ship could hold 5,227 people.[15] The date set for the maiden voyage was 8 June 1913. The ship was not filled to capacity. There were 2,850 passengers with about 1,100 crew to maintain the ship and to care for the passengers during the twelve days of sailing.[16]

Graph 3: Composition of the Imperator According to Class (in percentages)

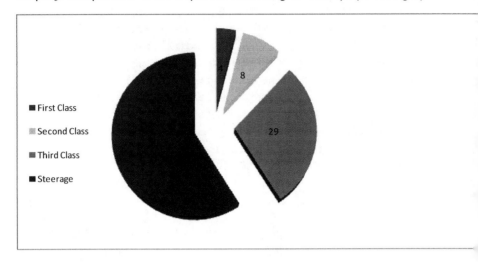

Source: *Staatsarchiv Hamburg, Archivband: 373-7 I, VIII A 1 Band 260*

Graph 3 shows that 88 percent of the passengers in the *Imperator* were migrants who traveled to the United States in third class and steerage, of which 1,679 were in steerage and 834 in third class.

Graph 4: Distribution of the Passengers in Steerage on the Imperator According to Country of Origin (in percentages)

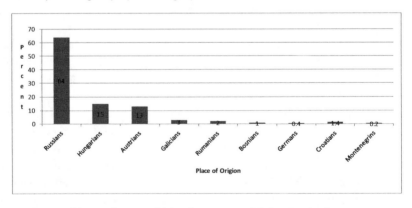

Source: *Staatsarchiv Hamburg, Archivband: 373-7 I, VIII A 1 Band 260*

Graph 4 shows that the majority of the migrants (64 percent, or 1,064 migrants) were from Russia, with far fewer from Hungary, Austria, Galicia, and Rumania. The graph does not show the number of Jews who sailed on the ship because the

GUR ALROEY

HAPAG officials did not ask for the ethnic identity of the migrants. However, since Jews can often be identified by their personal and family names, a fairly precise estimate can be made. For example, Meyer Friedman and Israel Weintraub may well have been Jewish and Malke Lewitt and her children (Chaje, Rosa, Slata, and Bachewa) as well. For marginal cases in which the names are less characteristic, cross-reference was made with the computerized list of names at Ellis Island in which the ethnic identity of the migrants was indicated.

Graph 5: Proportion of Jews Among the Russian Migrants on the *Imperator*

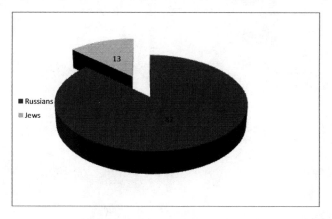

Source: Staatsarchiv Hamburg, Archivband: 373-7 I, VIII A 1 Band 260

About 13 percent of the Russian migrants who sailed on the *Imperator* were Jews. This proportion does not differ from the proportion of the Jewish population in the Pale of Settlement, which was calculated at 11 percent. The general assumption in research that the Jews migrated in a higher proportion than did the general population is not reflected in the numbers represented on the maiden voyage of the *Imperator*.[17] In absolute numbers, the ship had 124 Russian Jews and 940 Russians. The proportion of Jewish migrants in steerage was lower and was calculated at about nine percent.

Seventy percent of the Jewish migrants were men and thirty percent were women. This distribution of men and women among the Jews on the *Imperator* was lower than the general proportion of Jewish migrants entering the United States between 1899 and 1914. In those years, about one and a half million Jews entered the United States. Fifty-five percent of them were men and forty-five percent were women.[18] In comparison to other peoples entering the country in that period, there was a higher proportion of Jewish women than non-Jewish women, meaning also a higher proportion of Jewish children on the ship. Graph 7 below proves this. It examines the distribution of steerage passengers according to age.

Graph 6: Distribution of Jewish and Non-Jewish Migrants by Gender (in percentages)

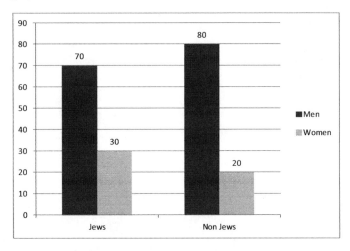

Source: Staatsarchiv Hamburg, Archivband: 373-7 I, VIII A 1 Band 260

Graph 7: Distribution of Jewish and Non-Jewish Migrants by Age (in percentages)

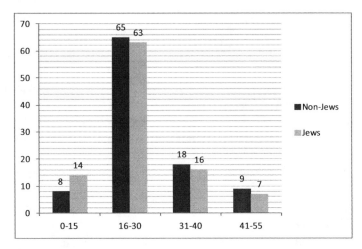

Source: Staatsarchiv Hamburg, Archivband: 373-7 I, VIII A 1 Band 260

The distribution of the 1,679 passengers according to age indicates a great resemblance in all categories except for those aged 0 to 15. Among the non-Jews, eight percent were children, while among the Jews, this was nearly double at 14 percent. An analysis of the demographics of the entire population that entered the

United States during the years 1899-1914, both Jewish and non-Jewish, points to the outstanding differences between the two migrant groups. A quarter of the Jews entering the United States were children aged fourteen years or younger, while for other migrant groups the proportion was far lower (12 percent) and slightly higher on the *Imperator*.[19] The difference between the Jewish and the non-Jewish passengers in the rate of children migrating can be explained by the fact that Jewish families migrated westward permanently, and thus the whole family migrated together. Conversely, the non-Jewish migration was temporary in aim, and people planned to return home. Naturally, fewer non-Jewish children migrated and instead stayed behind in the Old World.

Another important difference between the Jewish and non-Jewish migrants on the *Imperator* was their occupations. Seventy-nine percent of the Jews of working age (16 and older) had a profession, while only 21 percent did not specify any occupation to the shipping authorities. This number was significantly higher than the non-Jewish migrants who did not report any defined occupation.

The ship held within it a floating version of the Tower of Babel in which hundreds of travelers of different nationalities were mixed and merged together. It may be assumed that during the course of the voyage, ties were formed and the passengers came to know one another. The statistical facts of the *Imperator* do not provide any evidence of a system of relationships developing between the different migrant groups. But Edward Steiner described in his contemporary work, *On the Trail of the Immigrants*, colorful and fascinating encounters between steerage passengers sailing to the United States in 1906. Steiner writes that when the Slovaks burst into singing the song *Red Beer and White Cakes* the Slavs responded with a rousing war song. Folk singing in the depths of the ship created a gay atmosphere, and the migrants danced to the tunes of the accordion and harmonica. Each ethnic group, according to Steiner, presented its native repertoire:

> Greeks, Servians, Bulgarians, Magyars, Italians and Slovaks laugh at one another's antics and, while listening to the strange sounds, are beginning to enter into larger fellowship than they ever enjoyed; for so close as this many of them never came without the hand upon the hilt or the finger upon the trigger.[20]

Steiner then describes that the only ethnic group that did not take part in the singing and dancing in steerage were the Jews. Throughout the voyage the Jews kept apart from the non-Jewish migrants, forming a separate group that had no contact with them. Steiner writes that:

> No morning no matter how tumultuous the waves, but the Russian Jews will put on their phylacteries, and kissing the sacred fringes which they wear upon

their breasts, will turn towards the East and the rising Sun, to where their holy temple stood.[21]

In view of this description, one can only guess what the travelers in steerage thought when they saw the Jews wrapped in prayer shawls, wearing phylacteries, and praying towards the east to the rhythm of the rocking ship.

The apparent strangeness of the Jews as well as their segregation drew them closer to each other and led to their mutual support and assistance in steerage. The story of the migrant Sarah Leah Levin is one example of the brotherhood felt among the Jewish migrants. In April 1909, Sarah Leah Levin sailed with her three children from the port of Antwerp to be with her husband in America. A short while after the ship sailed, she became ill and died. As was customary in sailings, the captain wanted to throw her body into the sea. But a burial of this kind was completely contrary to Jewish tradition, and the Jewish migrants utterly refused to allow her to be buried at sea, insisting that she should be buried in a Jewish grave when they arrived in the United States. After much discussion with the captain, it was decided that the migrants would pay for the construction of an iron coffin at the cost of $250 in order to avoid the spread of disease that might be caused by a decaying body. This sum of money could not be raised among the migrants. With the help of an English-speaking Jewish migrant who argued their case, the captain lowered the sum to $100. In the end, the body of Leah Levin was not cast into the sea but was handed over to her husband in America.[22]

The voyage to the countries of destination was a turbulent event that aroused fears and apprehension. For most of the migrants this was the first time they had ever gone beyond the borders of their town. Encountering a steamship anchored in port, a gigantic steel monster that rose to such a height, and the boundless ocean that stretched before them left a powerful impression and awakened fears of the unknown. For the Jewish migrants, the twelve days on the ocean constituted a microcosma of their lives in their countries of origin. Their religious customs and the dietary laws (kashrut) divided the Jewish travelers from the other travelers and made it difficult for them to integrate into the daily routine of steerage. For them, the voyage was not much different from the life they had conducted in the towns of Eastern Europe with its complex system of relationships.

In order to relieve the concerns of all migrants, Jewish and non-Jewish alike, the steamship companies published booklets to provide migrants with information about what to expect during the sailing period. To give a hand to Jewish migrants in particular, the Nord-deutscher Lloyd for example was the first to issue a booklet in Yiddish entitled Durkh bremen keyn amerike mit den dampf shifen fun nord-deutscher Lloyd [From Bremen to America with the steamships of Nord-deutscher Lloyd]. It contained a detailed explanation of the steamship company, the fleet of ships, and the agents of the steamship company in Europe and the United States. It continued with explanations of how to reach Bremen from the

GUR ALROEY

border, along with details about the port city and the stay there. Finally, the conditions of the voyage and an explanation of the laws of entry to the countries of destination concluded the information. Naturally, Nord-deutscher Lloyd described the voyage as a positive experience, comfortable and without difficulties. In order not to frighten the migrant too much, life on board ship during the voyage was described in an ideal way as having no special difficulties.[23]

The information office of the Jewish Colonization Association (JCA) located in St. Petersburg, described a completely different reality. Representatives of the JCA went as secret reporters on the trans-Atlantic voyages to experience and report on them to the press. In the November 1909 issue of Der Jüdischer Emigrant, S. Bloch wrote an article on a voyage from Bremen to Argentina and back again. He described the conditions of the voyage. In his article, Bloch drew the attention of the reader to the distribution of sweet (drinking) water during the course of the voyage and the struggle over it. "Disputes frequently erupted over the use of sweet water."[24] The passengers on the intermediate deck had not received sufficient water. Bloch advised them to be stubborn and to demand an amount to which they had a right. Understandably, descriptions of this kind did not appear in the booklets of Nord-deutscher Lloyd. But what is interesting in the article by Bloch is not the struggle over the distribution of water but the necessity of explaining what sweet water was: "Sea water is salty and not fit for drinking. Therefore the ship has to be provisioned with drinking water from land sources – and this is called sweet water".[25] The very explanation shows the lack of general knowledge among readers of Der Jüdischer Emigrant. Many of them had never seen the sea and did not know what it was. Crossing the ocean was for them a turbulent experience. In their memoirs they also describe the voyage as traumatic. The Austrian-Jewish journalist and writer Joseph Roth, who was a native of Galicia, expressed very well the fears of the Jewish migrants about the voyage:

It's not America that frightens him, it's the ocean. He [the Jew] is well used to crossing large expanses, but never water. The Eastern Jew is afraid of ships. He doesn't trust them. For centuries he has been living in the interior. The steppes, the limitlessness of the flat land, these hold no terrors for him. What frightens him is disorientation. He is accustomed to turning three times a day toward Misrach, the East. It is more than a religious imperative. It is the deeply felt need to know where he is. To know his location [...] At sea, though, he doesn't know where God lives. He can't tell where Misrach is.[26]

Since a high percentage of the passengers were Jewish, and in order to enhance the economic profit derived from Jewish migration, the steamship companies began to prepare their kitchens for kosher food service. Sometimes there was even a Jewish kitchen worker authorized by a rabbi to serve the Jewish migrants during the voyage. In some of the ships departing from the port of Libau, there was a full-time *kashrut* supervisor.[27] In 1904, HAPAG began to offer kosher meals.[28] Nord-deutscher Lloyd followed HAPAG's example and also prepared its kitchens to offer kosher food during the voyage. The kitchens in some of Lloyd's ships were subject to the supervision of the rabbinate in Bremen, and they served four kosher meals that included vegetables, milk, grits, rice, soup, meat, and fruit.[29] On the other hand, the Belgian Red Star Line did not have kosher kitchens because "the guiding principle of the company was to offer equal care and consideration for the migrants of all nationalities." The migrants who refused to eat the food that was offered received bread, potatoes, and salted fish.[30]

The gap between the picture presented by the steamship company guidebooks and the conditions encountered on the voyage was considerable. Suffice it to say the migrants did not receive all the information necessary before sailing. The American immigration authorities were well aware of the conditions of the voyage and from the middle of the nineteenth century onwards, the American Congress began to pass a series of laws that obliged the shipping companies to provide better conditions for their passengers. The aim of these laws was to protect migrants from the arbitrary treatment of the shipping companies during the long voyage from Europe to America. These laws limited the number of migrants that were allowed to board the ship, and the shipping companies were forced to supply the passengers with suitable food and reasonable living conditions.

However, since the owners of the steamship companies wanted to make as much profits as possible, they did not obey the laws and continued to violate the rights of their passengers. For this reason, the American government sent undercover agents posing as migrants on the ships between Europe to America to check the conditions of the voyage. One of these undercover agents was Anna Herkner who sailed from Bremen to the United States. She gave a detailed report on the conditions of the migrants during the journey. The reports of Herkner and of the JCA information office[31] gives us a view into the difficulties of the voyage and shows the attempts of both the Jewish and non-Jewish migrants to cope with them.

Upon boarding the ship, the migrants were divided into three groups: women, women with children, and men. The crew, by means of temporary partitions, also divided the Jews from the other migrant groups, since the needs and demands of the Jewish migrants were different from the non-Jewish ones. The conditions of the voyage were not easy for any group. The beds in the ship were made of iron with a length of 1.80 meters (5.8 feet), and each berth had a straw mattress. The cabins were crowded. And because they were not properly aired, the lack of fresh air and stench in them were unbearable.[32] The ship had no place to store hand luggage, and the passengers had to place their baggage on the beds. The crowding was intense, and the rocking of the ship threw down and scattered the baggage in all directions. The floor of the ship was made of wood, and only rarely was it properly cleaned and thoroughly sanitized of the dirt and pollution that had accumulated from previous voyages.

Only two washrooms were at the disposal of the passengers in third class. The area of the washroom was 2.1 x 2.7 meters (7 x 9 feet), and the passengers had ten taps with cold seawater for washing. Only ten passengers could wash at the same time, a situation totally insufficient for the 1,500 passengers, and one that made it impossible to maintain a division between men and women. To wash during the voyage was a matter of "the first one wins." The condition of the toilets was far worse. From Herkner's report it appears that the women had six toilets and the men only five. Some 1,500 men and women were forced to use the eleven toilets that were only cleaned once a day in the evening hours, leaving them dirty for most of the day. Their stench spread throughout the living quarters, and it was difficult to remain inside.[33]

In order to escape from the crowding and the putrid smells in the ship's interior, many passengers spent as much time as possible on deck. Here it was possible to breathe clean air, to stretch, and to gaze at the endless horizon of the ocean. But during storms and bad weather, the passengers were not permitted to stay on deck.[34] The rocking of the ship during a storm made the lives of the crowded passengers hell. Seasickness, which affected most of the passengers, caused nausea and vomiting, and it is not difficult to imagine what occurred in the ship's interior when a storm rocked it up and down. Sheyne-Gadye Mendelson, who sailed from Bremen to Galveston, describes the difficult conditions of the voyage in a letter to her brother: "The first day, the weather was very beautiful, but after only a few hours in the sea air, I started to feel bad. The rocking of the ship and the unfamiliar sea air caused dizziness and nausea. I started vomiting and I was beginning to feel better by evening".[35]

Even meals were not a pleasant experience. Seven long tables with two benches on each side were provided for the passengers in the ship's dining room. Since the tables did not have place enough for all the migrants, they had to eat in sittings. The food was served in large cooking pots in the center of the table without any serving utensils, and the migrants had to manage by themselves. When a bell rang to signal the beginning of the meal, a tumult would break out and everyone would scramble for the food. Herkner writes in her report:

If the steerage passengers act like cattle at meals, it is undoubtedly because they are treated as such. The stewards complain that they crowd like swine, but unless each passenger seizes his pail when the bell rings announcing the meal and hurries for his share, he is very likely to be left without food [...] When I went for my breakfast, it was no longer being served. The steward asked why I hadn't come sooner saying, "the bell rang at 5 minutes to 7, and now it is 20 after," I suggested that twenty-five minutes wasn't a long time for serving 160 people, and also explained the real reason of my tardiness. He then said that under the circumstances I could still have some bread. However, he warned me not to use that excuse again.[36]

The sailing experience to Palestine was not different. "When we left Odessa the weather was cool and even snow fell; on the ship we wore winter clothes and did not take them off until we reached Constantinople," wrote David Smilansky:

As usual, the stoves in the third class of ships are not lit. The passengers living below quickly catch cold and are ill on the journey; they constantly have to suffer chills, cold and dampness. And they are always in a state of dirt and lack of sanitation. The ship authorities do not pay attention to such small matters, and the passengers of the third class are not taken into much account [...] Near the engine boilers that are fired with anthracite there are a few places for third class passengers. Only the lucky ones manage to enter these corners, and even this is done after much tussling. One cannot of course ensure comfort in this niche. You are first surrounded by the warmth emanating from the boilers, and at the next moment a draught attacks you from every side and you are swung between cold and heat.[37]

Herkner also wrote to portray the gap between the passengers in first class and steerage. She showed the sharp differences between those who sought a better life through emigration, and those for whom the journey was no more than a pleasure cruise.

Conclusion

From the moment that the migrant made his decision to emigrate until he reached the country of destination, a long series of complicated and torturous obstacles had to be overcome. In theoretical research literature on migration, these difficulties are called "intervening obstacles." The more these obstacles were solved, the more the stream of migration increased from the land of origin to the land of destination.[38] The ocean crossing was one of the main obstacles that lay before the migrants from Europe going to America. So long as the voyage lasted many weeks and the ship was dependent upon the mercies of the wind, with the crossing involving a danger to life, Europeans preferred to starve on their land rather than migrate *en masse* across the seas. The construction of steamships changed the voyage into a speedy, safe, and especially cheaper one for the migrants. The steamship companies significantly reduced the obstacles involved in crossing the Atlantic Ocean, and thus allowed millions to reach every corner of the globe and begin a new life.

Migration from Europe to America at the beginning of the twentieth century was a rich source of income for the owners of steamship companies. They understood the economic potential of migration and built large, fast ships that could carry the greatest possible number of passengers. The attempt to maximize profits led to a significant deterioration in the quality of the voyage. The greater the number of migrants crowded into steerage, the more difficult the travel conditions were, reaching levels that were almost unbearable. The viewpoint of the shipping magnate was not in line with that of the migrant. The former wanted to make a profit and reduce his expenses. The latter wanted to receive value for his hard-earned ticket. Though the interests of the shipping magnates and the migrants were at odds, their aim was the same: to allow millions of migrants to cross the ocean safely to realize their dreams. The magnates could not have made their millions without the migrants, and without the ships the migrants could not have realized their dreams.

This article has attempted to understand the importance and influence of the steamship companies on the migration from Europe to America at the beginning of the twentieth century. It has also highlighted the migration experience of the Jewish migrants from the moment they boarded the ship until they arrived at their port of destination. For some of the migrants this was the first time they had seen a large and threatening vessel that could swallow hundreds of people into its depths. The Jews formed a segregated group in the ship and had little contact with the non-Jewish migrants in steerage. In many ways, the ship was like a floating *shtetl* where you could find the Jewish way of life with kosher meals, three daily prayers, a distinct style of dress, and an embedded national distrust similar to life for Jews in Eastern Europe *vis-à-vis* the surrounding community.

The voyage was an important first stage in the journey of all migrants. For hundreds of thousands of Jewish migrants, the challenges they faced at their destinations were completely different from the difficulties that characterized their long trek from Eastern Europe towards the West.

Notes

1. The research studies of Pamela Nadell published at the end of the 1980s and the beginning of the 1990s were exceptions that do not prove the rule. See, for example, Pamella Nadell, "The Journey to America by Steam: The Jews of Eastern Europe in Transition," *American Jewish History* 71 (1981), 269-284. See also: Nadell, "En Route to the Promised Land," in *We are Leaving Mother Russia*, ed. Kerry M. Olitzky (Cincinnati: American Jewish Archives, 1990), 11-24; Zosa Szajkowski, "Suffering of Jewish Immigrants to America in Transit through Germany," *Jewish Social Studies* 39 (1977), 106-107. In recent years there has been a gradual increase of interest in this aspect of migration. See, for example: Tobias Brinkmann, "'Travelling with Ballin': The Impact of American Immigration Policies on Jewish Transmigration Within Central Europe, 1880-1914," *IRSH* 53 (2008): 459-484; Brinkmann, "Managing Mass Migration: Jewish Philanthropic Organizations and Jewish Mass Migration from Eastern Europe, 1868/1869-1914," *Leidschrift* 22.1 (2007): 71-90. See also: Gur Alroey, "Out of the Shtetl: On

the Trail of the Eastern Jewish Emigrants to America, 1900-1914," *Leidschrift* 22.1 (2007): 91-122.

2. Edward Steiner, *On the Trail of the Immigrants* (New York, 1906), 41. Steiner was a professor at Iowa College who researched immigration to the United States in the late ninetieth century and the early twentieth century. He was very involved with and connected to American officials who helped him obtain the relevant documents. About his unique methodology, see Edward Steiner, *The Immigrants Tide: its Ebb and Flow* (London, 1909), 5-8.

3. Philip Taylor, *The Distant Magnet: European Emigration to the U.S.A* (London, 1971), 133.

4. K. T. Rowland, *Steam at Sea: A History of Steam Navigation* (London, 1970), 131.

5. On the HAPAG shipping company, see Lamar Cecil, *Albert Ballin: Business and Politics in Imperial Germany, 1888-1918* (New Jersey, 1967). See also: Kurt Himer, *Die Hamburg Amerika Linie: Im Sechsten Jahrzeht Ihrer Entwicklung, 1897-1907* (Hamburg, 1907). Also see Arnold Kludas, *Die Geschichte der deutschen Passagierschiffahrt*, 5 Bands (Hamburg, 1986-1990).

6. On the Dutch shipping companies, see Ger Knap, *A Century of Shipping: The History of the Royal Netherlands Steamship Company, 1856-1956* (Amsterdam, 1956).

7. On the Cunard Steam Ship Company, see Francis E. Hyde, *Cunard and the North Atlantic, 1840-1973: A History of Shipping and Financial Management* (London, 1975).

8. Lamar Cecil, *Albert Ballin*, 18.

9. Finsk, Atlantic Express, Navig Italiano, Austro-American Line, Anglo Continentalle.

10. Part of the data in the present article is based on statistical data from information bureau files of the Jewish Colonization Association (JCA), now located in the JCA section of the Central Archives for the History of the Jewish People in Jerusalem. Three databases have been constructed using the records of JCA information bureaus that operated in the Pale of Settlement and Poland. The first is an aggregate database of more than 150,000 applications made to the information bureaus during the years 1910-1912; the second is a statistical report compiled by the information bureaus in 1910 based on 30,000 Jews who both applied to the bureaus and emigrated. The third (in the present article) contains the names of 6,000 Jews who immigrated to various countries overseas in the period 1906-1914.

11. See *Hamburg und die HAPAG: Seefahrt im Plakat*, Museum für Hamburgische Geschichte (Hamburg, 2000).

12. *Der Jüdischer Emigrant* 21, 16 December 1910, 19.

13. *Durkh Bremen, Keyn Amerika mit den Dampf Shifen fun Nord-deutscher Lloyd* (Bremen, 1909), 5-8.

14. The sailing of the *Imperator* is a representative case of many other steamers that sailed from Europe to the Americas at the beginning of the twentieth century. I would like to thank Jürgen Sielemann who helped me to obtain the list of passengers on the *Imperator*. On the passenger list of the *Imperator*, see Hamburg Staatsarchiv, Archivband: 373-7 I, VIII A 1 Band 260.

15. See Staatsarchive Hamburg, 373-7 I Auswanderunsamt I, vi 9 Nand 1. On the process of building the ship, see Peter Zerbe, *Die Grossen Deutschen Passaguerschiffe: Imperator, Vaterland, Bismarck* (Hamburg, 1999). The superbly illustrated book by Zerbe describes the construction process of the ship from planning to sailing.

16. See Hamburg Staatsarchiv, Archivband: 373-7 I, VIII A 1 Band 260.

17. See Gur Alroey, *Imigrantim: Ha-agirah ha-yehudit le-Eretz Israel bereshit Ha-mea Haesrim* (Jerusalem, 2004), 15-16.

18. Liebman Hersch, "International Migration of the Jews," in *International Migrations*, eds. Imre Ferenczi and Walter Wilcox (New York, 1931), 474.

19. Ibid. 485.

20. Steiner, *On the Trail*, 43.

21. Ibid. 45.

22. S.n., "Oyfn yom," *Der Jüdischer Emigrant* 8, 28 April 1909, 7-8.

23. See *Durkh Bremen keyn Amerike mit den dampfshifen fun nord-deutscher lloyd, Veg Vizer fun di Yiddshe Reisender* (Bremen, [1909?]), 5-12.

24. S. Bloch, "Fun Bremen kein Argentina," *Der Jüdischer Emigrant* 21, 28 November 1909, 6.

25. Ibid. 3.

26. Joseph Roth, *The Wandering Jews* (Juden auf Wanderschaft 1927) (Reprint New York, 2001), 97-98.

27. Die libauyer Shifen, *Der Jüdischer Emigrant* 8, 14 May 1909, 12.

28. Staatsarchiv Hamburg, Auswanderungsmat I, II A IVc Nr 5.

29. *Durkh Bremen keyn Amerike mit den dampfshifen fun nord-deutscher lloyd*, 38-41.

30. Alexander Harkavy, 'Diary of a Visit to Europe in the Interests of Jewish Emigration,' AJHS, Harkavy papers (1906-1907), 5.

31. Reports of the Immigration Commission: Steerage Conditions, 61st Congress 3d Session, Doc. No. 753, Washington 1911.

32. Bloch, "Fun Bremen," 3. See also: Steerage Conditions, 14.

33. Steerage Conditions, 14.

34. Ibid. 7.

35. Gur Alroey, *Bread to Eat and Clothes to Wear: Letters from Jewish Migrants in the Early Twentieth Century*, (Detroit, 2011), 97.

36. Steerage Conditions, 18.

37. David Smilansky, *Ir Noledet* (Tel Aviv, 1981), 22.

38. See Everett Lee, "A Theory of Migration," *Demography* 6 (1966): 47-57.

Off the Beaten Track

The Transatlantic Voyage as a Translational Process: What Migrant Letters Can Tell Us

Cecilia Alvstad

Translational processes are part of a migrant's reality, and such processes are closely related to the migrant's changing identity.[1] In the case of transatlantic migration in the early twentieth century, the translational process started long before the migrant arrived in the new continent. Whether they were on the train to the harbor or on a ship over the sea, migrants met other passengers speaking to them in unknown languages. To understand how migrant identities may be related to and negotiated in translation, one must start by studying the process of transit.

Letters home are one of the best sources for understanding migrants' translational practices and their transitions in identity. This paper studies translation in relation to the process of transit by describing the translational practices in two series of letters written by two young Swedish men on their way to Argentina: Axel Lundberg (1894-1958) and Eric (Eduardo) Mellberg (1909-?).[2] Both men later decided to stay in Argentina, married Argentinians and had children there. Focusing on how the letters depict their new realities, I address the following questions: how do the letter writers make sense of the foreign? What transitional processes do they go through? In what way and how much do they interact with others?

By highlighting the intimate link between translational processes and the migrant's changing identity during the journey and beyond, and by demonstrating that translation changes together with the migrant's identity, I wish to add to previous scholarship on the epistolary practices of international migrants.[3] Furthermore, and contrary to a common assumption about translation, I argue that a knowledge of the foreign is not a requirement for translation to take place. Migrants engage in translation while traveling to their intended destination, in their first encounters with the foreign.

An analysis of the two series of letters helps our understanding of linguistic and cultural translational processes in relation to migrants' changing identities. Migrant narratives and their depictions of linguistic and cultural encounters with the foreign, as well as the negotiation of identities, may be staged differently, depending on the authors' changing identification with the targeted audience, in this case the family at home.

No two transatlantic journeys are alike. In addition to individual circumstances, the journeys vary according to the given route of migration. The vast majority of Scandinavian migrants in the early twentieth century migrated to the United States. In fact, this migration was so considerable, it has been claimed that practically all Swedish households received letters from the United States in the late nineteenth and early twentieth centuries.[4] At this time there was also emigration from Northern Europe to other parts of the world, for instance, Latin America.[5] Our focus here is on migrants to Latin America rather than the United States. Lundberg and Mellberg provide an especially interesting locus for the study of translational processes, since less was known about Latin America in Sweden and because they would have been in the minority on the ship going to the new continent. Most of their co-passengers came from Southern Europe, and questions arise as to how easily they mixed with them. These Northern Europeans who, just like the migrants in Vik's and Ritz-Deutch's chapters were "off the beaten track," did interact with other nationalities on the ship. They were more or less forced to engage in translational processes, and they presumably felt an urge to share these processes with those at home. If virtually all Swedish households received letters from the United States, this was not the case with letters from Latin America. Thus, Latin America is likely to have been conceived of as a less familiar place for the ones back home, a circumstance that required a higher degree of translation. The two series of letters analyzed here are, to the best of my knowledge, the only Swedish series of letters presently available in Swedish archives that depict the journey to South America.

Despite the narrow focus on migrant letters written on the passage to Latin America, the discussion here is relevant for scholars studying other geographical areas and for scholars working on similar materials, such as travel books and migrant diaries. Lundberg and Mellberg's letters provide a framework for approaching textually negotiated linguistic and cultural translational processes. Furthermore, the discussion is of interest to translation studies scholars in general as it, following Sakai,[6] approaches translational issues by emphasizing the ambiguous status of the foreign as alien, but "already in transition to something familiar."[7] Initially I will discuss transit as a translational process with both cultural and linguistic qualities. And then I present the two migrants and analyze their letters in relation to the theories presented.

Transit as a Translational Process: Points of Departure

Transit and translation are intimately related. People leaving the place where they were born will, by definition, meet unknown realities and unfamiliar ways of speaking. When they try to make sense of this, they engage in a translational

CECILIA ALVSTAD

process. Either they will figure out the new for themselves, or they will get help from mediators to negotiate the unknown, both languages and cultural practices. Mediators who help to translate the unfamiliar may be official, such as interpreters working for immigration authorities, or unofficial, such as a helpful person pointing out the right train. Translational processes are a part of a migrant's reality.

The relationship between migration and translation is nevertheless understudied with regard to contemporary perspectives as well as historical ones. We have yet to discover the subtleties of migrants' translational processes and how they may change together with the migrant's identity. Malena noted this in 2003, in a special issue of TTR: Traduction, Terminologie, Redaction on translation and (im)migration, by writing that the relationship between translation and migration "is only beginning to attract the attention of translation scholars and cultural theorists."[8] She also noted that the broad call for her special issue mostly generated submissions on literature. From this she concluded that the field of translation studies still needed "to expand and diversify in order to venture into most of these areas."[9] By focusing on experiences during transit in particular, this article is a late answer to Malena's call to study the relationship between migration and translation in non-literary materials.

Malena draws attention to the physical movement of migrants and the shift in language(s) they use:

> Migrants are translated beings in numerous ways. They remove themselves from their familiar source environment and move towards a target culture which can be totally unknown.[10]
> Migrating individuals [...] become bi- or polylingual along a complex translation process which while ensuring their survival, also transforms their collective identity.[11]

Along similar lines of thought, and inspired by Malena, Cronin notes:

> Implicit in this movement of people in a multilingual world is a shift between languages and cultures. [...] The condition of the migrant is the condition of the translated being. He or she moves from a source language and culture to a target language and culture so that translation takes place both in the physical sense of movement or displacement and in the symbolic sense of the shift from one way of speaking, writing about and interpreting the world to another.[12]

Both Malena and Cronin highlight that migrants become bi- or polylingual, but neither of them address proper linguistic translation, the movement of linguistic items from one language into another. The same appears in Gentzler, even though he explicitly states that translation is more than a metaphor or trope:

> These immigrants, migrants and refugees are always in the process of translating, both as a means to conform to the ways prevalent in their new locations and as a means to resist assimilationist pressures. The Americas are primarily made up of immigrants, migrants and refugees, and thus translation operates in the America not as an isolated linguistic or literary activity, nor as a postcolonial metaphor or trope, but as a concrete, historical movement with the power to include and exclude.[13]

Malena, Cronin, and Gentzler mention language but do not seem to refer to translation as a movement of linguistic items. For them, translation is cultural rather than linguistic, if by cultural translation we understand a translational process in which an agent makes sense of new realities.

Cultural translation is commonly described as a process that does not require a fixed source text or target text. Pym phrases it in the following way:

> 'Cultural translation' may be understood as a process in which there is no source text and usually no fixed target text. The focus is cultural processes rather than products. The prime cause of cultural translation is the movement of people (subjects) rather than the movements of texts (objects).[14]

One can therefore assume that cultural translation occurs in letters written by migrants while on their journey. A transatlantic voyage certainly involves the movement of people, and, as is customary in cultural translation, there is no fixed source text. Rather, the source is constituted by the letter writer's observations and experiences and, ultimately, by what he decides to write. In a sense, it is the writing of the letters themselves that produces the source.

When analyzing migrant letters, however, it is insufficient to approach the ongoing translational processes solely as cultural translation. Writing creates a target text, i.e. the letters. These letters or actual texts we may call, borrowing Pym's words, fixed objects. Letters consist of words – i.e. linguistic material – and this linguistic material is a translation not only of new realities and experiences, but also of new realities experienced in another language or languages. We are dealing not only with cultural translation but with linguistic translation as well.

That there is a linguistic component in translation does not imply that a deep knowledge of the foreign language or languages is required for translation to take place. Rather, as recently argued by Sakai,[15] it is the translational process itself that produces differences between languages. We distinguish different languages because we translate between them. We cannot know what the foreign is until we

CECILIA ALVSTAD

begin to translate it, and once we begin to translate it, "it is already *in transition* to something familiar":

> If the foreign is unambiguously incomprehensible, unknowable and unfamiliar, it is impossible to talk about translation because translation simply cannot be done. If, on the other hand, the foreign is comprehensible, knowable and familiar, it is unnecessary to call for translation. Thus the status of the foreign must always be ambiguous in translation. It is alien, but is already *in transition* to something familiar.[16]

This translation, rather than being something that bridges gaps between different languages and cultures, is a process of drawing borders. In Sakai's own words, "translation is not only a border crossing but also and preliminarily an act of drawing a border, of *bordering*."[17] Translation is, in other words, "not only a process of overcoming incommensurability; it is also a process in which difference is rendered representable."[18]

If one produces the foreign when translating, it signals that translation does not require a deep knowledge of the foreign. One may ask, therefore: what is required? What urges the concrete translational process, the letters from migrants? Sakai suggests that someone can only be summoned to be a translator "when two kinds of audiences are postulated with regard to the source text, one for whom the text is comprehensible, at least to some degree, and the other for whom it is incomprehensible."[19]

That two kinds of audiences are required for translation to take place and that translation has more to do with a drawing of borders than a crossing of borders – this is crucial for understanding the translational processes that take place during a migrant's journeys. I analyze the letters on the basis of these ideas and suggest that migrants may loosely identify these two audiences as "the ones at home" and "the ones that are part of the new culture." Furthermore, and again inspired by Sakai, I suggest that an internal split within the translating migrant may arise, an internal split that

> [...] reflects in a certain way the split between the translator and the addresser – or the addressee, and furthermore the actualizing split between the addresser and the addressee themselves [...] this internal split within the translator is homologous to what is referred to as the fractured I, the temporality of 'I speak' which necessarily introduces an irreparable distance between the speaking I and the I that is signified, between the subject of enunciation and the subject of the enunciated.[20]

On the basis of these ideas, I assume that during their journey, migrants move from identifying themselves with those at home towards identifying with those of the new environment. This means that the migrants are on the move, not only in a physical sense from one continent to another, but also between two audiences. They may begin by translating "others" for themselves and the ones at home, but they soon start translating "themselves" for the ones at home.

In the first letters of Lundberg and Mellberg, they identify themselves with the audience at home, for whom the foreign is incomprehensible. As they start to make sense of the foreign, they move towards the other audience for whom it is already comprehensible. It is precisely this change in identification that is linked to a change in translational practice. In a sense, the family and friends at home become the new 'others.' Inspired by Sakai's idea of translation as a drawing of borders, I test the hypothesis that to translate while traveling is a way of engaging in bordering. At first the writers are engaged in drawing borders between themselves and the unknown and then, together with a change in their identity, they instead turn to establishing borders between themselves and their family and friends at home.

The Transatlantic Migrants Lundberg and Mellberg

Axel Lundberg's transatlantic passage took place in 1912, when he was eighteen years old. His first letters home were written on the transatlantic steamer *Cap Ortegal* on the way from Hamburg to Buenos Aires. Buenos Aires was not Lundberg's final destination. He was heading further south, to Trelew and San Martín, where he was to work for a Swede named Lundkvist. Lundberg traveled together with three others who were also going to work for Lundkvist.

Eric (Eduardo) Mellberg's transatlantic journey took place fourteen years later, after the First World War. The year was 1926, and Mellberg was then seventeen years old. Similar to Lundberg's letters, Mellberg's first letters home were also written on the transatlantic voyage, in this case on board the *Sierra Cordoba* from Bremen. He was traveling on his own, but he had family in Argentina an uncle, Axel Zedoff, and cousins who picked him up when he arrived in Buenos Aires.

There are similarities between Lundberg and Mellberg. They were both born in Sweden, both traveled to Argentina in their late teens in the early twentieth century, and they already had a connection to the place where they were going. The most striking difference is that Lundberg traveled together with three other Swedes, whereas Mellberg traveled on his own. This has important consequences for how they portray their encounters with the foreign in their letters home.

Lundberg's and Mellberg's Tales of Transit

Axel Lundberg's first letter home is addressed to "Dear parents and siblings and grandmother" and is dated 1 March 1912. He starts by saying that he had not planned to write on the boat, but that he had been told that he could send letters from Boulogne, France, where they would arrive that same night. He recounts how he and his travel company arrived in Hamburg and what they did and ate there. The letter is written in Swedish, with a few German words like *Bahnhof* appearing untranslated in the text. A few other German words appear with an explanation in Swedish, for example "*Grose Grasbrok = inskeppningshallen.*" Similarly, Lundberg tells that he had a good dinner that cost '75 *fennig* = 70 *öre*.' The foreign lexical items stick out in the text and indicate that he is writing in a foreign environment and that another language is spoken there. Their presence in the text works simultaneously in two ways. On the one hand, these foreign lexical items help render the unfamiliar more familiar. On the other hand, they are the first signs of a distance being created between Lundberg and his family at home, a distance produced by the fact that the translational process is given visibility in the letter.

This first letter also tells about his first experiences on board the *Cap Ortegal*. His fellow passengers are described in the following terms:

> We almost backed away when we saw the co-passengers we were getting. There were many different languages. Almost all of them were riffraff with tattered quilts and mattresses under their arms, dirty kids and tiny sucklings, old men and old women with tattered and filthy clothes.[21]

The way this is phrased may appear rather shocking. A clear distance is signaled towards the other passengers, and the migrant's identification seems to be with the audience at home and not with the people being described. The following passage works in a similar way, but there are also clear signals that linguistic translation is taking place:

> When we arrived on board, we were stowed away in the hold, where 160 beds were set up where we were supposed to lie. A noxious air rose up towards us, it was almost impossible to breathe it. We hurried as quickly as possible up to the deck to get some fresh air. [...] We got Anders to go to the manager and ask to get another, smaller room. After lengthy negotiations we were allowed, at the cost of 20 marks each, to live in a cabin for 8 people, the other four in the cabin were German.[22]

The negotiation that leads to the successful change of quarters must have taken place in another language than Swedish, presumably German, even though this is not made explicit. The way the passage is written may also suggest that the man referred to, Anders, functioned as an interpreter.

The references to other languages being spoken on board is clear in the following quote:

Here on board there is a Babylonian confusion. The Germans sit in one place and sing patriotic songs, the Jews sit in another place and sing and yell, Gypsy women with sucklings sit in yet another place and vomit. We're doing relatively well on the ship.[23]

The depiction suggests that the different national and ethnic groups stick together. Lundberg seems to be ranking the different groups on board on the basis of race and ethnicity, from Germans that sing to Gypsies that throw up. This passage creates a difference between the people described. This passage is also a bit shocking – a description of reality influenced by prejudice. Read from another angle, even though the description is both stereotypical and condescending, one may note that the young Swedish migrant at least observes the others on board. He notices that they do not all speak one single language. This is a first step in negotiating the unfamiliar and of trying to understand it. Whether it is read in one way or the other, a distance is created with fellow passengers and not with the ones at home. A similar formulation appears in the next letter, dated 8 March:

We are now 500 passengers on the middle deck, the ship is really teeming. Since the Spaniards came on board in Vigo, the deck looks like a pigsty and it smells terrible. There are at least ten or so languages that are spoken here on the ship.[24]

This passage marks a distance from the Spaniards, similar to the distance to the Jews and Gypsies in the previous quote. And even though Lundberg does not explicitly blame the Spaniards for the deck looking look a pigsty, this is implicitly suggested.

In contrast, the Germans are described in quite different and much more positive terms. Lundberg and the other Swedes with whom he travels affiliate themselves with them. The four Swedes are, for example, allowed into their coffee club:

Regarding coffee, 10 of the better Germans on board have formed a club, one of the Germans is the same kind of businessman as Lundkvist, to whom we are traveling.... This club has also admitted 'der fiere Schwede,' as they call us. We have chipped in with ½ a mark each and bought roasted coffee, sugar and cream and we also cook our coffee ourselves. This coffee tastes like the one we used to get at home.[25]

When Lundberg writes about the Germans on board and of himself as belonging to this same group, he again introduces a German phrase, *der fiere Schwede*. This can be interpreted as a bordering between himself and the ones at home. He distances himself from them rather than from the ones on board whom he describes. The act of drawing a border is intensified by using a foreign expression. Someone with a better knowledge of German than the one Lundberg himself evinces will notice that the Germans probably called the four Swedes *die vier Schweden* rather than *der fiere Schwede*, but this is irrelevant for how the words function in the Swedish letter targeted at people who presumably did not have a knowledge of German.

In the following passage, no such foreign expressions are used except for the mention of German currency. The passage describes the customary ritual baptism upon passing the Equator, and again the Spaniards are depicted negatively:

> The next day the customary baptism took place, we were 18 people who had signed up on a list for participating in the party, it cost 3 marks... An unpleasant incident took place during the party. For the Spaniards had become furious because they weren't allowed to join the party. A Spaniard went for the boatswain's jugular and had him on his back, but John Ericsson, our companion from Stockholm, took the Spaniard by the neck and held him as in a vice until the able seamen arrived. We dropped to our knees and then Neptune read out loud a long litany, and then he grabbed a large brush and dipped it in water and slapped our faces with it, and then we received a beautiful diploma signed by the captain and then we were baptized.[26]

The conflict in this passage can be understood in several ways. The letter writer is sure that his audience shares his perspective. The border drawing that takes place is twofold: between the letter writer and implicitly the ones at home, and between the letter writer and the Spaniards. But one can also read the passage as contrary to the author's intentions and see the ritual itself as an ostentatious way of establishing a difference between passengers; those who are permitted to take part and those who are not at the party. The crossing of the imaginary line between North and South would then be an act of drawing borders. The letter itself works in the same way. It creates a distance between the letter writer and those who are soon to be his new Argentinean compatriots. The depiction of the Germans and the Spaniards, as well as the respective affiliation and antagonism towards these groups, creates a duality in this letter between identifying with the ones at home and with the ones in the transit environment.

While still on the ship, Lundberg is unaware that, once he arrives at the unknown continent, he will in fact have to interact with people in Spanish. However, after his arrival at port but while still en route to his final destination in San Martín de los Andes, Spanish words begin to appear in the letters instead of German ones. The following quote shows this. Here the Spanish loan words have the same spelling as in the Swedish letter:

This meal is called 'potjäro,' and then we drank 'matte,' a drink that is used here instead of the coffee we drink back home. It is prepared with 'jerva,' which we call Paraguayan tea, as well as warm water in a large cup in which you put a straw, then the cup gets passed around until the water runs out, then you add more water, and so it goes on until the jerva has lost its force.[27]

The passage describes a typical Argentinean dish, a meat-based stew, called *puchero*, which if spelled as it sounds in Swedish is spelled "potjäro." The passage then continues by describing the most typical of all Argentinean rituals, *mate* drinking. Just as the passage tells us, *mate* is prepared in a cup, generally a calabash gourd, with *yerba mate* (which written as it sounds in Swedish would be spelled 'jerva' and 'matte'). And, Lundberg writes, everybody drinks from the same straw. This typical ceremony is described almost as if it were a tourist brochure or an ethnographic account. Foreign elements are used but explained, and they function as a way to mark affiliation with the ones at home rather than with the ones being described. The tone is much less hostile than when the Spaniards on the boat were depicted, though it is not as congenial as the depiction of Germans on the ship sharing coffee. He draws borders between himself and the Argentinians, not between himself and the ones at home.

The other letter writer, Eric (Eduardo) Mellberg, leaves Sweden fourteen years after Lundberg, in 1926. Since he travels on his own, he has problems understanding others and making himself understood, something he experiences right away on the train to Bremen, where he is to board the *Sierra Cordoba*. There is no other Swede to help him negotiate what is happening around him.

His depictions of others are softer and less focused on conflict than Lundberg's. Even though a certain national stereotyping takes place in his letters, his judgments are based on the personal characters of those he meets and the ways in which he sees them as part of a group. He recounts his difficulties in understanding the Germans on his way to Bremen in the following way:

... and then he said something in German that I did not understand. It was even worse later on when I was about to get on the train for Hamburg. Nobody understood Swedish so that I could get to know what to do. But then I saw the ticket collector and asked him. At first he did not understand what I meant, but then he walked towards a train and made signs for me to follow. I obeyed, but before we got there, it left. At first I became very anxious and thought, even though it wasn't that late in the day yet, that I was going to arrive too late [i.e. for the ship]. But the train was merely switching tracks.[28]

My companion in the compartment was an old German man, who soon started talking to me. I learned later on that Germans are very talkative and that they cannot sit next to somebody for five minutes before starting to talk, something I myself experienced later on. The old man asked me quite a few questions in German, but then I explained to him that I spräckte no deutsch.[29]

The way Mellberg addresses his difficulties in understanding others and his own reactions is depicted with some humor. Just like Lundberg, he introduces a few German words, but interestingly, and in contrast to how the German words function in Lundberg's letters, these do not create distance from the ones at home. Rather they produce affiliation. He says that he does not speak the language of the old German man who addressed him. This is funny, and also helps draw a border between himself and the foreign, not in antagonistic terms, but rather, as if he sees himself as the one being strange and lost, not the others.

The following passage, which depicts the routines for meals on board, works in a similar way. Through his description we can still today, eighty-five years later, appreciate how difficult it must have been for this young boy. With hardly any knowledge of foreign languages, he had to figure out when and where he was to eat:

After I had been on the deck for a while, I went down to the dining room to eat. I was quite naughty and sat down at a table without considering that there were certain rules. When a waiter walked by, I hailed him and knocked on the table to signify that I wanted some food. He then walked over to me and said something that I of course didn't understand. He then summoned a couple of waitresses who were walking past and said something to them. They started talking in yet another language, one that I also didn't understand.

Then they summoned the man who takes care of things down in the dining room, a kind of overseer. He looked like a nice guy, which he also was. He asked me to follow him and then we went to his office. He asked me in English whether I could speak English. 'Yes, a bit,' I answered in that language. Then he asked me for my ticket, tore off a piece of it and gave it back to me along with a small piece of paper, on which was written the number of the table, and similarly in one of the corners the number 2, which I at the time did not know the meaning of. But it meant the second time they were going to eat. Perhaps you don't understand what I mean, but you understand that there are so many people, and there isn't room for everyone at the same time. That's why they've divided it up into several times instead. All in all there are four servings.[30]

Mellberg describes how he uses body language as a way of obtaining the information he needs, and he writes that the overseer ultimately must use writing and numbers to get the message across. Even though Mellberg, judging by his description, did not understand the situation completely, he received enough information to understand the system of seatings. In this case, the successful translation did not occur through verbal languages but through body language and numeric symbols, knowledge that both parties shared.

In this letter the border that Mellberg draws is between himself and the ones of the new environment and not between himself and the ones at home. Indeed, we can still read the passage as explicative of Mellberg's situation. He makes us see it as he himself saw it, from the perspective of someone who had not before been on this kind of transatlantic ship. It is noteworthy, however, that the border between himself and the foreign is marked by curiosity and a lack of familiarity rather than by the negative distancing that Lundberg displayed. Another example is the following quote:

> After a few days we arrived at Vigo in Portugal. You can believe it was beautiful there. We stayed in the city of Vigo almost all day. I bought some oranges and bananas from the natives, who came up on deck with their goods. I thought they were a very funny people and very indecent.[31]

The tone of this passage is a bit exoticizing, and it depicts the foreign in positive terms as different. The border drawing is clearly between himself and the "funny people" of Vigo, not between himself and the ones at home. Furthermore, it is a case of exhibiting the foreign rather than of a negative distancing from it, which is what colored Lundberg's description of the people who came on board in Vigo. Lundberg did get more of his facts right, Vigo is indeed part of Spain, not Portugal, an indication in itself that Mellberg may have had greater problems in understanding what was happening around him.

When Mellberg starts describing what happened to him after arriving at his uncle's home in Argentina, his narrative style changes. His funny descriptions of difficult language situations disappear. He is now among people who speak his own language and who help him realize that he must confront the language issue and learn Spanish. This is how he describes his first dinner with his Argentinian family:

> Later on at the dinner table they spoke to me about how I should read. First I am going to learn the Spanish language. Then I am going to study other things that will be useful for me.
> So I'm really busy and am studying all I can. Sigrid [the cousin] is reading Spanish with me.
> Sometimes we guys go into town and have a good time. When I had been there a week, the guys and I went into town and visited the zoo. It was very enjoyable for me to see it. Then we visited the city and took a closer look at it.
> Axel has bought many clothes for me so that I might look stylish when I go out with them. I've gotten a nice straw hat, a pair of white pants, 3 pairs of

drawers, 2 ties and a pair of really nice shoes. You must know that he's very kind.[32]

This description is much less vivid than the ones from the ship. We no longer get the many details that made it possible to figure out what life on board must have been like. What he now provides are details of a much more enumerative kind, and Mellberg has problems describing his new life. The border is being drawn to the ones at home, not the ones of the new environment. This is also clear in the following quote: 'Yesterday I was back in Buenos Aires again and went to the cinema. I've been to the cinema twice already and I understand quite a lot.'[33]

He does not relate how they get to the city, what film they saw or what it was like to be in an Argentine cinema. He says that he understands quite a lot, but he does not seem able to transfer what he understands to his audience at home. The internal split within the translator-migrant seems complete and we see another kind of translational practice. Now he is narrating for those who do not know. He himself is already part of the other audience and the new environment.

Conclusion

This article has examined the translational processes of two Swedish teenagers who migrated to Argentina in the early twentieth century. Both wrote home to their families about their journey and arrival. These letters are analyzed in this article. The letters contain strong elements of cultural translation, but linguistic translation appears ubiquitously in them as well. The two Swedish migrants en route are translators, still largely unfamiliar with the cultural phenomena they encounter and translate, and who do not yet speak the language of "the others." The two young men clearly engage in translational practices in their letters home, even though they have a very limited understanding of their fellow passengers and the new environments of multicultural trains and boats.

Their translational processes change along the way. In the beginning, the two letter writers seem to translate for themselves. In their early letters home, they share a similar perspective as the ones at home and tell about the new things they encounter from a distance. The perspective gradually changes and the young Swedes, still en route, start to translate for their addressees at home rather than for themselves. They establish distance from their family members rather than between themselves and what they write about. These migrants are not only involved in a process in which they bridge the gap between the well known and the foreign; they also draw borders between the ones they write about and the ones they write for. Despite important differences between the two letter writers, this pattern is common to both of them.

Regarding the abovementioned differences, it is noticeable that one of the letter writers is more tolerant towards the foreign. It is worth recalling that he is the one who traveled alone, whereas his compatriot was accompanied by a few other Swedes. In a larger study it would be interesting to explore whether his being more tolerant was related to him traveling alone. To be able to understand how life on the boat works, he was forced to communicate, despite the lack of a shared language, and it is possible that this interaction itself contributed to making him more tolerant.

The more "hostile" migrant seems to have interacted with others mainly through one of the other Swedes. He does not recount his own attempts to communicate but rather those of his travel companion. The fact that he was part of a small group that confirmed his Swedish identity may have contributed to him being more hostile to others. His letters show that while on board he never directly interacted with non-Swedes. To learn more about how belonging or not belonging to a group of compatriots affects the process of transit, a future study is in order. It would be of great interest to compare the letters studied here to letters from South European migrants traveling to South America or North European migrants traveling to North America –i.e., migrants more usually seen as "on the beaten track."

Notes

1. Anne Malena, "Presentation," TTR: Traduction, Terminologie, Redaction 2 (2003): 9; Michael Cronin, Translation and Identity (London: Routledge, 2006), 45; Edwin Gentzler, Translation and Identity in the Americas (London: Routledge, 2008), 7.

2. The letters are archived at the migration museum 'Utvandrarnas hus' in Växjö in southern Sweden. The letters from Mellberg are archived as 15:14:6F and the letters from Lundkvist as 22:16:8P.

3. See, for instance, the contributions in Bruce S. Elliott, David A. Gerber and Suzanne M. Sinke (eds.), Letters across Borders: the Epistolary Practices of International Migrants (New York: Palgrave Macmillan, 2006).

4. Hans Norman and Harald Runblom, Amerika-emigrationen (Uddevalla: Cikada, 1980), 11.

5. This part of Scandinavian emigration history is an extremely understudied field, and more studies therefore need to be conducted. The only academic studies as yet have been María Bjerg's study about Danish immigration to Argentina and Gunvor Flodell's studies on a group of Swedish migrants to Brazil (of whom many died, some ended up in the province Misiones in the north of Argentina and about 500 were transported back with support from the Swedish state in 1912); Bjerg, Entre Sofie y Tovelille. Una historia de la inmigración danes en la Argentina, 1848-1930 (Buenos Aires: Biblos, 2001); Flodell, "Brasiliebreven berättar," in Ord i nord. Vänskrift till Lars-Erik Edlund 16 augusti 2003, eds. Gunvor Flodell et al. (Umeå: Umeå University, 2003); Flodell, 'De verkar te å gå bakåt': språk, etnicitet och identitet belyst utifrån emigrant- och dialektmaterial (Umeå: Kulturgräns norr, 2002); and Flodell, Misiones-svenska: språkbevarande och språkpåverkan i en sydamerikansk talgemenskap (Uppsala: Uppsala University, 1986).

6. Naoki Sakai, "How Do We Count a Language? Translation and Discontinuity," *Translation Studies* 2.1 (2009): 71–88.

7. Ibid. 83 (his italics).

8. Malena, "Presentation," 9.

9. Ibid. 10.

10. Ibid. 9.

11. Ibid. 11.

12. Cronin, *Translation and Identity*, 45.

13. Gentzler, *Translation and Identity in the Americas* (London: Routledge, 2008), 7.

14. Anthony Pym, *Exploring Translation Theories* (London and New York: Routledge, 2010), 144.

15. Sakai, "How Do We Count a Language?" 71.

16. Ibid. 83.

17. Ibid. 83 (his italics).

18. Ibid. 83.

19. Ibid. 83-84.

20. Ibid. 83-86.

21. The quotes from the Swedish letters have been translated into English for this article. The original Swedish phrasings are provided in notes. "Vi nästan ryggade tillbaks när vi sågo vilka medpassagerare vi skulle få. Det var många olika språk. Nästan bara slödder med trasiga täcken och madrasser under armarna, smutsiga ungar och små dibarn, gamla gubbar och käringar med trasiga och lortiga kläder." (Lundberg, 1 March 1912; 22:16:8:P).

22. "När vi kommo ombord stuvades vi ner i lastrummet i vilket var uppställda 160 sängar där vi skulle ligga. En osund luft steg emot oss, den var nästan omöjlig att inandas. Vi skyndade så fort som möjligt upp på däck för att hämta frisk luft. [...] Vi fingo Anders att gå till förvaltaren och be att få ett annat mindre rum. Efter en längre underhandling fingo vi komma mot en ersättning av 20 mark vardera, bo i en hytt för 8 personer, de andra fyra i samma hytt voro tyska." (Lundberg, 1 March 1912; 22:16:8:P).

23. "Här ombord är en Babylons förbistring. På ett ställe sitta tyskar och sjunga foster-landssånger, på ett annat sitta judar och sjunga och skrika, på åter ett annat sitta zigenarkäringar med dibarn och spy. Vi hava det jämförelsevis bra ombord." (Lundberg, 1 March 1912; 22:16:8:P).

24. "Vi äro nu 500 mellandäckspassagerare, det riktigt myllrar ombord. Sedan spanjorerna kom på i Vigo, ser det ut som en svinstia på däck och det luktar förfärligt. Det är då åtminstone en 10-tal tungomål som talas här ombord." (Lundberg, 8 March 1912; 22:16:8:P).

25. "Angående kaffet så har 10 stycken av de bättre tyskarna ombord bildat en klubb, däribland en tysk, som är samma sorts affärsman, som Lundkvist vi skall till, [....]. Denna klubb har också intagit 'der fiere Schwede', som de kalla oss för. Vi hava tillskjutit en ½ mark var och köpt och bränt kaffe, socker och grädde också kokar vi vårt kaffe själv Detta kaffe smakar som det vi fick hemma." (Lundberg, 8 March 1912; 22:16:8:P).

26. "Dagen efter ägde det sedvanliga dopet rum, vi voro 18 personer, som hade tecknat sig på en lista för att deltaga i festen, det kostade 3 mark. [...] Ett obehagligt uppträde

inträffade under festen. Spanjorerna hade nämligen blivit förargade över att de ej fingo deltaga i festen. En spanjor flög båtsmannen i strupen och hade omkull honom men John Ericsson, vår Stockholmskamrat, tog spanjoren i nacken och höll som i ett skruvstäd till matroserna kom. Vi fingo falla på knä och så läste Neptunus upp en lång ramsa och sedan tog han en stor pensel och doppade den i vattnet och slog oss i ansiktet med den och så fick vi ett vackert textat diplom undertecknat av kaptenen och så vore vi döpta." (Lundberg, 8 March 1912; 22:16:8:P).

27. "Denna rätt kallas 'potjäro' därpå drucko vi 'matte' en dryck som användes här istället för kaffet hos oss. Den tillredes av 'Jerva' hos oss kallat paraguayte, samt varmt vatten i en stor kopp i det man sticker ned ett sugrör, sedan får koppen gå laget runt tills vattnet är slut, då fyller man på mera vatten och så fortgår det tills jervan mist all sin kraft." (Lundberg, 26 June 1912; 22:16:8:P).

28. "och så sade han något på tyska, som jag inte förstod. Men värre var det sedan när jag skulle på tåget, som gick till Hamburg. Ingen förstod svenska så jag kunde få veta vad jag skulle få göra. Men så fick jag se konduktören. Och frågade honom. Han förstod inte först vad jag menade men så gick han mot ett tåg och tecknade att jag skulle följa med. Jag lydde men innan vi hann fram så gick det. Jag blev först mycket skraj och tänkte, fastän klockan inte var så mycket än, att jag kom försent. Men det skulle bara växla."(Mellberg, 25 November 1926; 15:14:6F.).

29. "Till kupékamrat fick jag sällskap med en tysk gubbe, som snart började prata vid mig. Jag fick senare reda på att tyskarna är väldigt pratsamma och inte kan sitta tillsammans med någon i fem minuter förrän de börjar prata, som jag själv fick pröva på sedan. Gubben frågade mig en hel del frågor först på tyska men så förklarade jag för honom att jag inte spräckte deutsch" (Mellberg, 25 November 1926; 15:14:6F.).

30. "När jag varit på däck en stund gick jag ner till matsalen för att äta. Jag gick helt fräckt och satte mig vid ett bord utan att jag tänkte på att det fanns några regler. När en kypare kom förbi så kallade jag på honom och slog på bordet och mente att jag skulle ha mat. Då gick han till mig och sade något som jag naturligtvis inte förstod. Då ropade han på ett par flickor, som gick förbi, sade något till dem. De började prata på ännu ett annat språk som jag inte heller förstod mig på.
Då kallade de på den som sköter om sakerna nere i matsalen en slags uppsyningsman. Det såg ut att vara en hygglig karl., som det också är. Han bad mig följa honom och så gick vi till hans kontor. Han frågade mig på engelska om jag kan tala engelska. 'Ja lite', sade jag på samma språk. Så bad han mig om min biljett, rev av den ett stycke och gav mig den tillbaka jämte en liten pappersbit, som det stod bordets nummer på, och likaledes i ena hörnet en 2, som jag inte då visste vad det betydde. Men det skulle vara andra gången de åt. Ni kanske inte förstår vad jag menar, men förstår ni det är så mycket folk, och de får alla inte rum på samma gång. Därför har de delat upp det i flera gånger istället. Det går ända till fyra gånger." (Mellberg, 30 November 1926; 15:14:6F.).

31. "Efter ett par dagar kom vi till Vigo i Portugalien. De kan tro det var vackert där. Vi låg i staden Vigo hela dagen nästan. Jag köpte några apelsiner och bananer av infödingarna som kom upp med sina varor på däck. Jag tyckte det var ett mycket lustigt folk och mycket oanständigt.' (Mellberg, 26 December 1926; 15:14:6F.)

32. "Sedan vid matbordet talade de om för mig att jag skall läsa. Först ska jag lära mig spanska språket. Sedan skall jag studera annat jag ska ha nytta av. Så jag är i full gång och studerar allt vad jag kan. Sigrid läser spanska med mig. Ibland åker vi pojkar till staden och har roligt. När jag hade varit där en vecka åkte vi pojkar in till staden och besökte zoologiska trädgården. Det var mycket roligt för mig att se den. Sedan var vi och besökte staden och tittade lite närmare på den. Axel har köpt mycket kläder åt mig för att jag skall vara fin när jag är med dem ute. Jag har fått en fin halmhatt, ett par vita byxor, 3 par kalsonger, 2 slipsar och ett par finfina skor. Ni ska tro att han är väldigt snäll." (Mellberg, 26 December 1926; 15:14:6F.).

33. "Igår var jag inne i Buenos Aires igen och var på en biograf. Jag har varit två gånger på biografen redan och jag förstår rätt mycket." (Mellberg, 26 December 1926; 15:14:6F.).

Decisions in Transit: The Case of Scandinavian Immigrants to Argentina

Elisabeth Vik

How do migrants decide whether to stay or go, where to go, and where to settle? Research on Norwegians in Argentina indicates that decision-making may be understood as a process in transit and not always an act made at one point in time nor necessarily prior to departure. Statistics on the arrivals of Norwegians and Swedes in Buenos Aires between 1882 and 1940[1] suggest that the majority of these immigrants did not embark directly from their country of origin but had passed through other countries and continents before traveling to Argentina. The same statistics also show that many traveled back and forth and arrived several times in Argentina. Their destination was thus not always clear upon departure, and their initial intention was not always to emigrate. Analyzing the letters and stories of three Scandinavians in relation to these statistics illustrates how decisions may be understood as ongoing processes subject to change and turns in directions while in transit.

Thomas Faist supplements rational choice theories and migration-systems theories by introducing a meso-level between the individual (micro) and structural (macro) levels in a social relational approach.[2] He suggests three levels of analysis: the structural, relational, and individual levels. The relational level is understood as the "density, strength and content of social relations between stayers and movers within units in the areas of origin and destination."[3]

Faist's basic assumption is that "potential migrants and groups always relate to other social structures along a continuum of degrees of freedom."[4] Faist points out that "potential migrants can reorganise both in the country of origin *and* in the new country of settlement."[5] The use of "potential migrant," however, gives the impression that factors influencing a decision, like social networks, collectives, and relationships, exist prior to the migration and before the journey starts. It is not enough, however, to specify the existing relations before departure to understand decision-making as informed by social ties and networks. Decision-making is also open to influence and affected by the possibilities, opportunities, and misfortunes offered by people and circumstances along the way. Decision-making may then be understood as an ongoing process as the social ties and networks are also in a process of transition as events unfold and plans change while in transit.

To illuminate how decisions are made as a process in transit, individual stories are more helpful than a macro-focus on economic and demographic conditions in the country of origin. While macrostudies are useful for an overall study of large-scale emigration and immigration, actual stories of decisions by individuals may contradict assumptions made on the macrolevel. These individual stories illuminate other paths taken towards the final destination of migrants. The stories of three Scandinavians in Argentina presented here and the statistics on Norwegian and Swedish arrivals in Buenos Aires provide examples of how decision-making may be understood as a process.

Oscar, Otto, and Solveig

For Oscar, Otto, and Solveig,[6] we see how serendipity, circumstance, and particular encounters contributed to their choices and transition to immigrant status in Argentina. Their stories are presented through excerpts from Oscar's travel biography, Otto's letters to his mother and sister before, during, and after the journey, and Solveig's narration of the journey and arrival in Argentina.[7] Oscar, Otto, and Solveig are examples of migrants who were not considered emigrants at the moment of departure but became immigrants to Argentina at a later stage. All three took the decision to stay in Argentina after a while – either because a temporary stay turned into a permanent one or because they stopped on their way to somewhere else.

Oscar was a Swedish sailor[8] sailing on a Norwegian ship who, after two years at sea, decided to stay in Argentina. In the introduction to his travel biography, Oscar describes how he ended up in Argentina and the circumstances that brought him to Buenos Aires in the first place:

> It was December 1898, and I was 20 years old. I remember I was on duty on deck the night before we maneuvered into the harbor of Buenos Aires, and I felt convinced that I would stay in this country. The lights from the city called out to me and said: 'Here is your destiny, young man'.
> I don't know where this feeling came from, because I knew nothing about Argentina and I still hadn't set foot ashore. In Cape Town and New Orleans, where I had been stuck for weeks, I went ashore and got to know the surroundings, but I found nothing that attracted me and I felt absolutely no need to try life on land.
> And it was just a coincidence or a stroke of luck that brought me to La Plata. At the harbor in Mobile there were quite a few Norwegian ships, and at night the boys were rowing between the ships to say hello. One of those nights I met a guy, an able seaman just like me, who longed for Norway and his girlfriend. My ship was leaving for home, something I was sad about, so we went to our

respective captains and opened our hearts, and happily and hurriedly changed ships.

This easily is a man guided onto the path of his destiny.[9]

A brief encounter and a heartbreak provided Oscar with a change in his plans and prolonged his time at sea. But it was not the reason for his immediate attraction to Buenos Aires. His initial attraction was not enough to keep him in the capital, however, and after a few days he found a job possibility in the south of Argentina.

Almost 40 years later in August 1935, Otto left for Uruguay but ended up in Argentina. Otto was 19 years old and wrote to his parents during his journey. He had left Bergen and was about to leave Norway:

> I have arrived in Kristiansund and from here we leave for Buenos Aires, this afternoon, they tell me. The passengers are mostly Danish and most of them are headed for Brazil. We are only three Norwegians. The third is 29 years old and has a job at the same place as the father of the girl who was at the passport office. As you might have read in the papers, on our way from Bergen we were hit by another steamship. The anchor split the side of the ship and threw the girl out of her bed, but otherwise she was unharmed... [10]

Otto was traveling on a commercial steamship by the name of Norma with the Norwegian South America Line. Commercial ships were allowed to bring along 12 passengers. The Danish passengers left the ship in Santos, while the three Norwegians continued to Buenos Aires. The 14-year-old girl made quite an impression on Otto, as she was the victim of the accident on their way from Bergen to Kristiansund.

I was able to trace this same girl, whose name was Solveig, more than 70 years later when she was 90 years old and living in Buenos Aires. I gave her a copy of the letter Otto had written about their common journey. She remembered the incident on board. She read the part about the accident over and over, confirming it was her, and she told me she wasn't hurt but "would you believe the commotion!" She told me that Lien was the last name of the third Norwegian passenger on board. He continued from Buenos Aires to Patagonia where he worked for Solveig's father for several years in the oil business. In the 1940s he moved to Canada. Solveig was just 14 years old and traveling alone on that journey in 1935, but her first trip to Argentina was in 1926, with her mother. They went to see her father for the first time. He had left Norway in 1920, after marrying Solveig's mother, but before their daughter's birth.

The Exception To the Rule

Oscar, Otto, and Solveig belong to a small group of Scandinavians in Argentina. The vast majority of the Norwegians and Swedes who left during the period 1820-1930 migrated to North America. Only a few thousand went to Argentina. Being the exception to the rule, their cases may tell a different story. They did not just leave their country; they also went in a completely different direction from the larger group.

There is abundant research on Nordic emigration to Canada and the United States. Almost no attention, however, has been paid to those who chose to migrate elsewhere. The southern destinations are hardly mentioned except for the occasional comment. One exception is Gudmund Stang's work on Scandinavian emigration to Latin America between 1800 and 1940[11] and his study of the transatlantic dispersion of Scandinavian engineers between 1870 and 1930. This work includes a section about engineers working and living in Argentina.[12] Stang himself was born in Buenos Aires of Norwegian parents and re-migrated to Norway, first to carry out his military service in 1951, and later to work as a historian at the University of Trondheim.[13]

In Argentinian literature, immigration is the focus rather than emigration, as Argentina was the receiving country for many nationalities from the turn of the nineteenth century. Among these various nationalities, most of the literature concentrates on the largest groups of immigrants – the Spaniards and the Italians.[14] There are, however, studies on smaller groups like the Welsh, Polish, and Danish immigrants and their agricultural communities in Argentina.[15] Recently, Alicia Bernasconi at the Center for Latin America Migration Studies (CEMLA) wrote about the minority group of immigrants from San Marino. This group is even smaller than the Scandinavians, and hopefully the usefulness of studies of smaller groups of migrants is becoming increasingly recognized.

Although a small group in total numbers,[16] the largest group of Norwegians in South America ended up in Argentina. This study is a beginning attempt to uncover knowledge about the Norwegians in Argentina. The exact number of Scandinavians that were in Argentina is uncertain, as estimates and the numbers from different registers vary a lot. In the case of Norwegians, from 1882 to 1950 there were 3,142 arrivals registered through the port of Buenos Aires.[17] This does not include missing records, people entering through other ports, or arriving by river, land, or airplane. Between 1882 and 1905, 381 Swedes arrived and probably more afterward. Because of the Swedish-Norwegian Union (1814-1905), Norwegians might have been registered as Swedish before 1905.

Some immigrants were registered more than once because they traveled back and forth several times. This reduces the overall number of unique individuals. The registers from the years 1933-1937 were not included at the time and are now inaccessible.[18] Otto's arrival and Solveig's second arrival are not included in

ELISABETH VIK

the statistics because this was in the period of the missing records. There are several known individuals who do not appear in these records although they all arrived in Buenos Aires between 1882 and 1950. This is not just a case of missing records. Oscar is not listed among the Swedes. He might not have gone through immigration since his status at arrival was as *tripulante*. All of this suggests that the real number of immigrants might be considerably higher than the official number. We also know that there were Swedes and Norwegians in Argentina before 1882.

The Norwegian commercial fleet had long been active in South American ports as a result of British and German trade, bringing with it sailors-in-transit, shipping agents, and import/export businessmen. The Norwegian-Swedish consulate was established in Buenos Aires only a few years after Argentina's declaration of independence from Spain.[19] Norwegians were employed in the construction of infrastructure like railroads and channels during the 1870s and 1880s. All of this indicates that there was a higher number of Norwegians in Argentina than we find documented in the arrival registers, which only start in 1882. From 1914 onwards, the community increased because of the establishment of the Norwegian South America Line, which facilitated direct commercial relations and travel between the two countries.[20] Argentina also attracted adventurers drawn to the great unknown, the vast loneliness of Patagonia and the pampas. Scandinavians signed up for work in unwelcoming climates and participated in work to build infrastructure, map territories, and chart waters. They even introduced skiing as a mode of transportation, and later leisure, in the South of Argentina. Work, business opportunities, and adventure, or preferably all of the above, were aspects of attraction. But in spite of all the attractive opportunities, the number of Scandinavians remained small, and for those who stayed, there were other aspects that influenced their choices, as will become clear from the stories of Oscar, Otto, and Solveig.

Individual and Professional

As with Solveig, Oscar, and Otto, most Norwegian and Swedish migrants to South America were traveling individually. More than half (1700 or 54 percent) of the arrivals were single, divorced, and widows or widowers.[21] It is uncertain whether those who are listed as married (830 or 26 percent) actually traveled with their families.

While one of the main economic reasons for emigrating from Scandinavia was the overpopulation and scarcity of farmland,[22] exceptionally few Norwegian farmers went to Argentina. Only 90 individuals are listed as farmers or agricultural workers, which is less than 3 percent. The most common occupations were merchants, engineers, and seamen, and most of the occupations are connected to some sort of urban life: businessmen, engineers, architects, craftsmen, employees, artists, and positions within the service industry.

As a group, they seem to be best characterized as skilled and educated people who already had job offers or business ideas to put into motion once they arrived. Almost half of them traveled first class or on commercial ships as opposed to the common arrangements for most migrants on passenger ships in second and third class. Their emigration was not an escape from poverty or overpopulation. This movement involved people with resources and professions, especially engineers and merchants who set out to make the most of their connections in both countries. Oscar, Solveig, and Otto also traveled individually, and their journeys were not an escape from conditions in their country of origin.

Deciding on Argentina

The decision to leave their country of origin did not at the time include immigration to Argentina. Oscar worked his way to Argentina over the course of two years. His decision to stay was guided by a desire for more adventures and an emotional experience. His process of making decisions took place a long way from home. At no point did he actually decide to become an immigrant, but the sum of all the people he met and intervening circumstances made him stay in Argentina at least until 1914.[23]

Like Oscar, Solveig's father planned to see the world for a couple of years and return to Norway. Solveig's mother got tired of waiting for him and, six years after he left home, she brought their daughter to Argentina with the idea of bringing her husband home. Neither Solveig's mother nor her father had the intention of migrating.

Solveig left Norway twice. The first time was not her own decision since she was a child. She and her parents returned to Norway a few years later so that Solveig could go to a Norwegian school. Her parents, however, missed Argentina and left Solveig with her aunt to return to Patagonia the following year. The second time she went to Argentina, it was Solveig's own decision. After finishing primary school, Solveig was given the choice at age 14 to study further and stay in Norway with her aunt or leave school to migrate to Argentina to be with her parents. There were no further possibilities for her education in Comodoro Rivadavia. Nevertheless, she missed her family, wanted to see her newborn sister, and decided against education to reunite with her family.

Otto, on the other hand, wanted to emigrate, but still had not decided upon a destination. In his letters prior to departure, he first looked at Australia, Spain, or Uruguay as possible destinations.[24] Because there was less bureaucracy in Uruguay, he asked his parents for permission to leave school and Norway in 1935. He wrote that they wanted him to wait until he finished school the following spring, but he wanted to leave earlier partly against his parents' wish. Otto decided to leave although he had possibilities of a livelihood in Norway. His father was about to buy a farm for Otto where he could raise cattle. Otto, however, was not interested in such a job. He was then 19-and–a-half years old and wanted to leave before he reached 20.[25]

Transmigration

Otto and Solveig are among the few Norwegians who left directly from Norway. Only 552, or 17 percent, of Norwegian arrivals embarked from a Norwegian port, about half of them (267) in Kristiansund.[26] Kristiansund was the main port for the export of bacalao from Norway to Latin American countries. All of the Nordic ports together (Finland, Sweden, Norway, and Denmark) account for 772 of the Norwegian arrivals to Buenos Aires, or 24 percent. The rest of the arriving emigrants are listed as coming from ports of origin outside of the Nordic countries.

France (119), Germany (382), and England (453) together account for 30 percent of Norwegians traveling to Argentina from their respective ports, almost twice the total number from Norwegian ports. Excluding the Nordic countries, Europe accounts for 1,152 Norwegians or 36 percent who traveled to Buenos Aires. Seven hundred and fifty Norwegians embarked from countries and continents outside of Europe, which is a larger percentage than those traveling from Norway. Among these individuals, 202 traveled from the U.S. and Canada, with fully 184 travelers embarking in New York. This is more than the total number of travelers leaving Oslo/Christiania.[27]

Comparing the arrival registers in Argentina with the emigration protocols in Norway may shed light on the travel patterns of migrants and the various steps of their journeys. So far, the points of departure suggest that a large part of the arrivals were transmigrants, those who first left Norway for another country, spent time in several countries, and then continued onwards to Argentina. If their intention was to migrate, Argentina was, more often than not, not the first stop.

Unlike the standard narrative of the farmer emigrant who sold everything and left his country of origin to start a new life in the U.S., Norwegians in Argentina seldom decided to emigrate before leaving Norway. Generally, it seems that the initial idea was to work abroad for a few years or set up a business and then return to Norway once it was up and running. The decision to stay in Argentina seems to have been made after a while, after trying life elsewhere, sometimes many years after their first journey from home or after several journeys. This last aspect is also true for the many sailors who decided to stay. They first intended to work and return home, but later decided to settle. As a result, their period of transit became very long – sometimes years or even decades.

For Otto, Buenos Aires was supposed to be a stop on his journey to Uruguay. He had planned to leave the next day for Uruguay, but there were no travel connections because it was a Sunday.[28] At the Norwegian Seamen's Church, the pastor advised him to stay at the German Seamen's Home in Buenos Aires. The pastor there would look after his letters and money. Two months after his arrival in Buenos Aires, Otto wrote that he had a job at a Danish hotel owned by friends of the Norwegian pastor in Tres Arroyos further south in Argentina. Otto wanted to continue his travel and did so for three years. Then he returned to Buenos Aires to settle. He had learned Spanish and had tried out several lines of work for a few months at a time. In the end, he never followed his original plan to go to Uruguay. He deviated from his plan as a result of the Sunday transportation situation, but also because his extra days in Buenos Aires at the Seamen's Church brought him other acquaintances and opportunities.

For Oscar, the city of Mobile was his fork in the road, while Buenos Aires also functioned as a stop on the road where he took advantage of the opportunities the city offered. In La Boca, a cartographic expedition to Patagonia that set out to determine the borders between Chile and Argentina recruited Oscar, and he was soon on board a ship again, this time on his way to Puerto Madryn in Patagonia to serve at the Comision 8 Chubut.

Solveig traveled directly to Comodoro Rivadavia to be reunited with her parents and to meet her little sister for the first time. This time she stayed with her family until she was married, and it was not until 1948, when the couple had two children, that they decided to return to live in Buenos Aires.

Places of Transit: Social Network, Reunion, and Identity

Oscar, Otto, and Solveig provide us with just a few examples that illustrate how the end result may deviate completely from the original plan. How things turn out depends on possibilities, obstacles, aquintances, and new connections. These processes have multiple outcomes that are affected by multiple factors including adaptation to changing circumstances, coincidences, and luck. Sometimes they completely contradict conventional assumptions about how macro conditions drive migration flows.

Faist's meso-level with its focus on interpersonal relations brings us to a better understanding of individual people's decisions. Economic possibilities and hopes for a better future may start a journey, but then decisions are subject to changing possibilities or constraints, good luck or misfortunes, emotions, acquaintances, and new friends along the way. Although there are examples of Norwegians emigrating to Argentina with economic expectations of a better life, this was not always the case. Oscar left a job only to wind up broke three days later. Otto decided to leave a secure livelihood in Norway for an insecure future of adventure. Solveig decided against education in order to live in a place where her family was and no education was possible.

Many stories recount people who were initially regarded as travelers, workers, adventurers, and tourists. Their decisions not to return to Norway were informed not only by the social networks to which they belonged before departure but by new social contacts and ties they formed while in transit. Oscar, Solveig's father, and Otto are examples of adventurers who decide in the moment to diverge from their original plan as an impulsive reaction to offers from people they met on their path. By contrast, Lien, Solveig's mother, and Solveig traveled to Argentina as a result of a social tie across the sea.

One way to study networks and social relations formed during travel and transit is to study the places of transit themselves.[29] The Norwegians established churches, clubs, and associations in Argentina but did not establish agricultural communities as the Danes did in Argentina. There were many more Danish immigrants – about 13,000[30] – and they formed entire communities where the main language was Danish and that had Danish schools, libraries, newspapers, churches, and so on. The Swedes played a central role in the founding of the city of Oberá in the tropical Misiones in the North. Later this would become the host city of the traditional immigrant festival where most of the ethnic communities in Argentina currently are represented.[31] A few Norwegians attempted to form a community in the south of Argentina, in Magallanes, but it was short-lived. Because of their relatively small number, there are no communities, villages, or cities mainly associated with Norwegians. Most of them, nevertheless, did manage to stay in contact with other Scandinavians in Argentina through the Norwegian and Scandinavian clubs and associations. The Scandinavians were not exceptional in the establishment of clubs. Almost all ethnic communities in Buenos Aires had a social club or sports clubs, and most of them are still active today. As recently as 2003, an umbrella club called Club Europeo or European Club connected a number of international identity-based clubs into one network.[32]

One such place of transit was the Norwegian Seamen's Church in Buenos Aires, established in 1888. It was first located by the Riachuelo River, where all the ships arrived, and was able to offer an alternative to disreputable and potentially dangerous establishments near the harbor. As the first Scandinavian church in Buenos Aires, it was a place for sailors from all the Scandinavian countries who were passing through to go to. Although the church targeted mainly sailors, it also remained an important place of social reunion for whalers, visitors, immigrants, and permanent residents in Buenos Aires of Scandinavian, Nordic, and Baltic origins. For almost one hundred years, the Norwegian Seamen's Church in Buenos Aires was a place of transit and reunion. It functioned as the first step into other clubs, institutions, and arenas where networks were established and expanded.

The church held Protestant religious services, an alternative to the mainly Catholic church in Argentina. And it functioned as a network bridge and facilitator allowing for the cultivation of new social ties with others in the same situation who spoke the same or a related language and had similar cultural backgrounds. Consequently the networks made in such an arena influenced and helped people to make decisions whether to stay in Argentina, to move on further within Argentina or beyond, or to return to their countries of origin.

The Seamen's Church became a connection point also as a center of logistics for people, jobs, and goods. To the Scandinavians, the church was not just a church. It was also a bank, post office, library, employment agency, and "Santa Claus," distributing letters and gifts from mothers in Norway. At times it was a sports club, especially when Sverre Eika was a pastor there. He was fondly called the football pastor. It was often the first place for someone recently arrived to meet other countrymen who could inform them of job oportunities, social activities, and other clubs. From there, they could form their own social network. The Swedish-Norwegian consulate before 1905, and both the Swedish and Norwegian consulates after 1905, cooperated with the church and pastor in order to locate people and their next of kin. There was also an exchange of information between the church and consulate with regard to job opportunities for Scandinavians.

Other places to find fellow countrymen were the Norwegian Association of La Plata[33] and the Scandinavian Rowing Club.[34] Both were in close contact with the church and the consulate. The La Plata association was founded with the objective of organizing a celebration of Norwegian Constitution Day on May 17th of every year. It provided a meeting place for Norwegians, mostly men. It also organized an aid fund directed at helping fellow countrymen in need of economic assistance.[35]

Return, Visits, and the Norwegian-Argentine Association

While Norwegians worked to keep in contact with their countrymen in Argentina, they also stayed in touch with those in their country of origin. Those who left and those who stayed behind in Norway maintained family ties, informed each other about educational and job opportunities, gave news of business relations and cultural connections, and had exchanges of political information. There was also a substantial return of migrants, which strengthened the transnational connections between the two countries.

In the country of origin, contact was kept up with the social network the immigrants had before they left and also with new people who shared their experiences in Argentina. These connections materialized in yet another association, this time in Norway. The Norwegian-Argentine Association,[36] based in Oslo, was established in 1935 by Norwegians who had returned from Argentina. Together with the La Plata association and the Scandinavian Rowing Club, it was an arena for reunion in both countries for people who had experienced life in Argentina. Likewise, Danes who returned to Denmark established their own Danish-Argentine Association, and the two associations traditionally invite each other's members to their yearly *asado* events. The Norwegian association celebrated its 75-year anniversary in 2010 and continues to unite Norwegians and Argentinians in Nor-

ELISABETH VIK

way to share that certain something about Argentina that it seems is impossible to lose.

Conclusions

Individual stories of Argentina migrants from Norway contrast with the conventional perspective of migration as a one-way exodus. Like Oscar, Otto, and Solveig, many traveled individually, either in first class or by working their way across the Atlantic. Most believed they had embarked on a temporary journey. Only later did it turn into a permanent settlement. Some traveled back and forth many times and settled in Argentina after several journeys. For these examples the choice of Argentina as a destination seemed to have been taken after spending time in Argentina and not only before departure from Norway.

As Thomas Faist so optimistically puts it: "Looking at moving and staying as both interpersonal and an intertemporal process, we can analyse first-time moves, repeated migration and return migration with the same conceptual tools."[37] Adding in the places of transit, social arenas, and institutions that facilitate social networks and ties to people and countries might bring us closer to an understanding of "what exactly happens in networks and collectives that induces people to stay, move and return."[38]

In the case of Scandinavians, as with most migrant groups, social contact was kept across the sea, business relations upheld, cultural traditions preserved, and political information exchanged. All of this, in addition to return migration, contributed to transnational connections between those who left and returned, and those who stayed, and in turn facilitated changes in plans and decisions. It is fair to say that migration is not just a movement going one way but rather a flow of information, goods, people, and ideas in both directions and beyond, thus influencing social networks in both countries a little bit with every exchange. The Norwegian Seamen's Church was one such place of transit – a reunion and connection point. There, new ties were formed, old ties and national identity maintained, and connections with other institutions made – all while providing for possible alternatives of decision.

The perspective of decisions as a process in transit helps us understand that actual decisions may contradict the standard narrative of the migrant and the conventional view of migration as a one-way exodus. Within the largest immigrant group in Argentina, the Italians, it was common to work seasonal jobs and go back and forth every year. They were called *golondrinas*, the name of a migratory bird with a specific seasonal route. Ute Ritz-Deutch also mentions how Germans in southern Brazil lived entire adult lives between Brazil and Germany. Øverland notes that "there were no rules or patterns for immigrant behavior or careers and there were as many experiences of transition as there were immigrants."[39]

The particular Scandinavian stories analyzed here serve as examples and suggest one way of looking at migratory decisions that can supplement the perspective on mechanisms driving the major migratory flows. These stories show how decision-making must be understood as a process in transit, something that can change along the way, not as a once-and-for-all decision taken prior to departure but as a process that is influenced by changing practical circumstances and the social connections and networks established prior to and during the time in transit.

Notes

1. Centro de Estudios Migratorios Latino Americanos (CEMLA): Base de datos 1882-1950: Suecos entrados por el puerto de Buenos Aires 1882-1906 y Noruegos entrados por el puerto de Buenos Aires 1882-1950. List of Norwegians and Swedes extracted from CEMLA's database of immigrant arrivals based on arrival immigration registers in Buenos Aires 1882-1950. The research is in progress and the results presented here are to be regarded as preliminary and may be subject to change and further discoveries.

2. Thomas Faist, "The Crucial Meso-Level," in International Migration, Immobility and Development, eds. T. Hammar et al. (Oxford and New York: Berg Publishers, 1997), 187-217: 194.

3. Ibid. 195.

4. Ibid. 197.

5. Ibid. 198.

6. I have chosen to only use the first names of Otto and Solveig to protect their families. Their particular identities are not important to understand the main argument of the paper. Their stories are true and function as illustrations in this context. Oscar's book is published and his full name may be found in the bibliography list, but for the sake of equal appearance I name all three migrants only by their first names in the text.

7. Oscar Lundquist, Hårda Tag i Argentina (Stockholm: Albert Bonniers forlag, 1946). Otto's letters to his mother and sister between 1935 and 1938 are part of a private collection owned by the family. Interview with Solveig Wallem Rodriguez in Buenos Aires, July 2007. Both Oscar and Solveig tell their story years later; Oscar published his book almost 50 years after his first arrival in 1898, and Solveig is looking back after spending her whole life in Argentina. Otto's letters start already from the port of Kristiansund in Norway. His letters to his family in Norway provide therefore the most immediate impression, while the other two accounts are colored by later experiences and memories.

8. Although Oscar was Swedish, he was one of the very few sailors who wrote about his journey and life in Argentina. His account of his meeting with Argentina and Buenos Aires may be similar to that of other sailors on Norwegian ships at the time.

9. Lundquist, Hårda Tag, 13.

10. Otto's letter to his mother dated: Kristiansund 22. August 1935. (My translation from Norwegian to English).

11. Gudmund Stang, "La emigración Escandinava a la América Latina, 1800-1940," in *Jahrbuch für Geschichte von Staat, Wirtschaft und Gesellschaft Lateinamerikas* 13 (Köln Wien: Böhlau Verlag, 1976), 293-330.
12. Stang, "The Dispersion of Scandinavian Engineers."
13. Mörner and Schwartz, "Gudmund Stang (1933-2002)," in *Hispanic American Historical Review* 82 (2002): 762-764.
14. See, for example, A. E. Fernández, J. C. Moya and B. Bragoni, *La inmigración española en la Argentina* (Editorial Biblos, 1999); Maria Liliana Da Orden, *Inmigración española, familia y movilidad en la Argentina moderna* (Editorial Biblos, 2005); J. C. Moya, *Cousins and Strangers: Spanish immigrants in Buenos Aires 1850-1930* (University of California Press, 1998); Arnt Schneider, *Futures lost: nostalgia and identity among Italian immigrants in Argentina* (P. Lang, 2000).
15. See, for example, M. T. Dittler, *De sol a sol: inmigrantes polacos en la Patagonia* (Prometeo Libros, 2007); A. Matthews, *Crónica de la colonia galesa de la Patagonia* (Editorial Raigal, 1954); M. Bjerg, *Historias de la inmigración en la Argentina* (Editorial Edhasa, 2009); M. Bjerg, *El mundo de Dorothea* (Imago Mundi, 2004).
16. Ingrid Semmingsen, *Veien mot Vest* (Oslo, 1950), 291; Gudmund Stang, "The Dispersion of Scandinavian Engineers 1870-1930 and the Concept of an Atlantic System," in STS *Working Paper* No 3/89, 1989.
17. Centro de Estudios Migratorios Latino Americanos (CEMLA): Base de datos 1882-1950: Suecos entrados por el puerto de Buenos Aires 1882-1906 y Noruegos entrados por el puerto de Buenos Aires 1882-1950. Extracted from the immigrant arrival database owned by CEMLA, based on the arrival protocols, ships' registers and immigration protocols in Buenos Aires 1882-1950.
18. The protocols from the years 1933 to 1937 were transferred to Archivo General de la Nación (AGN) before they were copied to the database and are, according to officials at CEMLA and the AGN, currently inaccessible.
19. Eilert Sundt, *Nordmenn i Argentina* (unpublished, 1948). According to Eilert Sundt in an unpublished manuscript from 1948, the Swedish-Norwegian consulate was already established in Buenos Aires in 1828 and maintained its offices there until today, except for the period under Juan Manuel de Rosa's violent rule 1835-1853 when they had to move office to Montevideo in Uruguay. Different versions or copies of the manuscript are archived at Det norske utvandrersenteret in Stavanger, Norway, and in an unordered collection of documents from La Asociacion Noruega-Argentina which is privately owned, as well as at the Norwegian Emigrant Museum and among diplomatic documents also in an unordered collection currently in the possession of the Norwegian Foreign Ministry, soon to be handed over to The National Archives of Norway. The versions differ in dates but not much in content.
20. The Norwegian La Plata Association, *Det norske La Plata Samfund 1896-1936* (Buenos Aires, 1936), 1.
21. 1,585 single, 30 widows or widowers, and 75 divorced individuals.
22. Orm Øverland, *The Western Home: A Literary History of Norwegian America* (Northfield: Minnesota, 1996). The Norwegian-American Historical Association: 4.
23. His account ends with the outbreak of the First World War. It is fair to assume that this news would make him stay also after 1914.

24. Letter from Otto to his family dated: Stend 14.11.1934.

25. Letter from Otto to his family dated: Stend 29.01.1935.

26. CEMLA: Base de datos 1882-1950. There is a large number of unknown ports of departure, 382 Norwegian arrivals in Buenos Aires are registered with unknown port of departure.

27. Oslo 55, Christiania 78. Oslo and Christiania is the same city, it changed names back to its original name Oslo in 1924.

28. Letter from Otto to his family dates: Den tyske sjømannsheimen (The German Seamen's Home in Buenos Aires) 20.09.1935.

29. This approach was suggested by the organizers of the conference in Belgium: Tales of Transit: Narrative Migrant Spaces in a Transatlantic Perspective 1830-1950.

30. Per Agertoft, Danskhed på Pampaen (Historisk Specialeafhandling: Aarhus Universitet, 2005), 37.

31. http://www.fiestadelinmigrante.com.ar/; http://www.fiestadelinmigrante.com.ar/paises-nordicos-la-colectividad/paises-nordicos-historia/; http://www.misionesvive.com.ar/obera/historia_obera.html.

32. http://www.clubeuropeo.com/index.php?PN=introduction.

33. Det Norske La Plata Samfund, founded in 1896.

34. Club Remeros Escandinavos, founded in 1912.

35. Den norske Hjelpekasse, The Norwegian Aid Fund.

36. Norsk-Argentinsk Forening, The Norwegian Argentine Association.

37. Faist, "Crucial Meso-Level," 216.

38. Ibid. 188.

39. Øverland, The Western Home, 10.

German Colonists in Southern Brazil: Navigating Multiple Identities on the Brazilian Frontier

Ute Ritz-Deutch

What a topsy-turvy world! The sun shines from the North. The cold wind is from the South. Spring starts in September. Christmas is supposedly the hottest time of year. The waxing moon I observed last night, did not have the form of half a C but rather the shape of a boat, and when trying to steer the horse to the left, one has to pull the reins to the right. What else do I have to relearn!
Gustav Stutzer reflecting on his arrival in Blumenau, Brazil, 1882.[1]

Over there [in Germany] one lives by the past and for the future: here [in Brazil] one only lives for the present. The country does not yet have a past. Nobody is concerned about the future.
Therese Stutzer reflecting on their life in Blumenau, 1886.[2]

When the Protestant pastor Gustav Stutzer and his wife Therese arrived in the well-known German colony of Blumenau, Santa Catarina, they were trying to make sense of their new world. When compared to Germany, it seemed to be turned upside down. In southern Brazil, the Stutzer family was indeed *off the beaten track*, in a place so unfamiliar that even the celestial bodies took different positions in the sky. The books Gustav Stutzer published on his experiences in Brazil, which also contain letters written by his wife Therese, speak to these early and ongoing struggles of adaptation. Their reflections on life in Brazil show a German-Brazilian ethnic identity in transition, always prompting them to relate their experiences in Brazil to those in Germany and vice versa.

Even after years in Brazil, the Stutzer family still experienced an identity in transit, showing that the process of acculturation is a translational, circular, and continuing movement rather than an initial transition followed by a linear progression toward assimilation. In many ways they remained in transit, always negotiating between both worlds.[3] While the experiences of the Stutzer family do not necessarily reflect those of all Germans in Brazil, they represent a group of German community leaders who were vocal and widely published and consequently had a disproportionate influence on the discourse about German Brazilians on both sides of the Atlantic. Stutzer's writings are a way to understand the experience of those Germans who, like himself, traveled back and forth between the two countries, living in each for several years at a time. These individuals straddled both worlds and often shared their experiences by publishing articles, papers, or books, introducing Brazil to a German readership.[4] Many of them were Germans who kept their German citizenship (*Reichsdeutsche*), although in this body of literature it is difficult to ascertain the citizenship status of the authors. The term German Brazilian was generally a cultural term, referring to German speakers living in Brazil. In fact they could be German citizens, Brazilian citizens, or persons who were neither.

Gustav Stutzer, whose initial goal as pastor in Blumenau was to guide the German Protestant community there, also actively promoted German emigration to Brazil, without completely immersing himself in the immigrant experience.[5] His books are part of the larger German colonial literature that helped shape the image of Brazil and of German Brazilians, and promoted the preservation of German culture. These authors were a point of reference and an authority on the conditions in Brazil for their readers on both sides of the Atlantic. For prospective emigrants, the German communities in Santa Catarina – especially in Blumenau and Joinville – were of particular interest. Articles about them appeared in colonial publications and periodicals, including the *Handbook of Germandom Abroad* (*Handbuch des Deutschtums im Auslande*) and newspapers such as Berlin's *Vossische Zeitung*.[6]

Monographs by Gustav Stutzer, José Deeke, Dr. Wettstein, and others were also an important source of available information.[7] These private accounts often echoed the attitudes and prejudices readers found in professional journals and official reports published in Germany. They saw Germans as "hardworking and efficient" in contrast to Luso-Brazilians.[8] However, this literature was more than a guide for prospective emigrants. It also promoted German identity and the preservation of so-called Germandom in the context of nation-building in Brazil as well as Germany.

Immigrant letters such as the ones penned by Therese Stutzer are an important supplement to monographs and political publications. They offer insights into particular moments of the migration experience. These personal accounts give voice to those who were uprooted in a way that official statistics or macro-analysis of migration cannot. As Kathleen DeHaan has noted in her study of Dutch immigrant letters, such means of communication provide a forum through which immigrants try to understand and translate national differences "while simultaneously articulating an emergent, complex sense of their transitional identity."[9] By narrating daily experiences, describing new situations, and explaining differences between the old and new world, authors engage in multiple strategies that substitute for face-to-face encounters. Letters "provide a site where immigrants construct, articulate and deliberate their knowledge of the world."[10] These writings allow them to make sense of what they have left behind and what they have gained in their new world – in this case, southern Brazil.

German immigration to Brazil is of great significance especially in the three southern states of Rio Grande do Sul, Santa Catarina, and Paraná. At the end of the nineteenth century more than 90 percent of German immigrants went to North America, and only 5 percent settled in South America. Total numbers are therefore modest. By the eve of the First World War, only an estimated 350,000 Germans resided in Brazil, around 100,000 of them in Santa Catarina.[11] Although many of the farmers had settled in areas that were sparsely populated, they nonetheless represented a significant percentage of the total population.[12] At the turn of the twentieth century in Santa Catarina, one out of every five residents was German-born or of German descent. Due to natural increase, German Brazilians now comprise one-third of the total population in southern Brazil. Indeed, the influence of Germans in southern Brazil should not be underestimated, since they created a region of ethnic composition and social structure different from the rest of the country.[13]

In many ways, it was easier for Germans to adjust to the United States than Brazil. In Brazil, conditions were harsher, and the cultural differences between Luso-Brazilians and German Brazilians were great. Nonetheless, several German propagandists at the time argued that migration from Germany should be redirected to southern Brazil despite the difficulties because Germandom had a better chance of surviving there. Germandom as a term was not clearly defined in the late nineteenth century but generally meant the preservation of German language and culture. Some contemporaries also conflated it with political loyalty to Germany.

The degree to which Germans in southern Brazil managed or failed to "assimilate" has been one of the more studied aspects of the German immigrant experience. It has received considerable attention in the Brazilian scholarship.[14] Giralda Seyferth notes that assessing the overall impact of Deutschtum (Germandom) in Brazil, or of Brasilianerdeutschtum (Germandom of Brazilians) is difficult because of the anti-German prejudices that existed in many communities. Furthermore, immigrant experiences are situational, and considerable differences exist from one context to the next or from one individual to the next.[15] Even in Blumenau, where Stutzer's Protestant congregation was located and where the German presence was particularly strong, ethnic identity among Germans was hardly monolithic. In Blumenau, the newspaper Der Urwaldsbote tended to promote the preservation of German culture, whereas Die Blumenauer Zeitung was more likely to advocate assimilation, claiming in one article that the rapid integration of Germans in the United States was a favorable model.[16]

While the Stutzer family undoubtedly became more familiar with southern Brazil over time, it would be wrong to speak of their adaptation as being a completed process. Later in life after he had already returned to Germany and committed his memories to paper, Stutzer reminisced about the disorientation he experienced when he first arrived in Blumenau in 1882. His brother, who introduced him to the area, had lived in southern Brazil for thirty years and was considered a community leader there. Like most travelers, Gustav Stutzer made constant comparisons between Germany and Brazil, marveling at the new environment and often being dismayed at the social conditions he found. It was a strange world (*verkehrte Welt*) indeed, where the sun shines from the north, the cold wind comes from the south, spring starts in September and Christmas time is during the hottest season of the year.[17]

Brazil was intriguing as well as unsettling for Stutzer. His critiques are attempts to understand his new home and also reflections on how deeply anchored he remained in his German upbringing and world-view. As a German who stayed in Brazil for two decades but ultimately returned to Germany, Stutzer represents a vocal minority among German Brazilians. Indeed, in southern Brazil, many of the leaders of the German community never intended to stay permanently. This was particularly the case among German businessmen, government officials such as embassy personnel, and Protestant pastors and teachers, who were at least partially financed from Germany. Unlike immigrant farmers who had come to Brazil to start a new life and generally did not have the means to return, many including Dr Blumenau, who founded the colony that bears his name, stayed for years or even decades, only to return to their old *Heimat*.

Germans who first set foot on Brazilian soil experienced profound culture shock. Adjusting to a new climate and ecological environment proved challenging, even in southern Brazil, where the climate is subtropical. This presented numerous challenges for farmers from northern Europe, who had to plant different crops and adjust their farming practices. Many of them succumbed to tropical diseases. Not surprisingly, many authors tried to caution German farmers about the hardships they would encounter if they chose to emigrate to Brazil.

Adjusting to a new climate, flora, and fauna was only half the battle. Stutzer was not alone in describing Brazil as a comparatively lawless country that was lacking in order and discipline. Clearly not all of the virtues Stutzer considered quintessentially German prevailed in Brazil, and he especially complained about the lack of work ethic among Luso-Brazilians. "The main purpose of the Brazilian worker and colonist is to be idle."[18] He described men sitting in front of their huts all day long until they were driven into action by the threat of starvation. Brazilian women supposedly shunned work as well. Stutzer found their way of life rudimentary, even primitive, and claimed that in Germany not even chickens were given such miserable huts to live in.[19]

The lack of Protestant work ethic in Brazil is a common theme found in many books and articles written for various German colonial societies. The message was clear. Germans who went abroad and maintained a high work ethic could make it in places like Brazil, where they presumably competed against people of lesser character and weaker wills. Of course, there was also the danger of going to Brazil and failing, simply because conditions were so difficult. Stutzer's advice on this matter was straightforward. Only sober and hardworking Germans should venture abroad. Drunkards and lazy people, on the other hand, should not emigrate to Brazil, because it could completely destroy a man.[20]

In some ways the image of Brazil as a land of opportunity but also as an untamed wilderness and lawless place where people on the frontier take matters into their own hands sounds reminiscent of the way the "Wild West" of North America was described to European readers. Undoubtedly, pioneers took risks if they settled on the frontier, where landownership was in dispute and where conflicts with American Indians were inevitable.[21] German immigrants must also have experienced a similar sense of alienation rooted in the unfamiliar in being isolated and far from one's birthplace, especially if one lived in the sparsely settled interior of the country.

Themes of cultural disorientation are prevalent in the literature generated by immigrants to both North and South America.[22] However, immigration is complex and multi-faceted, taking on different forms depending on the context. Undoubtedly, German immigrants living in New York City had different experiences from those who became farmers in the Midwest.[23] A similar range of conditions also existed in Brazil. German immigrants who went to São Paulo to work on the coffee plantations or in industry had different experiences from small-scale farmers in rural communities further south, where Germans had settled since the 1820s after a royal decree permitted the settlement of non-Portuguese groups.[24]

After Brazil became independent, Emperor Pedro I and his Austrian wife Leopoldine created favorable conditions for German immigrants. The Brazilian government encouraged and financially supported the settlement of German-speaking farmers to the southern provinces which later became the states of Rio Grande do Sul, Santa Catarina, and Paraná. The immigration projects in the South are consequently peculiar and unlike those in the rest of the country.

The Brazilian government had several reasons for encouraging German settlement in the South, which was at that time only thinly populated. The goal was to develop the region by bringing more land under cultivation, to "whiten" the nation, and to create a buffer zone to the La Plata states to the south and west.[25] Between 1824 and 1859, the Brazilian government gave over 20,000 German settlers various forms of aid to relocate to southern Brazil. This type of government involvement had no parallel in North America.[26]

Unfortunately the Brazilian government was not consistently nor sufficiently supportive of these new immigrant communities. Especially in the early days of colonization, many of them failed. Germans, and later Italians who settled in the South, were given land grants in isolated mountainous regions where transportation was difficult. Soil depletion and erosion posed numerous challenges and often forced farmers who adopted slash-burn methods from native peoples to move further into the interior every few years. Land titles were often disputed, and in some areas, local Indians would periodically attack settlers, who in turn hired Indian hunters to carry out revenge raids.[27]

Under these conditions, many European colonists felt abandoned by the state and federal government, which had also failed to provide for adequate schooling. German farmers who settled in southern Brazil therefore found themselves dealing with the problem of schools. If they were able to raise the necessary funds, they hired teachers and Protestant pastors from Germany. Private German schools in Santa Catarina, including in Blumenau, outnumbered Portuguese schools by ten to one.[28] In many households, German was still the mother tongue after four or five generations. Because of the nature of German settlement in the agrarian areas of southern Brazil, the preservation of German culture and language was therefore much more successful than it was in the United States, where the assimilation process was more or less complete by the second generation.

This divergence in the acculturation process influenced how people thought and wrote about the German presence in southern Brazil. Authors like Dr Blumenau, Gustav Stutzer, and José Deeke tended to elevate the accomplishments of Germans in Brazil. The same can generally be said about publications that promoted German colonialism. Blumenau and Joinville were considered the two most successful German colonies in Santa Catarina and were frequently heralded as places where German language and culture were better preserved than anywhere else.[29] The colonies were repeatedly described as striking examples of Germandom abroad and as the embodiment of the German diaspora in Brazil. Not surprisingly, Luso-Brazilians were often suspicious of these German communities and questioned the patriotism and loyalty of German Brazilians to the Brazilian state, especially during times of war.[30]

These realities played an important role in the daily lives of German Brazilians and their standing within the larger Luso-Brazilian society. The success of their settlements influenced the Germans' own ethnic identity and also shaped the way Germans in Germany assessed the importance of the colonies. Germany's continued interest in these communities is reflected in the works of well-known advocates of German colonial expansion. Both Otto Tannenberg and Friedrich Fabri favored Brazil as the most "important center of German influence in South America."[31] These publications were available in Germany and in Brazil. Educated Brazilians were keenly aware of the literature, which periodically gave rise to anti-German sentiments.

Some of the views on the supposed superiority of German culture, its work ethic, and love of order – views expressed by German colonial propaganda – can also be found in the writings of Gustav Stutzer. He remained deeply rooted in his attachment to Germany and the German emperor. Indeed, one of his main complaints about Brazil was the supposed lack of "great authoritarian powers" to give

UTE RITZ-DEUTCH

the individual and the nation a spirit of obedience and discipline.[32] Stutzer complained that military service, which he saw as a "great national educational institution," was almost completely absent in Brazil.[33] Moreover, seemingly to Stutzer's regret, the Brazilian Emperor, Pedro II, was considered merely a representative of the sovereign will of the people and not treated with the respect he deserved. Later, Stutzer would write that he was not surprised that Pedro II was forced to abdicate.[34] Clearly this was not a future he wished on Germany, where order and authority were presumably more forcefully maintained.

However, Stutzer's assessment of Brazil was not monolithic. He also acknowledged the positive potential of living in Brazil, even if his general assessment of Luso-Brazilian society was negative. Despite his desire for order and his disdain for the lower classes, he recognized the benefits of upward social mobility and described greater equality in Brazil. Men who were day laborers in Germany could actually become landowners in Brazil, an opportunity that was largely closed to them back home. As several propagandists pointed out, mass migration could solve real and growing social problems in Germany, including overpopulation and underemployment, a fact thoroughly debated in Germany in the late nineteenth century. In addition, emigration could potentially quell social unrest and political agitation.[35]

According to Stutzer, German immigrants in Brazil had everything they needed in life. Those who did not succumb to alcoholism did not complain. Stutzer, who heard few people express "socialist or social-democratic thoughts" in Brazil, saw this as a sign that people were generally comfortable, even if few managed to accumulate massive amounts of wealth. With regard to social unrest, imperial Germany seemed more politically volatile than southern Brazil, where according to Stutzer, political news rarely penetrated the isolated valleys of the hinterland.

The isolation of the interior, however, was not a blessing for everybody. In her letters home, Therese Stutzer wrote about being homesick and feeling trapped in Brazil. In Germany, one lived close to the train station and could travel everywhere, but in Brazil mobility was only possible for those who lived in the port city of Itajaí. The "impossibility of leaving" was oppressive to her, and being in the company of her children was not sufficient. For Therese, the wide openness of Brazil, the vastness of the country, and the wildness of the place were not liberating. Instead, she found it suffocating. Even nature in its untamed beauty seemed out of control, and she was longing for Germany "where the spirit of man had left its mark on nature."[36] In this regard, she clearly shared her husband's preference for order and control.

While Gustav Stutzer would write about the progress Brazilians and Germans were making in developing the region, Therese's letters focused on the daily struggle, which at times seemed overwhelming and depressing. She wrote that she was not blind to the poor conditions in Germany but, by comparison, found the struggle against the rainforest more oppressive. Furthermore, she suffered from what she described as a lack of spiritual and intellectual life, "*der Mangel an geistigem Leben.*"[37]

Therese Stutzer was not the only German in Brazil who found the lack of education and mental stimulus difficult. In fact, it was a very common theme, frequently discussed and analyzed in a wide array of letters, articles, and books. Education was considered to be an important signifier of German culture and a key component of German identity. Education in Germany was more than a matter of progressive government policy. It was also held in high esteem among the German population and therefore had considerable cultural value.[38] In Brazil, it was difficult to maintain an intellectual life, especially outside the urban centers, and the lack of educational opportunities created significant hardships for Germans who settled there. Having German books and German schools, attending German religious services and singing German songs was important for immigrants, who were trying to preserve a piece of the German *Heimat* in Brazil.[39]

Perhaps one of the most poignant comparisons Therese made between the two countries was her description of Germany as a place where people were grounded in the past and living for the future, whereas Brazil was a land that was too young to have a past, nobody was worried about the future, and everybody lived in the present. Seemingly all that mattered in Brazil was the daily struggle for survival.[40]

Undoubtedly, Brazil was not the place for everyone. As Gustav Stutzer reflected, only certain types of settlers could flourish there, those who were thrifty, hardworking, and sober. Clearly, not all Germans lived up to such expectations. While Stutzer extolled what he considered to be quintessentially German characteristics, he nonetheless recognized that not all Germans possessed them. Even those who were hardworking could expect considerable hardship, especially in the first generation.

This struggle for survival among those who left their home in search of a better life abroad is a universal theme applicable to immigrants everywhere. When Sabine Ludwig interviewed German Brazilians in Blumenau in the 1990s, one of her subjects presented her with a poem he believed summed up the German immigrant experiences in Brazil. "Death for the first generation, deprivation for the second and bread for the third."[41] Interestingly, this saying is well known and is frequently found in the literature of the Danube Swabians, German-speaking farmers who settled in southeastern Europe during the eighteenth century and were ultimately expelled at the end of the Second World War.[42] Clearly, some aspects of German immigration to Brazil, including the struggle for survival, apply more generally to immigrant experiences everywhere. Other aspects are, however, less universal and are rooted in the particular confluence of location, structural forces, and individual actors.

In order to gain a greater understanding of how German immigrant communities manifest themselves abroad, it is imperative to include the German diaspora in Brazil as a key component in the larger scholarship. Since more Germans emigrated to North America, it is not surprising that research has been more concentrated on that particular aspect of the overall immigration experience. Still, German communities in southern Brazil are of great significance. The work of Gustav Stutzer and his contemporaries make an important contribution to the literature generated by German Brazilians at the turn of the twentieth century. These publications shed light on the translational process of immigrant identity and deserve to be analyzed systematically as part of the growing field of German Brazilian studies.

Notes

1. "Was ist dies eine verkehrte Welt! Die Sonne scheint von Norden her. Der kalte Wind ist der Südwind. Das Frühjahr fängt im September an. Um Weihnachten herum soll die heisseste Zeit sein. Der zunehmende Mond, den ich gestern Abend beobachtet habe, hat nicht die Form eines halben C, sondern die eines Kahnes, und wenn man sein Pferd nach links leiten will, muss man den rechten Zügel gebrauchen. Was wirst du noch sonst alles umlernen müssen!" Gustav Stutzer, In Deutschland und Brasilien: Lebenserinnerungen (Braunschweig and Leipzig: Verlag von Hellmuth Wollermann, 1914), 203. The horse in question belonged to his brother, who introduced him to the back country of southern Brazil. Stutzer is generally not a person known for joking around, and I do not know whether or not the story of the reins is true, or how representative it may be of how horses were directed in the region. By the way, the name Blumenau can refer either to the city or the county (município). Blumenau was originally founded as a German colony in 1850 and named after its founder.

2. "Drüben lebt man von der Vergangenheit für die Zukunft: hier lebt man nur [sic] der Gegenwart. Vergangenheit hat das Land noch nicht. Für die Zukunft braucht Niemand zu sorgen." See letters from July to October 1886 in Teresa Stutzer, "Cartas de Famílias," Blumenau em Cadernos 39.8 (August 1998): 8. See also Gustav Stutzer, Meine Therese: Aus dem bewegten Leben einer deutschen Frau (Braunschweig: Verlag von Hellmuth Wollermann, 1916). The latter contains a more extensive selection of her letters. Portuguese sources spell her name Teresa but I have retained the German spelling of her name.

3. The Stutzers stayed in Blumenau from 1885 to 1887, at which point the family was compelled to return to Germany. They would return to Brazil in 1891, this time staying in the state of São Paulo until 1909 when they returned to Germany for good. Altogether, they spent two decades in Brazil. While Therese's letters date from their first stay in Blumenau, Gustav Stutzer wrote several of his books after his final return to Europe. These reflections late in his life speak to the fact that he was always trying to make sense of his experiences and that his identity was translational, even if it was fundamentally rooted in his German upbringing.

4. Some of the more prolific writers were also directors of German colonies in Brazil, for example Dr Blumenau, whose writings were at least partly intended to recruit new immigrants from Germany. Blumenau, like Stutzer, would ultimately return to Germany after the colony came under the direction of the state. José Deeke, Eugen Fouquet, and pastor Faulhaber also had leadership roles in German colonies and their works were similarly sought out. See for example: José Deeke, Das Munizip Blumenau

und seine Entwicklungsgeschichte in drei Bände [sic] (São Leopoldo, Brazil: Rotermund, 1910); H. Faulhaber, "Deutschtum in Südbrasilien," *Beiträge zur Kolonialpolitik und Kolonialwirtschaft* 1 (1899-1900): 435-438. The German citizen Eugen Fouquet ran the Blumenau newspaper *Der Urwaldsbote* for many years, which gave him the opportunity to shape the views of Blumenau residents.

5. Approximately two-thirds of German Brazilians were Protestants.

6. According to the *Handbook of Germandom Abroad*, the reputation of Germans in Brazil as hardworking and efficient (*fleissig und tüchtig*) was in large part based on Joinville and Blumenau. See W. Dibelius and G. Lenz, eds., *Handbuch des Deutschtums im Auslande*. 2nd ed. (Berlin: Allgemeiner Deutscher Schulverein zur Erhaltung des Deutschtums im Auslande, 1906) [hereinafter Dibelius], 375. Information about the German colonial projects and the German diaspora were published in a number of venues, including almanacs, denominational papers, and local newspapers in Brazil such as *Deutsche Zeitung, Der Urwaldsbote,* and the *Blumenauer Zeitung*. In Germany, newspapers also periodically ran articles on German Brazilian communities. See for example, "Amerika: Die Deutschen in Brasilien," *Vossische Zeitung* (VZ) 228.2. suppl., (17 May 1907). In colonial publication, the official colonies received more attention than Brazil but there was nonetheless sustained interest over the years. See Gustav Meinecke, ed., *Koloniales Jahrbuch: Beiträge und Mitteilungen aus dem Gebiete der Kolonialwissenschaft und Kolonialpraxis* 11.3 (1898): 177-211; Karl Ballod, "Die Bedeutung von Südbrasilien für die deutsche Kolonisation," *Jahrbuch für Gesetzgebung* 23 (1899): 631-55; Hans von Berlepsch, "Deutsche Kolonien und koloniale Bestrebungen in Paraguay, Rio Grande do Sul und S. Paulo," *Deutsche Kolonialzeitung* 4 (1887): 271-280; A. Geffcken, "Deutscher Kolonialverein: Die Auswanderungs- und Kolonisationsfrage," *Deutsche Kolonialzeitung* (1884): 69-72; Alfred Hettner, "Das Deutschtum in Südbrasilien," *Geographische Zeitschrift* 8.11 (1902): 609-626; Robert Jannasch, "Die praktischen Aufgaben der deutschen Auswanderungspolitik," *Verhandlungen des Deutschen Kolonialkongresses 1902 zu Berlin* (Berlin, 1903); and R. Sernau, "Zur Frage der Auswanderung," *Deutsche Kolonialzeitung* 3 (1886): 133-134.

7. See Dr. phil. Wettstein, *Brasilien und die Deutsch-Brasilianische Kolonie Blumenau* (Leipzig: Verlag von Friedrich Engelmann, 1907); and Gustav Stutzer, *Das Itajahy-Thal und die Kolonie Blumenau in Süd-Brasilien, Provinz Santa Catharina* (Goslar am Harz: L. Koch, 1883). The Itajahy is the river flowing through Blumenau, where it is presently known as the Itajaí-Açu. It empties into the Atlantic approximately 50 km downstream.

8. The term Luso-Brazilian usually refers to Brazilians of Portuguese ancestry. However, in the German literature it can also more broadly mean Brazilians that are not of German heritage. Hence German Brazilians saw themselves in contrast to Luso-Brazilians, who represented the general population.

9. Kathleen A. DeHaan, "Negotiating the Transnational Moment: Immigrant Letters as Performance of a Diasporic Identity," *National Identities* 12.2 (June 2010): 108.

10. Ibid.

11. Population statistics for Brazil in general are notoriously difficult, not just to establish how many immigrants came to Brazil but also how many emigrants left Germany, especially if they left through foreign ports. Some people believed they were leaving for a temporary business assignment and ended up staying abroad. Of those who

intended to migrate to Brazil, only those who came through Brazilian ports were counted, which excludes over-land migration. Sometimes it was assumed that only ship passengers in the second and third class were immigrants and first class passengers were not recorded. Today the population in Santa Catarina consists of 35 percent German Brazilians and 33 percent Italian Brazilians, with the remaining one-third divided among other ethnic groups. Nationwide, 10 percent of Brazilians claim at least one German ancestor, whereas in the United States people of German ancestry represent between 20 percent and 25 percent of the population. For various statistics see Leslie Bethell, ed., *The Cambridge History of Latin America*, Vol. V (Cambridge University Press, 1986), 779 and 782-3.

12. According to Sowell, as late as 1882, "the entire pioneering zone of southern Brazil" was still 71 percent German-speaking. Several statistics are noteworthy. In Rio Grande do Sul, Brazil's most southern state, Germans constituted a staggering 87 percent of all immigrants between 1844 and 1874. See Thomas Sowell, *Migrations and Cultures: A World View* (New York: Basic Books, 1996), 83-84.

13. See for example: Gottfried Pfeifer, "Deutsch bäuerliche Kolonisation in den Vereinigten Staaten und Brasilien. Konvergenzen und Kontraste," *Kölner Geographische Arbeiten* 13 (1973), 43.

14. See for example: Giralda Seyferth, "A identidade teuto-brasileira numa perspectiva histórica," in *Os Alemães no Sul do Brasil: Cultura, Etnicidade, História*, ed. Cláudia Mauch and Naira Vasconcellos (Canoas: Ed. Universidade Luterana do Brasil, 1994) and Arthur Blasio Rambo, "Nacionalidade e cidadania," in the same volume. I use the term 'assimilation' with caution, fully realizing that ethnic minorities never become fully absorbed by the majority but that the interaction between them tends to be more multi-directional, influencing all groups even if unevenly. I prefer the term acculturation or integration, although assimilation is the more prevalent term in the literature of the late nineteenth century.

15. Sociologist Emílio Willems has analyzed the willingness of Germans in Brazil to 'assimilate' along class lines, showing that middle-class Germans resisted assimilation most and were also more bound to the Protestant Church and the General School Association, which were antagonistic to assimilation efforts (*assimilationsfeindlich*). Furthermore, *Reichsdeutsche*, who often considered their stay in Brazil as temporary, also disdained Brazilian citizenship and Brazilian identity. Emílio Willems, "Zur sozialen Anpassung der Deutschen in Brasilien," *Kölner Zeitschrift für Soziologie*. New series of the Kölner Vierteljahrshefte für Soziologie 1 (1948/9): 320.

16. See "Die Deutschbrasilianer und Nordamerika," *Blumenauer Zeitung*, 24 February 1906. The *Blumenauer Zeitung* was the first newspaper established in the Blumenau colony in 1881. Two years later, the *Immigrant* was founded but was published for less than a decade. The second *Immigrant* was sold in 1893, at which time the name changed to *Der Urwaldsbote*. Both of the papers initially published weekly and later several times a week. Few of the German newspapers during that time reached readers outside of their immediate geographic area, but *Der Urwaldsbote* was one of them. I have not been able to ascertain what the circulation of the paper was. However, according to the *Handbuch des Deutschtums im Auslande*, only about ten German newspapers in Brazil published more than 1,000 copies and none of them over 3,000. It is reasonable to assume

that *Der Urwaldsbote* falls within that range. It should be noted though that each paper was passed around numerous times, which makes it difficult to assess how many readers there actually were. See Dibelius, 403. Also: Hans Gehse, *Die deutsche Presse in Brasilien von 1852 bis zur Gegenwart* (Münster in Westfalen: Aschendorffsche Verlagsbuchhandlung, 1931), 63; Karl Fouquet, "Deutsche Presse in Brasilien – ein Überblick," *Globus* 6 (1974): 7; and Ursula Brigitte Crofton, "Blumenau: A City of German Origin in Brazil" (MA thesis, San Francisco State College, 1972), 57.

17. Stutzer, *In Deutschland und Brasilien*, 203.

18. Stutzer, *Das Itajahy-Thal*, 20.

19. Ibid.

20. Ibid. 140ff.

21. I am aware that Indian is a misnomer but there are several reasons for using it. It was the most commonly used term in the primary source documents and has become common usage since. The American Indian Movement (AIM) used it, as did the Smithsonian with its *National Museum of the American Indian* (NMAI).

22. For a general comparison of migration, see Sowell. The chapter on Germans around the world includes data from the United States as well as Brazil but is not based on individual experiences. For a comparison of ethnic tensions and backlash against German communities in Brazil and the United States during the First World War, see Frederick C. Luebke, *Germans in Brazil: A Comparative History of Cultural Conflict During World War I* (Louisiana State University Press, 1987). For a comparison of agricultural communities in Brazil and North America, see Pfeifer, who points out that there was no uniformity in settlements but that considerable regional diversity existed on both continents.

23. For the diverse experiences of German immigrants in North America, see for example: Don Heinrich Tolzmann, *The German-American Experience* (New York: Humanity Books, 2000); also Kathleen Neils Conzen, "Germans," in *Harvard Encyclopedia of American Ethnic Groups*, ed. Stephan Thernstrom (Cambridge, MA: Belknap Press of Harvard University Press, 1980); Jeremy W. Kilar, "Germans," in *American Immigrant Cultures: Builders of a Nation* (New York: Macmillan Reference, 1997).

24. See Hartmut Fröschle, ed., *Die Deutschen in Lateinamerika: Schicksal und Leistung* (Tübingen and Basel: Horst Erdmann Verlag, 1979), 808-810. Conditions on the coffee plantations in São Paulo were so harsh, in fact, that the Prussian government was compelled to intervene. In 1859 the Heydtsche Reskript came into effect, forbidding agents to operate on Prussian soil to recruit Germans for emigration to Brazil. The Reskript was frequently referred to as an emigration prohibition (*Auswanderungsverbot*) but was in fact only forbidding solicitation. The Heydtsche Reskript was finally lifted in 1896, but only for the three southern-most states. See Horst Gründer, ed., '. . . *da und dort ein junges Deutschland gründen:' Rassismus, Kolonien und kolonialer Gedanke vom 16. bis zum 20. Jahrhundert* (München: Deutscher Taschenbuchverlag, 1999), 218.

25. According to Oberacker, German farmers were invited to southern Brazil because the country had previously failed to establish a thriving middle class and because the Portuguese supposedly were not adept as small-scale farmers. Karl H. Oberacker and Karl Ilg, "Die Deutschen in Brasilien," in *Die Deutschen in Lateinamerika: Schicksal und Leistung*, 183. As I have argued in my dissertation, some of the prejudicial views about Luso-

Brazilians represented by authors at the turn of the twentieth century have since then been reproduced in the works of Karl Oberacker and Carlos Fouquet, who almost idealized German contributions, while shying away from more critical analysis. See further Karl H. Oberacker, *Der deutsche Beitrag zum Aufbau der brasilianischen Nation* (São Paulo: Herder Editora Livraria, 1955); and Carlos Fouquet, *Der Deutsche Einwanderer und seine Nachkommen in Brasilien 1808-1824-1974* (São Paulo: Instituto Hans-Staden, 1974). Since few comprehensive monographs on German Brazilian communities are available, these two works and Fröschle's are still considered standards, although they are now dated.

26. Sowell, *Migrations and Cultures*, 83.

27. The involvement of German communities in these raids was discussed in a lively and contentious trans-Atlantic discourse that influenced the creation of the Brazilian Indian Protection Service. See further, Ute Ritz-Deutch, "Alberto Vojtěch Frič, the German Diaspora, and Indian Protection in Southern Brazil, 1900-1920: A Transatlantic, Ethno-Historical Case Study," (Ph.D. dissertation, Binghamton University, 2008).

28. At the turn of the twentieth century, the county of Blumenau had 10 state schools and 113 private schools enrolling 520 and 5,011 children respectively. As late as 1916, an estimated 40 percent of all schools in Santa Catarina were private, although the number is likely to be even higher. Approximately 80 percent of these schools taught exclusively in German. See Luebke, *Germans in Brazil*, 51. There were approximately 3,000 German schools abroad, 1,000 of which were in Brazil. About 700 of these were in Rio Grande do Sul. See Dibelius, 40.

29. See Dibelius, 375; also, "Amerika: Die Deutschen in Brasilien."

30. This was especially the case during the First and Second World Wars, when Germany and Brazil fought on opposing sides. See Frederick C. Luebke, "A Prelude to Conflict: The German Ethnic Group in Brazil, 1890-1917," *Ethnic and Racial Studies* 6.1 (Jan. 1983).

31. See Otto Richard Tannenberg, *Groß-Deutschland: die Arbeit des 20. Jahrhunderts* (Leipzig: Bruno Volger Verlagsbuchhandlung, 1911); and Friedrich Fabri, *Bedarf Deutschland der Colonien? Does Germany Need Colonies?* Eine politisch-ökonomische Betrachtung von D[r. Theol.] Friedrich Fabri. 3rd ed., trans. and eds. E. C. M. Breuning and M. E. Chamberlain, *Studies in German Thought and History*. Vol. 2 (Lewiston: The Edwin Mellen Press, 1998).

32. "Dazu kommt, dass die grossen autoritativen Mächte fehlen, die einem Volke und jedem Einzelnen den Geist des Gehorsams unter der Zucht, und damit der Kraft, fast unbewusst einflössen." Stutzer, *Das Itajahy-Thal*, 23.

33. "Militärdienst als grosse nationale Erziehungs-Anstalt" Ibid.

34. Stutzer, *In Deutschland und Brasilien*, 198.

35. See Arthur J. Knoll and Lewis H. Gann, *Germans in the Tropics: Essays in German Colonial History* (New York: Greenwood Press, 1987), 4.

36. Teresa Stutzer, "Cartas de Famílias," 8-9.

37. Ibid. 8.

38. Sowell, *Migrations and Cultures*, 54.

39. On the significance of the German *Lieder*, see Arthur Blasio Rambo, "Nacionalidade e cidadania," in *Os Alemães no Sul do Brasil: Cultura, Etnicidade, História*, ed. Cláudia Mauch

and Naira Vasconcellos (Canoas: Ed. Universidade Luterana do Brasil, 1994), 48. As several authors in that volume have noted, the word *Heimat*, meaning more than just reference to a place, has no equivalence in Portuguese.

40. Teresa Stutzer, "Cartas de Famílias," 8.

41. 'Der ersten Generation der Tod, der zweiten die Not, und der dritten das Brot.' See Sabine Ludwig, *In Blumenau und Pomerode: Bei Deutschen im Süden Brasiliens* (Würzburg: Bergstadtverlag Korn, 1997), 49.

42. Many of the Danube Swabians (*Donauschwaben*) ended up publishing books about their villages after they were expelled from the Balkans. The poem in question is frequently cited in such works with minor alterations. "Dem Ersten der Tod, dem Zweiten die Not, dem Dritten das Brot," is the variation found in Johann Lorenz, *Unvergessenes Kischker, 1786-1944: Ansiedlung, Entwicklung, Untergang* (Karlsruhe: Selbstverlag des Heimatausschusses, 1980), 118.

Traveling Between Languages and Literatures: A Spatial Analysis of *The Family Tree* by Margo Glantz

An Van Hecke

Autobiography and Family History

Autobiographies can catch a reader in a surprising and profound sense of intimacy, drawing the reader to participate in the personal feelings of the author. Autobiographies can also give the reader a new and different view of the historical and political context experienced by the author. Often, worlds unknown to the reader are opened up to them. Some autobiographies, especially those of well-known writers, captivate the reader because of the tension between these alternating perspectives. This is precisely what characterizes the autobiography of the Mexican writer, Margo Glantz (1930).

In her research, Glantz interviewed her parents and integrated their testimonies and insights into her own childhood memories. Thus, she enhanced the contrast between these perspectives. She published her autobiography *Las genealogías* in 1981. The first edition was followed by multiple re-editions revised by the author. In 1991, *Las genealogías* was translated into English by Susan Bassnett as *The Family Tree*.[1] In this autobiography, Glantz tells the story of her parents, Jacob Glantz and Elizabeth Shapiro, who migrated in 1925 from the Jewish Ukraine to Mexico, where she was born as the second of four daughters. The book is not only a recreation of the family's history, it is also a look at the collective history of the Jewish community in Mexico, and even of the Mexican cultural and artistic circles in which Jacob Glantz moved as a poet. It is this combination of private and public life, of individual and social life, which makes this autobiography so interesting and even inspiring for other writers.

An important aspect of the book is the inclusion of family photographs, such as those of the maternal grandparents (90), the mother with the two eldest daughters, Lilly and Margo (161), and also photographs of the father: "Jacob Mexicanised" (7) and "Jacob as a thinker" (88). In the original version, official documents such as passports and diplomas were even included, but despite the references to factual historical events which reinforce the effect of reality, the book has to be considered as "fictional", or more precisely as an "autofictional biography."

The author herself repeatedly expresses the struggle with memory in the book, especially of her father: "Yankl confuses all kinds of things, he reverses incidents and alters images. [...] the dates change every time he tries to remember. Never mind, the cloak of memory falls over writing [...]" (9). The problematic autobiographical character of the book is exactly what has been studied most by literary critics.[2] Unlike these studies, the focus of this analysis is on space and translation and how the different locations referred to in the book are represented. In this context, the question of language and translation is fundamental. This analysis also offers a comparative perspective and links the case of Glantz's autobiography to similar ones in Mexican literature.

Displacement and Migration: Traveling Between Literatures

Within the broader debate about migration and biculturalism, the concept of *transculturación*, "transculturation", as presented by the Cuban anthropologist Fernando Ortiz in the 1940s can still be applied. Among the multiple interpretations of the term, there is one in particular that works as a proper starting point. Transculturation "describes a promiscuous culture that proliferates the interplay between competing cultural discourses and perpetuates their irresolvable contradictions." It consists of an "open-ended process of mutual influence."[3] This is how Margo Glantz represents the process of the transit within her family. She writes of different cultural discourses conflicting with each other without resolving the contradictions.

The Jewish culture continues to be fundamental in the lives of both the parents and their children in Mexico. In chapter seven, Margo Glantz quotes the Jewish American author Isaac Bashevis Singer: "The Jews don't record their own history, they lack a sense of chronology. It is as though they knew instinctively that time and space are just an illusion." (22) Glantz observes that this is what happened in her parents' lives. The illusion of time and space, which is seen here as typically Jewish, actually reveals a basic problem. As we are dealing with an autofictional biography, it is necessary to distinguish between the geographical and the fictional space, between real places and the way Glantz focuses on them. The author makes quite a remarkable observation in the beginning, warning the reader that "geography has never been my strong point. I have always mixed up northern rivers with southern rivers [....]." (8) This geographical confusion is not an obstacle. On the contrary, it is exactly one of the many comments of the narrator that makes this text so charming. Paradoxically, the book is full of references to geographical locations.

The narrator explores several cities in Russia, the most important of which is Odessa, Ukraine, her parents' city of origin. There are also anecdotes that take place in the cities of Krivoy Rog, Kremenchug, Kiev, Moscow, and more. In Mexico, the reader follows Margo along innumerable streets of Mexico City as the

AN VAN HECKE

family moves from one house to another. It is striking, however, that references to a specific location – a country, city, or street – instantly evoke the name of an author or a quotation. The spatial perspective is marked by intertextual references. Geographical locations become literary locations. All the authors that emerge in the text, whether they are Russian, Mexican, or another nationality, enter as models, as guides who lead the Jewish Mexican narrator in search of her origins. She even states it explicitly herself: "I often have to turn to certain writers to be able to imagine what my parents remember." (20) Glantz sees the story of the migration of her family through the eyes of other writers. This intertextual perspective is the thread of the following analysis of space. I make a distinction between three moments in time: before the transit, the transit itself, and after the transit.

Remembering Russia: Echoes from Chekhov, Gogol, and Dostoyevsky

Glantz's parents were born in Ukraine and married in Odessa. We hear the stories about pre-revolutionary Russia and of the Revolution itself in 1917. The parents express some nostalgia for their land of origin. Especially Elizabeth, her mother, talks about the family and the Jewish high school where she received her education and a diploma as a medical assistant. (32) Elizabeth also learned to play the piano at the local music academy. (19) On the other hand, the father remembers the traumatic experiences. He talks of the pogroms, the persecutions of the Jews, the massacres (34-37), his active participation in the Russian Revolution, becoming a teacher of Marxism (30), and his arrest (40). Jacob also recalls the starvation that left many people dead in the streets of Herzon in 1922 (39). For Margo, Russia is the land of the unknown. When she tries to imagine the steppes her father frequently talks about, the image she envisions is influenced by her reading of Chekhov, Gogol, and even a poem of her own father, Jacob Glantz: "In the distance and all around and as far as the eye could see was the great plain of the steppes. Those steppes so admired by Chekhov and Gogol, the steppes that inspired my father to write when Lilly, my elder sister was born: 'The mountains of eternal snows are as strange to me as the flat lands of Ukraine are strange to my child.'" (10)

Gogol is also mentioned at the moment Jacob talks about Trotsky: "I remember him [Trotsky] before that, when he came with Lenin, with his *dziniel*, the great big cloak just like Gogol describes it, pulled up round his ears and all the people were shouting [...]." (43) Russian writers are also important references when talking about her personality. When Margo confesses that she is not that good in geography, she turns to Dostoyevsky to try to understand herself. "This fact [...] has made me feel like a Dostoievsky character and made me realize something about the contradictions within me, that something special which is my Russian soul blended with the Mexican." (8) The passion for Dostoyevsky leads the narrator to identify herself with Raskolnikov. She explains that in her adolescence she made the discovery "that I belonged (in some third corner of myself) to that Russian soul which could kneel down in a public square and confess out loud to the wind, as Raskolnikov did once (with very negative repercussions) and as I am doing now in these pages." (146) Chekhov, Gogol, and Dostoyevsky are just a few of the many Russian writers mentioned in the text. The references to the Russian Jewish writers such as Leivik, Opatoshu (108), and Isaac Babel (1, 13 etc.) are especially interesting. Babel was born in Odessa and was a close friend of Jacob Glantz.

Transit: Following the Tracks of Columbus and Cortes

In 1925, Glantz's parents tried to emigrate to the United States where Jacob's brothers already lived. They were denied permission to enter the country because of immigration quotas imposed by the U.S. Congress at that time. (40) They instead traveled from Odessa through Moscow to Berlin, and left from Rotterdam in the Dutch ship the Spaarndam for Mexico. This tale of transit has two versions, one from the father and one from the mother. When the couple waited in Amsterdam to board the Spaarndam, the father fondly remembers that moment: "I felt good in Amsterdam [...] everything was so clean." (59) In contrast, the mother expresses quite a different feeling: "We had very little money and a lot of anxiety." (59) The couple thus represents the typical ambiguity that we find in most migrant narratives: the hopeful view, the excitement of starting a new life, seeing the travel in a positive way, intermingled with worry and concern for an uncertain future. These divergent experiences of the father and the mother may also be due to their personalities. The father is depicted as more rational, whereas the mother is seen as more emotional.

In Amsterdam, they found a place to stay and received some money from Haias, the International Jewish Association (61). A photograph that represents the shif brider (ship brothers), taken in Amsterdam, is particularly revealing. The photograph was taken just before the trip to America. They are all Jews, from Poland and from Russia, except one goy (a non-Jew) from Poland. Margo expresses the particular appeal of the picture: "I have a lovely period photo, sepia coloured, with all the characters in a row, and their gentle trusting faces, photograph faces that nobody ever looks at now. They are the shif brider, the ship brothers, because besides blood brothers you can have all sorts of other kinds of brother and these are ship brothers." (58-59) There is undoubtedly a unique feeling that connected all these people on the long voyage on the ship. According to the narrator, "[t]he Dutch ship Spaarndam [...] is virtually a ghetto."[4] (59) The passengers finally end up in different destinations: Cuba, Mexico, the United States. One even went back to Russia, another went to Israel, and another to Australia. (59) When

I asked Margo Glantz directly about this photograph, she gave some details: "I only know that my parents traveled in third class [...], that my father went up and down from one class to another [...] that the passengers identified very much one with another, and that is why they considered themselves brothers, not of blood, but of the journey. [...] I can imagine that this brotherhood happened a lot between immigrants and went on for several years [....]."[5] In the book, the mother gives her impression of the voyage, and we read how common and mundane things of daily life on the ship affected her. The food was "awful," so she did not eat anything. (63) Then she remembers with an astonishing sense of detail the clothes she was wearing, the Russian clothes she had to sell, and the clothes she bought in Holland. (63) Jacob and Elizabeth anchored in Cuba in May 1925, but because it was terribly hot, they decided to move on to Mexico. Here again, the mother remembers the feeling of loneliness: "I really did feel very, very alone. We didn't know a soul and it was frightening." (62) The father expresses a similar feeling in Cuba: "I was really scared." (59) They continued to Mexico and disembarked at Veracruz. They passed customs thanks to the purser of the Spaarndam who lent them two hundred dollars. But they had to return this money immediately so that the purser could lend it again to other passengers without money. (60) From Veracruz, they took the train to Mexico City.

The book ends with a marvelous story of return. Margo travels to Eastern Europe, probably in the 1970s, in that "conscious and confused search for roots." She writes: "I went to Russia so as to be the first member of my (Mexican) family to retrace the journey my parents had undertaken in 1925." (170) She does not get to see the steppes her father remembered in his poem, but she meets a man called Perelman. From that moment on, the story is full of coincidences which, according to the narrator, only "happen in soap operas" (170) but are probably more comparable with the magical coincidences in the novels and stories of Julio Cortázar.[6] Perelman – Margo Glantz explained to me "this wasn't his real name"[7] – traveled with his parents in 1924 from Russia to Mexico on the same Dutch ship, the Spaarndam. She exclaims: "The soap opera has come true!" (172) Perelman tells her exactly the same story. They were refused visas by the U.S., stopped at Cuba before going to Mexico, and received two hundred dollars from the ship's purser. Unlike the Glantz family, the Perelmans went back to Russia because the mother was too homesick. (171-172) But Yasha Perelman, who had a Mexican girlfriend, missed Mexico a lot. He remembered Mexico City with nostalgia, continued to listen to Mexican songs, and decorated his apartment with Mexican objects. (173-174) Although the year is not the same (according to Perelman his family traveled in 1924, while the Glantz family traveled in 1925), this does not matter. The circle is closed for Margo. She made the trip in the direction opposite to that of her parents in 1925. Because of this encounter with Perelman, she can now "bring things to an end, at least for the time being."(183)

The story of the transit gets an extra dimension when we look at it in the light of the narratives of the discovery and the conquest of America. The comparison between individual migration and the first voyages of Columbus and Cortes is quite common in Latin American literature.[8] Glantz integrates both characters into her story and gives her personal interpretation of this comparison. "Everyone who emigrates to America thinks he's another Columbus and the ones who go to Mexico want to be like Cortes. My father preferred Columbus and, like the Cuban writer Carpentier he wrote an epic-lyric poem about the Genovese explorer." (106) The identification between Columbus and the father is justified by the poem dedicated to Columbus which earned him "a big name in Yiddish literary circles internationally." (108) Later on, when Margo tries to figure out how she herself can be situated in regard to these two great predecessors, the comparison turns out to be more complicated. "Twice in my life I've felt like Columbus." (135) She explains how she became ill on a trip to the Near East and had trouble pronouncing English words in New York. (136) The identification is even more interesting from a feminine perspective: "In all sincerity, as they say in Colombia, all women have something of the Columbus in them. We all have to tackle the question of which came first, the chicken or the egg [...]." (136) There are, of course, differences between the explorer and the narrator – for example, her "lack of avarice" and her travels which are "much more modest." (137) When Margo goes back to Russia, Columbus appears again: "I am another Columbus, with my grandfather Osher and my grandfather Mikail serving as navigators." (170)

How then does Cortes enter this story? Margo writes: "Sometimes getting around Mexico City involves long journeying," which makes her "almost feel like Cortes." She explains: "I feel like a female version, burning my boats or turning them round, when I finally turn my car onto the highway that is still under construction [...]." (137) Columbus appears when she talks about long travels in the past, Cortes becomes the reference when she comments on daily life in contemporary Mexico.

Living in Mexico: Lopez Velarde, Rulfo, and Pacheco

From 1925 onwards, Jacob Glantz and Elizabeth Shapiro stayed in Mexico. The children were brought up in Jewish traditions and customs, although Margo recognizes that she did not have a religious upbringing (2). One of the central sentences frequently quoted by the critics is: "So everything is mine and yet it isn't, and I look Jewish and I don't and that is why I am writing this – my family history [....]." (4) The family integrated quickly into Mexican life. Jacob and his wife tried to make a living in different ways, selling clothes or shoes. Jacob even worked as a dentist. All these job changes help explain the upheavals in Margo's childhood including the different schools she went to.

When we analyze the way Mexico City is focused in the text, we see first of all the places related to the Jewish community. The father tells about the first synagogue and graveyard (96) but also about the Jewish publishing houses. Jacob published a magazine *Die voi* and wrote a column in a Jewish newspaper for 50 years. (97) The active cultural life of the Jewish community, although a small one in comparison with New York or Buenos Aires, is also visible in the Yiddish theater: "In the daytime they all did other things, but they came together in the evenings to rehearse and watch plays." (101)

Secondly, I want to draw attention to the function of restaurants and cafés in Mexico City. For several years, Jacob and Elizabeth ran a restaurant, the *Carmel*, famous for its typical Jewish pastries and for the many intellectuals who gathered there. Jacob set up a gallery in *Carmel*, where painters and sculptors exhibited their works (113). The way Jacob establishes contact with the artists of that time, especially the great muralists Rivera, Orozco, and Siqueiros, is quite surprising. Being a poor immigrant struggling to become settled with his family in a strange city, he succeeds in socializing with them and he even considers Diego Rivera his "friend." (93) Besides his own restaurant, *Carmel*, there are also the cafés, principally the *Café Paris*, where the father meets numerous Mexican writers: Gonzalez Martinez, Mariano Azuela, and Villaurrutia, to name a few. Arriving in Mexico in the 1920s seems to have been very exciting for the young poet Jacob. It is also at the *Café Paris* that he gets to know the work of the poet Ramon Lopez Velarde whom he did not meet personally because he died in 1921: "They were always talking about him in the Café Paris [...]. He's so romantic... all that about trains looking like toys... everybody used to quote Lopez Velarde."[9] (76)

All these cafés and restaurants where the Jewish immigrants congregated can be seen as transit places in the way Shachar Pinsker described the cafes in the city of Berlin in the early decades of the twentieth century. Pinsker considers the cafés of Berlin, especially the so-called "*literarische Kaffeehäuser*," as "essential spaces" for immigrant writers and artists. They were attracted to the local urban cafés for several reasons. They were "emblems of Berlin modernity and modernism," they offered "refuge from harsh physical conditions," and they were favorite meeting places for writers. Interaction between Hebrew, Yiddish, and German writers "was inevitable and abundant." According to Pinsker, the literary café of Berlin can be seen as "a good example of a thirdspace," following the definition of Edward Soja, as it is located "between real and imaginary, the inside and outside, public and private."[10] This is definitely also the case of the cafés mentioned in Margo Glantz's autobiography. They are favorite places where Jewish and Mexican writers meet each other, where they observe and gain inspiration. Publishing houses, theaters, restaurants, and cafés – they are all represented as places where literature plays a central part.

Looking back on the places that impacted Margo directly, she remembers one of the streets where the family lived, "Niño perdido" (Lost Child) Street. (153)

Margo supposes that this name is the reason why she feels so close to abandoned children, and why she has always felt a bond with black sheep. "Someone once said that maybe it's all part of the feeling of belonging to the chosen people." (155) The feeling of being an abandoned child drives her "obsessively to read *Pedro Páramo*," Juan Rulfo's novel. (155) The reference to *Pedro Páramo* is not surprising, as its main topics of disorientation, solitude, and search of the origin are also fundamental in Glantz's autobiography. Finally, when Margo remembers the Mexico City of her childhood, her feelings seem rather contradictory. She becomes nostalgic, but strangely enough not for the Mexico she knew, but the Mexico at the end of the nineteenth century as it was painted by Velasco, "with the former crystalline magnificence of this region." (152) This is the moment when, again, Margo turns to literature to give way to the contradictions. Glantz quotes a final sentence of *Las batallas en el desierto* (*Battles in the Desert*), the novel by Pacheco: "Who could feel nostalgic about all that horror?" (153) There is nostalgia, especially when Margo considers the destruction of the city at the moment she writes this family history, but it is complex. There are mixed feelings about growing up in difficult times in a "place called Mexico." (153)

Traveling Between Languages

Hebrew, Yiddish, Russian, and Spanish are the languages involved in this collective history. Jacob spoke Yiddish and Russian and learned Hebrew at school in Ukraine. He taught Hebrew in Mexico. (65) Elizabeth spoke Russian and learned the Hebrew alphabet. (67) She did not know any Yiddish, although her mother had spoken Yiddish. (65) But to be able to communicate with other Jews at the club in Mexico, Elizabeth had to learn Yiddish. "We all had to use Yiddish because we couldn't manage any other way." (66) Elizabeth learned Yiddish from her husband, and decided to write a letter in Yiddish to her mother in Russia, who wrote back in a terrible state: "She didn't think it could be me, she thought I must be dead, so then I wrote back again to her in Russian and calmed things down." (67) The fact that Elizabeth did not speak Yiddish upon arrival in Mexico does not seem to have been uncommon. Michael Boyden revealed to me that "Abraham Cahan, the founder of the Yiddish newspaper *Forverts* in New York, did not speak Yiddish before his arrival in America."[11] When the couple arrived in Mexico they did not speak Spanish. Jacob's contact with Diego Rivera was partially due to Rivera's knowledge of Russian. For Jacob, a poet, language was a difficult issue: "When I arrived, neither Hebrew nor Russian were of any use at all [...]. Then I started writing in Yiddish, but that language wasn't very much used either." (95) His first poem in Yiddish was published in Mexico in 1927 (97), but after several years "Jacob suddenly starts writing poems in Spanish. He's a Spanish poet now." (126)

Margo spoke Spanish but did not understand Hebrew, Yiddish, or Russian. Her father wanted her to translate his poem "Columbus" into Spanish, but she couldn't because she did not know Yiddish, "except a few words relating to food and shouting at people." (137) Indeed, the words in the text in italics, in Yiddish or Russian, are mostly related to food, Jewish customs, or traditions. Margo sometimes gives a short translation in brackets or explains the concept in Spanish. In the English translation, Susan Bassnett adopts this same strategy, e.g., "*heder* (Jewish school)," (2) "*cholnt*, a stew made of tripe, meat, potatoes and beans." (3)[12] These foreign words do not disrupt the flow of the narrative. They give a certain exotic character to the text and reflect the multicultural background, the different worlds "in between" which Margo Glantz grew up. The words are conflictive but enriching at the same time. The narrator appears here as translator at a basic level; most of the time, only separate words are translated. This conflictive situation can be related to the definition of translation given by Naoki Sakai: "translation is not only a border crossing but also and preliminary an act of drawing a border, of bordering."[13] Actually, it is more about not being able to translate, as we have seen in the case of the poem "Columbus." It is about the frustration of not understanding, of being "lost in translation." The situations of the father and the daughter are very different. The father has moved from a multilingual to a monolingual environment. He had to learn Spanish. Margo speaks only Spanish and has lost touch with the languages spoken by her parents. In this context, it is interesting to notice the admiration that Margo expresses for her friend, Sergio Pitol. Pitol is an important Mexican writer and a translator, mainly from Polish and Russian into Spanish. There is a fascinating dialogue in which the father shows interest in the work of Pitol, but he resists believing that Pitol knows Russian. Margo has to insist twice, "Yes, Dad, he knows Russian well; he was in Russia too for several years." (72) Then again, "Does Sergio know Russian? -Yes, Dad, he knows it very well." (74) They talk about Pitol's translations of Boris Pilnyak and Chekhov. (72) These authors are important to Margo, and Pitol becomes a key figure in the whole process of understanding and writing her family history. The traveling between languages is a frequent phenomenon for many writers, especially those fundamental to this autobiography. Columbus wrote mainly in Spanish, but his texts are influenced by the languages spoken in Portugal, Galicia, Catalonia, and Italy, where he was born. The Cuban writer Alejo Carpentier, who is mentioned in the same chapter as Columbus, wrote some of his texts in French, and so on. The identification between Margo Glantz and these "in-between" authors has to be seen at this linguistic level.

Tales of Transit in Mexico: A Comparative Perspective

The critic Caleb Bach has clearly indicated the position and the role of *The Family Tree* within Mexican literature: "*The Family Tree* has been widely acknowledged as a pioneering work, a model for the many memoirs by women that subsequently appeared in Mexico."[14] According to another critic, Maiz-Peña, Glantz's autobiography can be considered a seminal text, a template for other women writers whose fictional narratives with autobiographical characteristics reveal the complex relationship between origin and gender.[15] Consequently, Glantz's text has been the subject of many comparative studies in Mexican and Latin American women's literature focusing on the genre of memoirs and autobiographies. The book has also been studied from a comparative perspective within Jewish literary and cultural studies.[16] All the comparisons with Mexican women writers, and especially Mexican Jewish women writers, are revealing. Equally revealing and interesting would be to broaden the view and place this book within the larger context of Mexican and Latin American literature in general, and the topic of migration in particular.

Many studies have been done on exile and migration in Mexican literature of the twentieth century. Special attention has been paid to the Spanish authors who emigrated in the 1930s and to Latin American authors who suffered exile from countries under dictatorships, such as Guatemala, Argentina, and Chile, and who found refuge in Mexico. It would be interesting to put Glantz's book within the context of migration literature to open other perspectives on her work. For instance, if we compare Glantz's case with other authors of the second generation of immigrants, we find an important characteristic in common. They are born in Mexico, but firmly express the need to know where their parents came from. Margo Glantz undertakes her search for her origin by writing a family history. In the process she travels back to Russia to retrace the steps they took in the migration. The Mexican writer Juan Villoro, whose father was born in Barcelona, lived in Barcelona from 2000 to 2004, so as to better know the land of his ancestors.[17] Villoro has not written an autobiography, but in his novels, short stories and essays, he develops this same question of the return and of taking a view from the outside. Glantz and Villoro, and no doubt other Mexican authors, have in common the fundaments of their work – migration and displacement. Through their writing, they create these elements within a constant and enriching dialogue between literatures of Europe and Latin America.

Conclusion

Nostalgia is a strange thing. The Russian Perelman is nostalgic about the Mexico of the 1930s, where he had a girlfriend and listened to Mexican music. The nostalgia of Margo is different. She is a second-generation immigrant and does not feel the same nostalgia for Russia as her parents do. Back in Mexico, when she tells her parents the whole Perelman story, Margo has a strange feeling of nostalgia, although she preferred to call it melancholia: "My sense of nostalgia grows and grows, keeping up with my new friend, in fact it isn't nostalgia, it's melanch-

olia, sweet, sticky and rose pink, like the song that Lara sang in the 1930s [....]."
(175) There is, of course, the nostalgia for the Russia of her parents and even for
the transit on the ship the *Spaarndam* evoked by the picture of the ship brothers
taken in Amsterdam. At the same time there is the nostalgia of that Mexico City of
the 1940s and 1950s, the place she grew up, and the magical period of cultural
and literary flowering despite the hardships of her childhood. This is where the
importance of the intertextuality in the text becomes clear.

If we look at the authors mentioned by Glantz, we can distinguish two types.
There are those who reinforce the nostalgia of the land. Among them are Russians as well as Mexicans: Gogol and Chekhov in their view of the steppes, and
the Mexican Lopez Velarde in his patriotic poem "Suave Patria." The other type is
the "in-between" author such as Columbus, Cortes, and Carpentier, and the Jewish authors in exile, with whom Glantz identifies. Both types of authors are
equally important to Glantz and reflect the many conflicts within her own life.
There is a strong identification with authors and with literary characters. At the
end of her book she compares herself with "The Idiot" (159) as she did earlier
with Raskolnikov (148) – both characters from Dostoyevsky.

The intertextual method throughout the analysis makes clear another distinction. Intertextuality is seen in the case of the author, and equally so in the case of
the father. For both, references to other authors form part of a strategy of self-
constitution, as a person and as a writer. There are some readings shared by
father and daughter, such as Russian literature, though each has their own unique preferences. The father knows many Mexican writers personally, but that
does not always mean that he has read their works. Margo seems skeptical when
asking her father about his readings of Lopez Velarde and Gonzalez Martinez.
(76) This is understandable since her father did not know Spanish when he arrived in Mexico. He is, however, an expert in literature written in Yiddish and
Russian.

Finally, if we interpret intertextuality in a broader sense, including plastic arts,
it is interesting to see how Glantz identifies herself with characters in great paint-
ings, just as she does with literary characters. Sometimes, when she sees herself
in the mirror "haggard and over-made-up," she feels as if she were the "incarna-
tion of some of those wretched women" of Orozco's frescoes in San Ildefonso.
(156) This is probably self-parody. She makes other comparisons typical of the
style Dorfman called "funny and enchanting."[18] When she talks about her hair-
styles, she thinks she looks like a "Gustav Klimt picture or an art deco model."
(165) Sadness and happiness alternate in this wonderful story that brings us back
and forth between Russia and Mexico City. *The Family Tree* by Margo Glantz is an
amazing voyage between the literatures, the languages, and the arts of Europe
and Latin America.

Notes

1. Margo Glantz, *Las genealogías* (México: SEP, Lecturas mexicanas 82, 1987). The latest edition has been published in Argentina (Buenos Aires: Editorial Bajo La Luna, 2010). This investigation is based on the Spanish text, considered to be the primary text. As this article is written in English, because of practical reasons, I use the English translation *The Family Tree* (London: Serpent's Tail, 1991). The purpose of this paper is not to make a comparison between the source text and the target text. Unless otherwise specified, all the references in this paper come from the English translation. When I quote from this book, I will only add the page.

2. For studies on the autobiographical character of the book, see the following authors: Rodrigo Cánovas, "Cuaderno de notas sobre *Las genealogías* de Margo Glantz," *Revista Chilena de literatura* 72 (2008): 115-125. Verena Dolle, "La construcción de sí mismo: memoria cultural e identidad en *Las genealogías* de Margo Glantz," in *Literatura-Historia-Política: Articulando las relaciones entre Europa y América Latina*, eds. Sonja M. Steckbauer et al. (Madrid, Frankfurt: Iberoamericana, Vervuert, 2004), 151-162. Sergio R. Franco, "Cultura visual y escritura autobiográfica en Hispanoamérica: tres usos de lo fotográfico," in *Cultura y cambio social en América Latina*, ed. Mabel Moraña (Madrid, Frankfurt: Iberoamericana, Vervuert, 2008), 403-420. Aída Nadi Gambetta Chuk, "Irreductible primera persona: la búsqueda identitaria en la narrativa de Margo Glantz," *Literatura Mexicana* 16.2 (2005): 173-183. Graciela Gliemmo, "Señales de una autobiografía: *Las genealogías* de Margo Glantz," *Monographic Review* 9 (1993): 189-198. Magdalena Maiz-Peña, "Sujeto, género y representación autobiográfica: Las Genealogías de Margo Glantz," *Confluencia: Revista Hispánica de Cultura y Literatura* 12.2 (1997): 75-87. Araceli Masterson, "Las genealogías de Margo Glantz: del Génesis al Distrito Federal," *Estudios Interdisciplinarios de América Latina y el Caribe*. 19.2 (2008), accessed 13 November 2009. http://www1.tau.ac.il/eial. Alida Mayne-Nicholls, "Necesidad de una genealogía," *Plaza Literaria*, 5 April 2010, accessed 8 September 2010. http://plazaliteraria.wordpress.com/2010/04/05/necesidad-de-una-genealogia/.

3. J. Hawley, *Encyclopedia of Postcolonial Studies* (Westport: Greenwood Press, 2001), 437.

4. The concept of the ship as a 'ghetto' has been analyzed by Adriana Kanzepolsky, "Escribir con la lengua. *Las genealogías* de Margo Glantz," *Biblioteca virtual Miguel de Cervantes*, accessed 6 March 2010. http://www.lluisvives.com/servlet/SirveObras/glantz/13548397012917617422202/p0000001.htm.

5. Margo Glantz, e-mail message to author, 3 June 2010 (my translation).

6. For Julio Cortázar, the concepts of chance, fate, and coincidence are fundamental and do not necessarily need an explanation as we can read in chapter seven of *Rayuela*. Julio Cortázar, *Rayuela* (Madrid: Cátedra, 1986), 160.

7. Margo Glantz, e-mail message to author, 3 June 2010 (my translation).

8. Among the many examples that can be given, I just mention one to illustrate this comparison. In *La flor de lis* by Elena Poniatowska, we read the story of the little girls who came from France to Mexico with their mother and when they are riding on horses, the narrator says: "Salimos a campo traviesa. Ni Hernán Cortés, ni Pizarro ni Núñez de Balboa, pisaron sus tierras con tanta soberbia." ("We went across the fields. Neither Hernán Cortés nor Pizarro nor Núñez de Balboa stepped on their lands with

AN VAN HECKE

so much pride," my translation). Elena Poniatowska, *La flor de lis* (Madrid: Alianza Tres/Era, 1988), 80.

9. In the Spanish original, the father quotes the verse of Lopez Velarde's most famous poem 'Suave patria': "El tren va por la vía... como juguetería." Margo Glantz, *Las genealogías* (México: SEP, Lecturas mexicanas 82, 1987), 81. It is a quote learned by heart, as this is the original text: "El tren va por la vía como aguinaldo de juguetería" ("The train is on the road as a Christmas toy," my translation). Ramón López Velarde, *La suave patria y otros poemas* (México: Alianza, 1994).

10. Shachar Pinsker, "Spaces of Hebrew and Yiddish Modernism – The Urban Cafés of Berlin," in *Transit und Transformation: Osteuropäisch-jüdische Migranten in Berlin 1918-1939*, eds. Verena Dohrn et al. (Wallstein Verlag GmbH, 2010), 59-62.

11. Michael Boyden, e-mail message to author, 11 January 2011.

12. Bassnett often changes the orthography of the original word: *heder* instead of *jeider* (in the Spanish version), *cholnt* instead of *tcholnt* (in the Spanish version), *vaymelke* instead of *yamelke* (in the Spanish version).

13. Naoki Sakai, "How do we count a language? Translation and discontinuity," *Translation Studies* 2.1 (2009): 84.

14. Caleb Bach, "A Human Body of Books," *Americas* 55.4 (2003): 46.

15. Magdalena Maiz-Peña, "Sujeto, género y representación autobiográfica: Las Genealogías de Margo Glantz," *Confluencia: Revista Hispánica de Cultura y Literatura* 12.2 (1997): 75-87. Maiz-Peña mentions the following books: *Las hojas muertas* (1987) by Barbara Jacobs, *Antes* and *Mejor desaparece* (1988) by Carmen Boullosa, *La flor de lis* (1988) by Elena Poniatowska, *La familia vino del norte* (1988) and *Héctor* (1990) by Silvia Molina, as well as some stories by Ethel Krauze and *La bobe* (1990) by Sabina Berman.

16. The Jewish background of the book has been studied by the following authors: Susanne Igler, "Identidades fragmentadas, fragmentos de identidad: Procesos de negociaciones culturales de escritoras judeo-mexicanas," in *Negociando identidades, traspasando fronteras: Tendencias en la literatura y el cine mexicanos en torno al nuevo milenio*, eds. S. Igler et al. (Madrid, Frankfurt: Iberoamericana, Vervuert, 2008), 99-110. Naomi Lindstrom, "The Heterogeneous Jewish Wit of Margo Glantz," in *Memory, Oblivion, and Jewish Culture in Latin America*, ed. Marjorie Agosín (Austin, TX: University of Texas Press, 2005), 115-129. Elizabeth Otero-Krauthammer, "Integración de la identidad judía en *Las genealogías* de Margo Glantz," *Revista Iberoamericana* 51.132-133 (1985): 867-873.

17. Juan Villoro quoted in Alberto Sánchez, "Mudarse para mejorarse. Entrevista con Juan Villoro," *La Jornada Semanal*, 23 September 2001, accessed 9 September 2010. http://www.sololiteratura.com/vill/villmudarse.htm

18. Ariel Dorfman, *The Family Tree. An Illustrated Novel*, translated by Susan Bassnett (London: Serpent's Tail, 1991), cover page.

Liminal Spaces

Steamships, Hospitals, and Funerals: Liminal Spaces in Nineteenth-Century Liverpool's Narratives of Transit

Ron Geaves

The following article is not a story of a nation or of a people that migrated, but rather of a group whose experiences in transit led to the establishment of Britain's first settled Muslim communities in the nineteenth and early twentieth centuries. The impact of Lascars (oriental seamen) on Muslim settlement in Britain has long been acknowledged in the history of migration studies in Britain. Ballard's classic four-stage theory of South Asian migration to Britain refers to Indian seamen during the nineteenth century and early decades of the twentieth as belonging to the "original pioneers" of settlement in Britain.[1] Fred Halliday explores the role of Yemeni seamen in establishing Britain's first settled Muslim communities in the seaports of Tyneside, Cardiff, and Liverpool.[2] Rozina Visram challenges Ballard's "original pioneers" thesis and demonstrates in her ground-breaking work that the presence of South Asians in Britain in the nineteenth century went far beyond a few courageous individuals. She shows us that there were a number of transit communities comprised of students, diplomats, wealthy travelers, entertainers, seamen, and the unfortunate ayahs.[3] More recently, Humayun Ansari has published a detailed history of Muslims in Britain in which he records the contribution of Lascars to the settlement and development of Muslim communities.[4] However, all these studies focus on the role of the seamen's settlements in the seaports where some of their number chose to open boarding houses or food outlets for their more transitory fellow sailors waiting for a passage back to the place of origin. These men often married British women and created one of the earliest forms of settled Muslim presences in Britain's expanding seaports. Thousands more remained in Britain for only short periods of time between ships. Their stories are virtually untold, yet they played a significant part in the movement of peoples during Britain's colonial era both on the transatlantic and oriental steamship routes.

Ansari calculates that the number of Lascars in Britain increased rapidly from 470 in 1804 to 1,336 in 1813. Around 3,000 arrived in 1842 and, according to an estimate, 10,000-12,000 in 1855. Salter calculated that 3,271 Lascars arrived on 40 ships in 1873, 1,653 were Muslims from India, Egypt, Malaya, and Turkey. Of the

7,814 Lascars surveyed in 1874, 4,685 came from India and 1,440 were Arabs, 225 Turks and 85 Malays.[5] Not all of these arrived in Liverpool. But this is the period when the city was becoming one of the busiest ports in Britain. Shipping grew from the mid-nineteenth century onwards at an impressive annual rate of 2.6 percent.[6] As trade and shipping with the Middle East, India, and Africa grew, people arrived from every corner of the Empire in search of opportunities. As the number of steam ships increased, the numbers of Lascars employed by the British merchant fleet grew, and by the early twentieth century Muslim seamen were a significant part of the migrant population in Britain and the dock areas of Liverpool.

The Lascars' recruitment into the British merchant marine in large numbers coincided with the period in which British colonialism was invoking a new patriotic discourse to justify imperial expansion. Fiction had become one of the primary tools for reaching the nation's youth, proclaiming racial pride, militaristic values, and heroic self-sacrifice. Although it would be analytically reasonable to describe the Lascars in terms of Marx's reserve army of migrant labor, the imperial context and the subsequent discourses of Empire insist that any exploration of the oriental seamen take account of the contemporary resonance of what Homi Bhabha describes as the "patriotic voice of unisonance."[7] The Lascars' visibility in British seaports would provoke hostility and racism not because of "the worn-out metaphors of resplendent national life,"[8] but rather precisely because such metaphors were new and vibrant in British cultural life, unlike the earlier period of colonization which had regarded British direct rule with some distaste.

The Lascars settled in numbers too small to fit into the category of "wave" migration, but they would have been under the gaze of the white European passengers on the steamships because they were recruited to serve above deck as shiphands. On shore, they were not only foreigners but part of a "migratory labouring underclass."[9] Robinson-Dunne reports that they were regarded on the same level as pedlars, vagrants, and petty criminals.[10] However, their color and exotic dress would have marked them out as "other" in a way not ascribed to the native denizens of the slums that surrounded the docks for both passengers and cargo to and from the East. The "otherness" of the Lascar rendered him more visible as both an object of desire and derision among the working classes of the seaports. Their desirability is demonstrated by the number of marriages that occurred when sailors "jumped ship" and married women from the lowest strata of dockland society. But they were also the victims of crime. Thus, articulations of difference were expressed in both racial and sexual terms, both functioning as "representations of difference" focused on a "fantasy of origin." Their life at the margins of a newly developing modern, industrial, and commercial nation can only be described in Bhabha's words: "wandering people who will not be contained within the *heim* of the national culture and its unisonant discourse, but are

RON GEAVES

themselves the marks of a shifting boundary that alienates the frontiers of the modern nation."[11]

The Lascar experience of migration could be described as one that originated and ended where ships came into port. This omits the millions who successfully negotiated Britain's seaports and went on to form major migrant population centers away from the ports of entry. (In)visibility was a feature of the Lascars' negotiation of the new cultural and geographic landscapes. They were visible on Britain's seaports as black, native, and exotic, but their invisibility is a major challenge when charting the journey of the Lascars to Britain and back to their places of origin. As a people of transit, the Lascars arrived in Cardiff, Tyneside, and Liverpool on board steamships. They passed itinerant weeks in cheap boarding houses in some of the poorest neighborhoods. The ships and the ports that received them could be described as transit places, but such sites normally figure only marginally in migrant narratives. The Lascars' invisibility was a condition of their itinerant lifestyle and also of their very low status in Britain's class structure. Moreover, the Muslim Lascars' invisibility was also physical. The steamship crews were stratified according to religious affiliation. Christians worked in the saloon. Hindus were usually deckhands, and Muslims worked in the engine room below decks.[12] Contemporary histories of Muslim life in nineteenth-century and early twentieth-century Britain indicate that the living conditions of the Muslim Lascars were harsh.[13] On board ship, they labored for wages that were up to one-third less than those of white British seamen, and on shore, they suffered unemployment, poverty, and sickness. Salter's research undertaken in 1873 noted that during the winter months, Lascars were often found frozen to death on the streets of London.[14]

Abdullah Quilliam as Cultural Intermediary

In the gaze of the contemporary scholar, Liverpool, which had grown to be the second city of importance in the British Empire in the nineteenth century, is a site of visibility *par excellence*. A window was to open from 1893 to 1908, when a convert to Islam, William Henry Abdullah Quilliam (1856-1932), a Liverpudlian lawyer of some renown, made himself the champion of the Lascars. He created a hostel for their accommodation, took care of their physical and spiritual needs, and conducted their rites of passage.[15] Quilliam was also a journalist. He edited a weekly newspaper, The Crescent, during this same period, and in its pages catalogued the experiences of the Lascars with whom he came in contact.

John Belchem describes Liverpool as the "shock city" of post-industrial Britain.[16] By the mid-nineteenth century, this city, where Quilliam was born, was already experiencing massive growth. During his lifetime, this expansion continued unabated. Even by the last quarter of the eighteenth century, it had been described as "the first town in the kingdom in point of size and commercial importance, the metropolis excepted."[17] Although not one of the new industrial centers like nearby Manchester, during the eighteenth and nineteenth centuries, Liverpool became the heart of the transatlantic trade. It was the link between Britain and Ireland, and after the invention of the steamship, the fulcrum between industrializing Britain and the remainder of the world, especially India and Africa.[18]

From a population of 7,000 in 1708, the city's population had expanded to 376,000 by the time Quilliam was born in 1856. Eighty percent of this population increase was due to migration. No other city in Britain can claim to have been formed by migration in quite the same way as Liverpool. Although the greater majorities were from North and South Ireland, Wales, and Scotland, the city had a flourishing Jewish community, the first Chinese quarter in Europe, and boasted the first registered mosque in the nation. There were also smaller presences of Greeks, Turks, Yemenis, Somalis, and South Asians who arrived in the city as sailors. The wealth of the city came from commerce, and the docks were the hub of Liverpool's activity. The areas adjacent to the docks teemed with sailors seeking a ship home or taking leave from ships in port. In addition, casual dock labor and entertainment industries flourished by supplying the needs of these transitory populations.

The tonnage of shipping had grown alongside the population, from 14,600 in 1709 to 4,000,000 in 1855. To cope with the burgeoning trade, the number of docks increased greatly. Seven new docks were built in the eighteenth and early nineteenth centuries, and that was before the period of Victorian expansion that saw the building of the most magnificent dock architecture in Britain. By the middle of the nineteenth century the annual value of exports was £55,000,000, accounting for half the exports of the nation. The influx of wealth and human capital resulted in a massive disparity of wealth between the commercial elite and the city's poor, mostly casual dock labor. Consequently, Power is able to say that the city was "moulded by the powerful forces of international trade, mass migration and appalling public health."[19]

William Henry Quilliam was a well-known Liverpool solicitor who had converted to Islam after visiting Morocco in 1887. The Liverpool Muslim Institute and British Muslim Association that he founded to promote Islam in Britain opened in September 1887, two years before the Woking mosque was built outside London. Although there may be disputes over the first building to be used by Muslims in Britain as a place of prayer, there is no doubt that the first attempt to promote Islam in Britain from within a mosque and Islamic center took place in Liverpool. Shaikh Abdullah Quilliam, as he was known to Muslims, was well placed to offer insights into the Muslim presence in Liverpool in the late Victorian and early Edwardian periods. Although Quilliam became renowned for his success in converting English men and women to Islam, the Muslim community in Liverpool was more than a group of Liverpool's middle-class converts. The renown of the British lawyer and his mosque in Liverpool spread to the Muslim world. It was promoted by word of mouth by returning travelers and through the circulation of *The Crescent* to more than eighty nations. The new railway linked Liverpool to Manchester and the rest of the nation. Wealthy upper-class Muslims had developed their own version of a world tour and arrived in Liverpool on steamships. They would use the city as a place of transit to visit London, Europe, and even the U.S. Many had heard of the mosque in the city and visited, often staying as a guest in Quilliam's villa. While there, they would attend *jum'a* prayers at the mosque on Fridays, sometimes even giving lectures on various aspects of Islam or Muslim culture and history.

Edward Said describes Oriental-European relations as Europeans "always in a position of strength, not to say domination."[20] But Said is more concerned to provide a definition of Orientalism that is an "exercise of cultural strength" in which the "East and everything in it is patently inferior to, and in need of corrective study by the West."[21] Adopting Said's classic definition of Orientialism as "a kind of western projection onto and will to govern over the Orient,"[22] it would be simple to condemn Quilliam as an orientialist engaging in Western projections and seduced by a romantic sentiment. However, Quilliam was a member of the English gentry and needs to be analyzed as someone who had been thoroughly mentally colonized by the Orient, enough to decide to convert to Islam. As such, he engaged in overturning the Orientalist's version of the Muslim world as backward, degenerate, and lacking in reason. Quilliam reversed the Orientalist paradigm by using the same terms of nineteenth-century Christianity and European culture, reflecting it back to the Muslim world by means of his journalism. The consequences for him would be eventual disgrace, loss of identity, and police files.[23]

Quilliam was also a philanthropist and social reformer who was known in the city for his work amongst the city's poor. His social activism consisted of temperance campaigning, reform of capital punishment, trade unionism, political lobbying against the Alien and Migration Acts,[24] satirical and political journalism, performance of mixed race weddings, and campaigning against racial discrimination in particular against slavery and the "negro" question. But it was his work championing the Lascars that provides the poignant tales of transit and offers insights into the condition of these men, some of whom went on to form Britain's first established migrant communities. As a lawyer he was able to represent them with the shipping agents and steamship companies that employed them. As a Muslim leader he provided a number of services including a hostel, free meals at the mosque, prayer and religious facilities, and correct performance of Islamic marriages and funerals. As a journalist and editor of a weekly newspaper, Quilliam provided regular narratives of individuals who sought or were in need of his assistance. The local hospitals in northwest England contacted him when Muslim seamen were in their care. Quilliam's reports on these incidents were often harrowing. His accounts are an extraordinary resource for researchers. A weekly newspaper directed at Muslim readers worldwide was significant in that it made the Lascars the subject of their own lives.

Many of the steamship deckhands ensuring the success of the British merchant fleet were Lascars. They were often in dire straits, stranded in port as they waited to contract a journey home. The invisibility of the Lascars was a facet of life even on board the ship where they disappeared below deck. For many of those in transit, the ship was a bridge that connected the homeland to the new location, but for the Muslim sailors it was a place that was territorialized. Their space was deep below deck where they remained invisible to both above- and below-deck passengers. Quilliam provided a fascinating glimpse of this liminal world in an account of his travels to Morocco in 1893. Quilliam was seen off at the Royal Albert Docks in Liverpool by four prominent Muslims visiting from London. Those on the dock included the converts Obeid-Ullah Cunliffe,[25] whose funeral the Sheikh would carry out on his return, and the Indian Muslims Imam Barakat-Ullah and Sheikh Fazil ud-deen Ahmed. The former would join Quilliam the following year and become the imam of the Liverpool mosque. Quilliam sailed on the P & O steamship *Arcadia* at 1pm.[26] By 10pm he had written a letter to the Muslims in Liverpool, conveyed to shore by the pilot. He stated that he was the only Muslim on board and that his fellow passengers were either returning to Australia or were military officers. Missing Muslim company, as the time of Maghrab prayers approached, he walked below deck wearing his fez to discover over forty Muslim crew members. He led them in prayer and they called him Abdullah Sahib. No more news was possible until the ship docked in Gibraltar. In fact, the Liverpool Muslims were to hear very little until their Sheikh returned two months later in April.[27]

Quilliam was one of the few to bridge the separated world of Victorian class and the social stratification of empire. His visit below deck revealed a liminal world where, periodically for the next twenty-five years, he entered as someone of his class and wealth on the one hand, and Islam's first leader in a western European nation on the other. Evidence of this unique ability to walk between worlds appeared in *The Liverpool Courier* in 1893. The newspaper reported that a funeral carried out by Quilliam was attended by Muslim sailors. It claimed that the Muslim funeral was the ninth to take place in the city and that eighty-eight Muslims were buried at the Necropolis cemetery. The majority of these would have been Lascars. The newspaper also noted that on this occasion, the funeral was conducted without incident unlike the previous one at which "rowdies" had attempted to push the mourners into the grave.[28]

The presence of Indian Muslim sailors at the funeral in some numbers indicates that even as early as 1893, the Lascars of Liverpool were aware of the Liverpool Muslim Institute and participated in its activities along with the converts. It also shows that Abdullah Quilliam was already involved with the Lascars and their affairs. During the first week of November 1893, Quilliam had received a letter from Birkenhead Union Hospital explaining that they had an Indian Muslim sailor as a patient. The Sheikh visited the sick, twenty-nine-year-old man at the hospital. The report in *The Crescent* of that week is instructive. It provides the details ascertained by the Sheikh at the sick man's bedside. The sailor was from Calcutta where his wife still lived. The article states that he prayed in the Ghowbara Masjid near Delhi Khan. He had departed on the SS *Daman* three months earlier. As with all the sick sailors met by Quilliam, their main concern seems to have been to receive Muslim funeral rites. An article in *The Liverpool Review* in February of 1898 commenting on a Muslim funeral performed by the Sheikh states that "it is amazing that the man was not afraid of dying but only that he would not receive a Muslim funeral."[29] The Sheikh relieved these hospital bed anxieties immediately, guaranteeing the sailors that full Muslim funeral rites and burial practices would be observed. In this case, the invalid was visited again on the following Sunday by both Quilliam and a party of Liverpool Muslims but the sick man fortunately seemed to have recovered.[30]

In 1894, it is possible to discern that Abdullah Quilliam continued his work on behalf of the sailors. Combining his role as the leader of British Muslims with his legal skills as a lawyer, he worked to defend Muslim sailors' rights. Quilliam became a renowned advocate for the Lascars. Significantly, his accounts also provide us with evidence of their condition. In October 1894, a Turkish Muslim sailor named Mahomet Ali suffered an accident aboard the SS *Dartmoor* where he was badly scalded by a steam pipe explosion in a boiler. A city police superintendent informed Abdullah Quilliam, who by this time had been appointed by the Ottoman authorities as their Turkish Vice-Consul in the city. Quilliam accompanied the Turkish Consul-General on a visit to the badly burned man in hospital, where they found him in a critical state. By the next morning he was dead.[31] The sailor was only thirty-seven years old and married. Abdullah Quilliam attended the coroner's inquest into the death on behalf of both the Ottoman Consul and the local Muslim community in Liverpool. He claimed that the man was not only a Turkish citizen but also a temporary Muslim resident under his jurisdiction and care as the officially recognized leader of the Muslims in the British Isles. As a skilled advocate, he was more than capable of cross-examining witnesses and was instrumental in winning the decision of gross negligence on the part of the steamship company. Quilliam had hoped to persuade the coroner to bring a verdict of criminal negligence.

There is another funeral of interest in Manchester in 1897. This funeral took place after the opening of the Manchester Ship Canal had permitted access to the city for sailors employed on the Clan Line and other companies trading with the Orient. An Indian sailor named Sheikh Hassan, who was employed on the SS *Imperialist*, was critically injured in an accident and had been admitted to Salford Royal Infirmary. Ibrahim Saleh, a member of the Liverpool Muslim Institute who resided in Salford, was asked to intervene as an interpreter. The sailor, only 21 years of age and from Bombay, admitted that he was a Muslim and personally requested the Sheikh al-Islam[32] of the British Isles because he feared he was dying. Quilliam was sent for and arrived in time to carry out the funeral in Manchester. The Sheikh was annoyed that the officers of the steamship company did not notify the sixty Indian Muslim sailors employed on their vessels in Salford Docks so that they could attend the funeral. This incident illustrates not only the networking that took place amongst British Muslims, but also that the Sheikh's reputation was known widely among Indian sailors.

There was a very good reason for Abdullah Quilliam to find out the precise details of the sailors' backgrounds. On 2 November 1903, a young Indian sailor named Rahim Buksh lay dying at Borough Hospital, Birkenhead. He was only twenty-two and in the last stages of tuberculosis. He had been in the hospital since June. On 14 November 1903, Quilliam and some British Muslims went to Bebington Cemetary to bury the young man. Quilliam discovered that he was due eight months' salary at the rate of sixteen rupees (approximately 15p at today's rates of exchange) per month. He took the details of the Charterers in Liverpool along with the address of the young sailor's relatives in Calcutta.[33] We read that the lawyer visited the shipping agents and ensured that the back wages owed to the sailor were sent to the relatives in India. Quilliam was hard to refuse, as his legal reputation in Liverpool preceeded him. On another occasion, when a sailor aged 51 named Munto Abbas of the SS *Rangoon* died without being able to inform Quilliam of his address in Calcutta, the Liverpool Muslim Institute took out advertisements in Indian newspapers to trace the family so that the wages could be sent to the appropriate next of kin.

Finances were a constant challenge to Quilliam. The Annual General Meeting for 1900 reported that Quilliam had once more subsidized the donations to the amount of £200. Indian Muslims had donated £30 towards the cost of a Muslim cemetery plot, but it was reported that the increasing arrival of destitute Muslim sailors in the city, docking either directly in Liverpool or arriving from other British seaports in Tyneside, Cardiff, or London, created a new challenge to the already meager finances of the Institute. The police were directing all destitute Lascars to the mosque. The Liverpool Muslim Institute found that it was not only looking after their accommodation but also paying for their passage home. In June 1900, the Institute was looking after the interests of over thirty such men. Some needed clothing and medical treatment, and the resources of the converts were being stretched to the breaking point. Quilliam advised the members that a proper hostel needed to be established by Indian Muslims to meet the needs of their compatriots. This was then added to the facilities of the Liverpool Muslim Institute in the opening years of the twentieth century.[34]

These incidents show that England in the nineteenth century was a dangerous place for Asian and African seamen who arrived in the nation's seaports. *The Crescent* further reports the death of two sailors who had died from the infectious illness beriberi in the Royal Southern Infirmary in Liverpool. They were buried by Quilliam at the Toxteth Smithdown Road Cemetery.[35] The newspaper recounts a tragic tale of a Berber from Morocco who had landed in Cardiff but traveled to Liverpool by train to search for a ship to take him to Egypt. Only 21 years old, he died of kidney failure through overexposure to the cold while homeless in Liverpool. Quilliam had visited him in hospital and read passages from the Qur'an to him. He was buried in Fazakerley Cemetery by the Sheikh.

The above incidents set a pattern for the fifteen years of the Sheikh's activities in Liverpool and further afield. Hospitals, the police, and workhouse authorities quickly learned that Abdullah Quilliam was the person to contact when sick or deceased Muslim sailors arrived anywhere in the northwest of England. These incidents deserve recounting, as they tell something about the nineteenth-century Muslim presence in Britain and the role of Abdullah Quilliam as a Muslim religious leader. The above accounts indicate the degree of pastoral care that became the pattern of the Sheikh's treatment of the sick and dying among the Lascars. He performed funerals for sailors from India, Yemen, Somalia, Zanzibar, and Morocco, and he ensured that not only British Muslim converts but also Muslim sailors present in the port attended these funerals. He was particularly keen that the deceased sailors' shipmates from the same line or vessel should attend.

Ansari reminds us that it was believed that, with the coming of steam, oriental sailors used to the climates of the tropics and the deserts were better suited to the heat generated by the furnace-like engine rooms below deck.[36] Although the pay may have appeared attractive to many young men and their families, there is compelling evidence that life was dangerous on board the steamships. Abdullah Quilliam became aware of the plight of these Muslim sailors, and he made them an integral part of the Liverpool Muslim community. In turn, the stories of the mosque in Liverpool and its English Sheikh spread through the Muslim sailor communities, drawing more men to the city and to the shelter he provided them.

Being an Asian seaman in Liverpool had always been hazardous. Salter reports visiting the graves of thirty Ottoman sailors buried in a Liverpool cemetery in the mid-nineteenth century, and Quilliam's detailed accounts provide more evidence of the hazards of their lifestyle.[37] Many of the diseases that hospitalized them and even ended their lives were contracted on board ship or were picked up while in Liverpool. The working conditions were dire, and the contracts of employment included only one-way passage. Quilliam provides accounts of young men walking in winter from Cardiff to Liverpool to seek a ship. He opened a khan (hostel) for them at the mosque and did what he could to ensure that these dangerous liminal spaces were crossed as safely as possible. His accounts of funerals reveal that these men were concerned about their wages being paid to their families and their funerals being carried out according to Muslim custom. Quilliam also performed marriages between Asian Muslim seamen and British women. These marriages were highly taboo, and the media attacked him. Angry crowds would gather outside the mosque, and occasionally violence would break out. The government even tried to use the Law Society to prevent Quilliam's activities, but the Society replied that he was not breaking any laws. These marriages were significant in that they showed that liminal spaces were being crossed and roots were being laid down for permanent British Muslim communities in the dockland areas of Liverpool. The marriages made the Lascars visible and changed their notion of homeland. These experiences were repeated in London, Cardiff, and South Shields, and these communities today remain the oldest permanent settlements of Muslims in Britain.

Conclusion

Homi Bhabha directs us towards the "concept of fixity in the ideological construction of otherness" central to colonial discourses.[38] But the discourses of nationhood equally develop an essentialized discourse. The peak period of recruitment for the Lascars coincided with the emergent Victorian nationalism that defined the nation in increasingly xenophobic discourses. As the Lascars gathered in British ports, they formed one of the first "*quasi colonial* presences."[39] Denied the myth of return articulated by settled migration and not able to develop narratives to describe their experiences, they sailed the high seas maintaining Britain's colonial enterprise. Occasionally they appeared in boy's fiction as "swarthy" sailors, often depicted as pirates. To some degree, they epitomized "the desolate silences of wandering people" described by Bhabha.[40] They were not completely silent. The white working women of the docks recognized reliable sexual partners free from the vice of alcohol that blighted their own men folk, and the resulting marriages formed Britain's first Muslim communities. The tales of these communities went back to homelands in Yemen, India, and Somalia and provided the family narratives that would lead to migration to Britain in the post-World War II era. In the final decade of the nineteenth century, Quilliam became the voice that the Muslims lacked, and his reports of meetings around such liminal spaces as hospitals, inter-class meetings below decks, marriages, and funerals demonstrate a sense of the perils that existed for such marginal presences. Du Bois's *quasi-colonial* fuses with Bhabha's understanding of marginal people to lead us towards a discourse that refutes "fixity."

As such, the classic anthropological thesis developed by Van Gennep with regards to rites of passage and the concept of liminality is a useful conceptual tool to contextualize the experiences of the Lascars. It posits movement rather than fixity.[41] Utilizing Turner's classic development of Van Gennep's ideas, where he extended the concept of liminality to include all forms of movement in social life, the Lascar seamen can be explored as "threshold people." They were liminal entities existing between positions assigned by law, custom, tradition, and convention. The liminal, the second of Turner's stages, is where the group or individual passes through a period that is "betwixt and between" located states and positions in cultural space. The third and final stage is the re-emergence of the group or individual to a new stable state described by Turner as possessing "rights and obligations vis-à-vis others of a clearly defined and structural type; he is expected to behave in accordance with certain customary norms and ethical standards binding upon incumbents of social position in a system of such positions."[42] Yet it is difficult to see how the oriental seamen employed by Britain's merchant marine could find a way out to a new stage of existence. The successful would find their way back to their homeland, re-emerging back into the first stage, the place of embarkation. It is not known how their journeys transformed them. Their memories of voyages and transit in Liverpool would inform a later generation of Yemeni post-World War II migrant settlers in the city. A minority stayed in the new land discovering how to live liminal lives in Britain's seaports and formed proto-communities for the second wave of settlers.

If the processes of migration can be compared to the stages of classic *rites de passage*, then it can be argued that Quilliam, in helping the Lascars establish their religious life and carry out their traditional rites of passage in Liverpool, provided them with new avenues to express their condition. In the Liverpool mosque they often sought the comradeship and egalitarianism that Turner notes marks the neophyte in *rites de passage*. Not always available in their transitory life, the Liverpool Mosque filled the need for *communitas*. It offered a sense of sacredness, homogeneity, and intense comradeship.

Unfortunately, the liminal stage in religious rites is frequently linked to death and wilderness. In Van Gennep's original analysis of rites of passage carried out by traditional peoples, neophytes are sometimes even disguised as monsters. Indigenous people recognized the perils associated with the liminal stage, where any kind of "fixity" is denied. Quilliam recognized this and in his role as the official representative of Islam in Britain helped the Lascars to negotiate truly dangerous spaces and transmigrate to safer, more secure spaces of settlement. The Lascars occupied a unique status in migrant labor, and their journeying was a site of transition and loss. They help us to understand that the processes of migration can begin aboard ship where unique communities of transit are formed. In the case of the Lascars, these shifting communities were extended to the seaports where the passengers and cargoes disembarked. In the first section of this volume, Yannis Papadopoulos claims that the transatlantic steamships functioned as spaces for creating links among migrants but also as symbolic markers for the presence of a "homeland" in American ports. The Lascars were denied even this consolation, as the ships they sailed in did not originate in their own land as had the ships that conveyed the Greek migrants.

Quilliam's accounts personalize the stories of the Lascar sailors. There are tales of hope and despair, individualizing experiences, something akin to the role of fiction in exploring individual identity. Quilliam's account of the rites of passage he performed on their behalf demonstrates how such rituals can lessen anxieties when any notion of essential identity has gone. Many of these men experienced border identities of extreme fluidity, caught as they were between land and sea, their place of origin and family a keen but distant memory. Only Islam offered a place of essential identity and certainty, and they clung to the British Muslim who offered them Muslim rites of passage conducted in the appropriate way. In performing the act of mimicry that the religious rite of passage contains, Quilliam restored the familiar and permitted a final restoration of identity and a way out of the sites of liminality.

Notes

1. Roger and Catherine Ballard, "The Sikhs," in *Between Two Cultures: Migrants and Minorities in Britain*, ed. J. L. Watson (Oxford: Blackwell, 1977), 21-56.
2. Fred Halliday, *Arabs in Exile: Yemeni Migrants in Urban Britain* (London: I. B. Tauris, 1992).
3. Rozina Visram, *The History of the Asian Community in Britain: 400 Years of History* (London: Pluto Press, 2002).
4. Humayun Ansari, *The Infidel Within* (London: Hurst, 2004).
5. Ibid. 30-35.
6. Ibid. 39.
7. Homi Bhabha, "DissemiNATION: Time, Narrative, and the Margin of the Modern Nation" in *Nation and Narration*, ed. Homi Bhabha (London and New York: Routledge, 1990), 315.
8. Ibid.
9. Sophie Gilliat-Ray, *Muslims in Britain* (Cambridge: Cambridge University Press, 2010), 31.
10. D. Robinson-Dunne, "Lascar Sailors and English Converts: The Imperial Port and Islam in Late-Nineteenth Century England," (paper delivered at the Seascapes, Littoral Cultures and Trans-Oceanic Exchanges Conference, Library of Congress, Washington D.C., 12-15 February 2003, *History Cooperative* website, accessed 15 January 2011, www.historycooperative.org/proceedings/seascapes/dunn.html, 2003), 2.
11. Bhabha, "DissemiNATION," 315.
12. R. Lawless, "Religion and Politics among Arab seafarers in Britain in the early twentieth Century," *Islam and Christian Muslim Relations* 5.1 (1997), 35-36.
13. See Gilliat-Ray, *Muslims in Britain* and Ansari, *The Infidel Within*.
14. Reported in Sophie Gilliat-Ray, *Muslims in Britain*, 30 from J. Salter, *The Asiatic in England: Sketches of Sixteen Year's Work among the Orientals* (London: Seeley, Jackson & Halliday, 1873).
15. Abdullah Quilliam's biography has been published by Ron Geaves, *Islam in Victorian Britain: The Life and Times of Abdullah Quilliam* (Markfield: Kube Press, 2010).
16. John Belchem, "Introduction" in *Popular Politics, Riot and Labour: Essay in Liverpool History 1790-1940*, ed. John Belcham (Liverpool: Liverpool University Press, 1992), 1.

17. R. Brooke, *Liverpool as it was during the last quarter of the 18th century, 1775-1800* (Liverpool: J. Mawdsley & Son, 1853).

18. M. J. Power, "The Growth of Liverpool" in *Popular Politics, Riot and Labour: Essay in Liverpool History 1790-1940*, ed. John Belcham (Liverpool: Liverpool University Press, 1992), 21.

19. Ibid. 21.

20. Edward Said, *Orientalism* (Harmondsworth: Penguin, 1978), 40.

21. Ibid. 40-41.

22. Ibid. 95.

23. In 1907, Abdullah Quilliam fled Liverpool for Constantinople never to return to Britain under the same name. In 1910, he returned to the North of England as Henri deLeon, an identity he maintained until his death in 1932. Files on Quilliam/De Leon were maintained by Scotland Yard, The Home Office and the Foreign Office (see Ron Geaves, 2010).

24. The Alien's Act of 1905 was passed after extensive campaigning by activists in the East End of London. Thomas Dewar and William Evans-Gordon were elected to Parliament with the aim of introducing legislation to limit alien (and especially Jewish) immigration. A Royal Commission into the effects of alien immigration into Britain was appointed in 1903, resulting in the first Aliens Act limiting immigration into Britain and categorizing some immigrants as 'undesirable'. The Act was designed to prevent paupers or criminals from entering the country and permitted deportation to those who slipped through. *Exploring Twentieth Century London*, Museum of London website accessed 15 January 2011, (http://www.museumoflondon.org.uk/English/Collections/OnlineResources/X2oL/Themes/1386/) and *Moving Here Migration Histories*, accessed 15 January 2011, http://www.movinghere.org.uk/galleries/histories/jewish/journeys/journeys.htm). The Act was supported by trade unions but resisted by most Liberals. Quilliam drew upon his resources as a journalist and lawyer to resist the passing of the Act.

25. An early Muslim convert who assisted Alexander Webb in promoting Islam in the U.S. He was the author of *The Disintegration of Christianity* and the poem "A Moslem Prayer" (see Umar Abd-Ullah, *A Muslim in Victorian America* (Oxford: Oxford University Press, 2006), 72.

26. The Peninsular and Oriental Steam Navigation Company (P&O) has a celebrated history dating back to the 1830s, although its origins go back to 1815. It was finally incorporated by a Royal Charter in 1840. The Oriental extension to their service occurred between 1840 and 1870 with voyages to Egypt inaugurated in 1840 by the 1,674-ton paddle steamer *Oriental*, and by 1842 regular services to India were available which involved a difficult overland journey to Suez where a second ship was boarded for the voyage to Calcutta. By 1845, services had been extended to cover Italy, Greece, the Black Sea, Ceylon, Madras, and China. After 1870 the shipping company went on to become Britain's premier shipping company and an Imperial institution. Aside from its normal trading activities, the company-chartered vessels to the government to be used as hospital ships and troop transports and in 1911 allowed the newly built *Medina* to be used as the Royal Yacht at the Delhi Durbar. Queen Victoria celebrated her Golden Jubilee in 1887 and to pay tribute to her and their own success, P&O built four

6,000-ton 'Jubilee' ships the *Victoria*, the *Britannia*, the *Oceania*, and the *Arcadia*. The size of the fleet had, by 1887, increased from 80,000 tons to 200,000 tons and the run to Bombay had been reduced by more than a week. Between 1870 and 1914, traveling on board a P&O steamship was an extension of living in the British 'Raj' for first class passengers. The crews were generally made up of Indians in the engine room, Lascars on deck, and stewards from the Portuguese colony of Goa. (*The Peninsular & Oriental Steam Navigation Company (P&O Line) Est. 1840* website accessed 15 January 2011, (http://www.oceanlinermuseum.co.uk/P&O2ohistory.html).

27. *The Crescent* (hereafter abbreviated to TC) 1.12 (8 April 1893).

28. *Liverpool Courier* (18 November 1893).

29. Reported in TC 266 (16 February 1898).

30. TC (5 November 1893).

31. TC 6.146 (1894).

32. The office of Sheikh al-Islam of the British Isles has only had one incumbent: Sheikh Abdullah Quilliam (1856-1932). The Ottoman caliph, Sultan Abdul Hamid II, granted Quilliam the position in 1894. The position had become prestigious in the Caliphate state of the Ottoman Empire and governed religious affairs of the state. Each of the territories governed by the Ottomans possessed a Sheikh al-Islam to control religious affairs. For an examination of Quilliam's appointment see Yahya Birt, "An enquiry into the statys of the Sheikh-ul-Islam of the Britisch Isles," (www.yahyabirt.com, 2008), 138, accessed 14 November 2010.

33. TC 521 (7 January 1903).

34. TC 389 (27 June 1900).

35. TC 466 (18 December 1902).

36. Ansari, *The Infidel Within*, 38.

37. Ibid. 30.

38. Homi Bhabha, *The Location of Culture* (London and New York: Routledge: 1994), 94.

39. W. E. B. DuBois, "Human Rights for all Minorities" (7 November 1945) reprinted in *W. E. B. DuBois Speaks: Speeches and Addresses 1920-1963*, ed. Philip S. Foner (New York: Pathfinder Press, 1970), 183.

40. Bhabha, "DissemiNATION," 316.

41. Arnold van Gennep, *The Rites of Passage* (1909), translated by Monika B. Vizedom and Gabrielle L. Caffee (Chicago: University of Chicago Press, 1960 and London: Routledge, 2004).

42. Arnold van Gennep's *The Rites of Passage* influenced anthropologist Victor Turner's research, particularly his text, *The Ritual Process: Structure and Anti-Structure* (Chicago: Aldine Publishing Company, 1969). The quotation is taken from Michael Lambek, *A Reader in the Anthropology of Religion* (Oxford: Blackwell, 2002), 359.

Heavenly Sensations and Communal Celebrations: Experiences of Liminality in Transatlantic Journeys

Babs Boter

The Kind of Family Sea Journeys Create

"I shat among strangers for six weeks to get to this land," Rebekka Vaark tells her servant in Toni Morrison's novel *A Mercy* (2008). Traveling alone from England to America around 1690 to "wed a stranger," sixteen-year-old Rebekka indeed was "among strangers" for weeks. She was assigned to the lower deck of the Angelus with seven other women who, despite their common state of being "exiled, thrown-away women," show remarkable differences.[1] With her fellow passengers, Rebekka has to stay in a "dark space below," next to the animal stalls.

> A tub for waste sat beside a keg of cider; a basket and a rope where food could be let down and the basket retrieved. Anyone taller than five feet hunched and lowered her head to move around. Crawling was easier once, like street vagrants, they partitioned off their personal space. [They were] huddled 'tween decks and walls made of trunks, boxes, blankets hanging from hammocks [...].[2]

Although Rebekka has to crawl in the dark, she is able to move around, and find room to enjoy her fellow passengers' singing, "alehouse wit," "quick laughter," and "know-how" that "lightened the journey."[3] In that dark space, lighted only by one small lamp, the women decide to have tea.

> The women scooted toward Rebekka and suddenly, without urging, began to imitate what they thought were the manners of queens. Judith spread her shawl on the lid of a box. Elizabeth retrieved from her trunk a kettle and a set of spoons. [...] with the care of a butler they poured [some rum] in the tepid water. Rebekka set the cheese in the middle of the shawl and surrounded it with biscuits. Anne offered grace.[4]

Firstly, this ritual, as focalized by Rebekka, suggests the possibilities of overcoming the "hideous" circumstances of the transatlantic journey by a collective resourcefulness, imagination, and play.[5] Secondly, as Rebekka reminisces later when she has established herself in America, the ceremony in the near darkness indicates the women's ability to overcome differences and become "the kind of family sea journeys create."[6]

Thus, the comforting and equalizing mock tea party turns the dark space at steerage level into a space of liminality. Penelope Ironstone-Catterall claims that certain spaces of traveling (she focuses on airports) are sites of liminality, offering "a state of being on the 'threshold' of or between two different existential planes."[7] Such spaces facilitate rituals, especially rites of passage, as described by Victor Turner, Ironstone explains, which involve some change for the participants, especially in their social status. The resulting liminal state is characterized by ambiguity, openness, and indeterminacy. Liminality is thus a moment and/or place of transition where normal limits to thought, self-understanding, and behavior are relaxed.

Experiencing the liminal moment of the tea party, Rebekka ponders the possibility that all women are blocking out, like her, their reasons for fleeing as well as their anticipations: "Wretched as was the space they crouched in, it was nevertheless blank *where a past did not haunt nor a future beckon.* [...] And when finally the lamp died, [...] *time became simply the running sea, unmarked, eternal and of no matter.*"[8] Following Rebekka's focalization, we detect here a shift from her collective experience of liminality to an individual awareness of it. As readers, we no longer visualize a mixed group of women who defy any notions of age and class differences; we see Rebekka herself experiencing timelessness and non-space, and the falling away of any perceptions of origins and prospects. Though immersed in the small, heterogeneous community of steerage travelers, Rebekka as focalizer shows her very personal experiences of travel and place. This is indicated as well by her reference to being both "mesmerized and bored by the look of [the sea] when she is allowed on deck."[9] Thus, Rebekka's account of her liminal condition in that transit space of the lower deck refers to a multifaceted experience of liminality.

The question here may arise whether such a literary representation of liminality is a mere literary tool or convention instead of being directly based on historical events and experiences. Rebekka's account clearly is a fictive one and not directly based on any historical documentation of transatlantic travel. Whereas Morrison has explained in a variety of texts that her inspiration comes not only from her imagination but also from historical research, she only roughly indicates which sources these are.[10] Many literary texts like Morrison's, ranging from ones by Charlotte Brontë, Eva Hoffman, and Marie Ndiaye, contain references to experiences of liminality and have been analyzed accordingly.[11] Neither these primary texts nor their analyses are explicit about any historical substantiation to prove the social basis of such experiences.

This essay is an attempt to find examples of such instances of liminality in historical accounts of transatlantic travel. Following a short introduction of the notion of liminality, I will first explore two published autobiographical accounts of transatlantic travel by emigrant women Burlend and Antin. Then I will look into other, less well-known historical accounts of transatlantic travel that use different generic forms, in order to be able to map out how liminal moments and spaces are being narrated and what their effects and limitations are.

Happy Hours on Deck

The liminal condition, explains Gilead, "symbolically generates those essential human bonds that transcend the social relations derived from the demands of structured daily existence." It is a state that exists "outside the ordinary classificatory systems."[12] Liminality, according to Fanetti, is present "in the space between rigid constructions of culture and identity."[13] In a liminal state, differences of social class are no longer significant and may even be invisible temporarily. In that in-between space, a social structure of communitas is possible where hierarchy makes room for equality and difference yields to an unrestrained and human companionship. Victor Turner, who wrote extensively on the topic of liminality, showed that pilgrims who have distanced themselves from various socio-economic classes will interact and communicate as if there were no social differences.[14]

To be sure, the emigrants whose texts I look at in this article were no Turnerian pilgrims. A number of published autobiographical emigrant accounts do, however, include references to some sort of communitas on board the ships. In the earliest example I was able to find, the narrative of a transatlantic journey from England to New Orleans in 1831 written by Rebecca Burlend, the female narrator at first describes the "community" and "neighborhoods" that were formed at sea through among other things joking, storytelling, cooking, and eating.[15] The passengers also collectively take care of the stowaway Jack who accidentally burns himself during the trip.

Rebecca, however, oftentimes shuns such familiarities with her fellow travelers, and often retreats to ponder her past and future. The sea allows her to do so:

> The sea [...] has its beauties and grandeur; but these are rather perceptible to the reflecting mind than the external sense. One evening I well remember when we were about half-way across the Atlantic, I was alone on the deck, pensively considering the peculiarity of my situation, and impatiently desirous to know what my future condition should be, when casting my eyes towards the east I beheld a most magnificent spectacle: the large full moon was just

clearing the watery horizon. [...] my whole soul was overpowered with ecstacy [sic].

The "highly imposing" and "magnificently splendid" appearance of the "broad disk" of the moon, which she regards as an old friend, make her realize "the insignificance of man and his noblest performances."[16]

A second case is offered by Mary Antin's well-known immigrant autobiography *The Promised Land* of 1912, which includes similar references to a transatlantic *communitas* but also to very individualized sensations and insights. At first, the adult narrator suggests her association with the other travelers aboard the ship that brings her from Polotzk (a town in what is now Belarus) to America, as she includes herself in the group of "inexperienced voyagers" and "frightened emigrants" who endure a storm at sea. She subsequently joins the others in the "happy hours on deck" which involve dancing, music, and fun. She also befriends officers and members of the crew. However, when Antin's young narrator writes to her uncle from the ship, she also emphasizes her very personal moments,

> Oh, what solemn thoughts I had! How deeply I felt the greatness, the power of the scene! The immeasurable distance from horizon to horizon; the huge billows forever changing their shapes [...].

Amidst the billows, the "gloomy clouds" merging with the waves, without "any object besides the one ship; and the deep, solemn groans of the sea," the narrator "so deeply" experiences "the presence of these things that the feeling became one of awe [...]. *I was aware of no human presence*; I was conscious only of sea and sky and something I did not understand."[17]

Both Burlend's and Antin's narrators, evoking Morrison's Rebekka, indicate a tension between their communal and individual experiences of the voyage. They narrate of the communities on board but also report their growing personal awareness that they themselves are but minute parts of the universe. Such revelations of feelings of a disengaged, transcendental self during the passage are rare in migrant writings. If we focus, for instance, on Dutch emigrant memoirs of transatlantic voyages, we find references to communal (religious) rituals on board, but they are not juxtaposed with personal reflections on spiritual experiences of transformation as presented in Burlend and Antin. The collection *Dutch American Voices: Letters from the United States, 1850-1930*, edited by Herbert J. Brinks, includes letters describing the transatlantic journey, but mostly report dryly on seasickness, sermons, and prayer services on board.[18] The Henry S. Lucas collection of memoirs of Dutch emigrants, written between 1846 and 1946, by and large holds accounts written from a first-person plural perspective. They were not meant to be personal reflections on the travel experience but were to be published in weeklies, yearbooks, and history magazines or to be "read at the Semi-Centennial celebrations in Holland [Michigan] in August 1897."[19]

A rare exception in Lucas's collection is "Journey of an emigrant family" written by Johannes Remeeus in 1854, based on the diary he kept during his journey from Middelburg, the Netherlands, to Boston. In this text, Remeeus refers to personal experiences of the voyage. In his entry of 21 July, he described a "beautiful sunrise."[20] The 20-21 June entry reads:

> Quiet weather. Snoep and I were on deck as late as 12 o'clock and we witnessed a fire at sea. It seemed as if our ship was sailing through a mass of fire [St. Elmo's fire]. A beautiful and imposing phenomenon which well might move the hardest among us and fill us with respect for him who said, 'Mine is the sea.'[21]

In other excerpts as well, Remeeus suggests that the sea journey was at least as much a personal as a collective experience. When the ship is still in Antwerp and other emigrants decide to go sightseeing, Remeeus occupies himself "all afternoon fixing up [his] berth."

> I used a coarse wallpaper for this purpose. I also put up curtains around the bed and did everything I could to make our quarters pleasing and comfortable for my family.[22]

The wallpaper and the curtain symbolically suggest the tendency in general, among both the crew and the other seafarers, to set up some sort of border between the self and others, between different nationalities, and between the healthy and the poor. Remeeus narrates how Hollanders were "placed on one side; the Germans on the other," and how one family which suffered from a "rash" was "left behind" in Antwerp.[23]

However, during the journey, all emigrants without exception join to celebrate Pentecost. Further, the Dutch emigrants link up with the German passengers in order to celebrate St. John's Day as well as a young man's birthday, which includes "a toast to the captain, the officers of the ship, and in fact everybody and everything."[24] Finally, at a fourth of July celebration on board, the American captain joins in the singing of a psalm.[25] These narrative sketches suggest some kind of liminal condition on board, where collective religious and spiritual experiences are possible.

At the same time, however, Remeeus indicates the limits of such a liminal condition. Although the passengers at times engage in the transnational, spontaneous, and warm comradeship that Victor Turner's pilgrims purportedly engaged in, the rules of the ship continue to set social standards and borders. An unmarried German couple is lectured, confined, and publicly put to shame for sleeping together, and a sailor is punished for talking with one of the passengers.[26]

Remeeus's text is a rare tale of transit in its very personal depiction of life on board. It is mostly travelers, not emigrants, who report personal and communal experiences on board. They are the journalists, artists, scientists, philosophers, ministers, and others who, following their journey to America between the late nineteenth and early twentieth century, published their accounts of the voyage. The differences between the two groups of transatlantic passengers – emigrants versus travelers – are of course many. For one thing, Krabbendam has pointed out that for emigrants, "the goal of the journey was different" than for other groups. "(I)nsecure rather than safe, their mood was anxious instead of curious, their destination permanent instead of temporary."[27] Among the emigrants, many of whom were traveling in steerage, a relatively large number were seasick, and the conditions of the third class left them little time and energy to reflect on their journey – let alone publish their accounts upon arrival.

Thus, it is mostly middle and upper-middle-class travelers, both male and female, who, watching from their first class decks, are able to observe not only the magnificent Atlantic waters and skies, but also those traveling third class – the emigrants. In the following sections I analyze the travelers' observations of the physical surroundings. Subsequently I examine their descriptions of their fellow passengers – both first and third class – in order to determine whether they were able to establish some sort of communitas amongst themselves or with those at steerage level.

Heavenly Sensations

In 1906, Henriëtte Kuyper, daughter of the former Dutch Prime Minister Abraham Kuyper, traveled to the U.S. In her travel account, Een half jaar in Amerika [Half a Year in America], she describes the air and the ocean as being one, presenting "glowing colors of metal, gold, silver, bronze, copper and steel. It is a party of colors."[28] Whereas Kuyper continuously groups herself among the "us" of her fellow first class passengers, as in "Fantastic, that free space around us. The sea below us – the heaven above us until the far horizon [...]," her descriptions clearly speak of her private celebration of colors.[29]

Evoking Burlend, who uses the metaphor of the "broad disk" for the moon, Kuyper employs phrases such as "filmy golden lines" and "fairy tale" and calls her environment solemn, "as if in a large temple of Roman style." She describes at length her observations of the stars, the planets, and the fluorescent marine plankton, which she refers to as large glistening diamonds on black velvet, a "repetition of the sparkling light [of the stars]." This all culminates in a lyrical description of the "glorious" rising sun. When Kuyper is finally able to behold New York City, "visible as a giant-like illumination," lines and colors merge, and a world of light is beaming. Light is shining from all stories of the skyscrapers. The ferryboats are large, lit-up gondolas of which the great lighting glow is reflected in the water. And on top of this all, the moon showers her with silver beams.[30]

On her second journey, Kuyper has by no means become blasé. The ocean's "foam glistens as sapphire," and the splendid colors of a doubled rainbow are especially magnificent where they are situated between the swaying waves and the "sapphire" of the water around the ship. The sun and the moon and stars obtain much meaning, she states, when one sees nothing other than water and air for days. Light and the movements of heavenly bodies, "created by God as signs of set times," were of special meaning for the seafarers of previous centuries, when they needed to travel without compass. However, in Kuyper's time, such spatial markers take on a different significance, it seems, as they turn into means of celestial beautification.[31]

Kuyper both echoes and anticipates other travelers' claims regarding the festive quality of their journey. In his travel account of his 1910 passage on the Atlantic, reverend Harm Bouwman, Dutch Professor in Theology at the Theological School in Kampen, refers to the ocean's foam as "an astonishing tissue, white as snow and fine as needlework."[32] Many years later, on her way to America in 1941, writer and journalist Mary Pos observes the "glittering effects of phosphor, as if chunks of stars had fallen down, around the ship. [...] the ocean sparkled as emerald." Approaching Manhattan at dawn, at the end of her journey, she describes the growing light of the sun and rejoices in the "festive" quality of the sky. Her travel back to Europe also includes a mother-of-pearl sky.[33]

Thus, using the metaphors of personal revelry and decorative gems, Kuyper, Bouwman, and Pos reserve space in their travel accounts to express their feelings of ecstasy and wonder when traversing the Atlantic. Like Morrison's Rebekka, and like Burlend and Antin, they most poetically convey their feelings of being spiritually immersed in a larger scheme of life.

Much of Kuyper's writing space in her 1907 account is reserved for descriptions of her personal and spiritual experiences on board. In no less than four chapters out of a total of thirty-eight, she ponders the sublime views from the *New Amsterdam*. Only in one instance does she invite the female passenger who shares her cabin to join her in a "nightly expedition" to see the sun rise.[34] Bouwman, in his turn, describes how he, on his own, delights in the "powerful impressions of the miraculous creations of God, the majestic sea," and suggests that as a "small man" he feels very insignificant.[35] Finally, Pos notes "the murmuring of eternity" around her, and "space, space." Standing on deck during a storm, she feels that her clothes are dripping with ocean water, her lips tasting of salt, and flakes of foam cover her hair. She now feels one with the elements that are breaking loose.[36]

Observing, and Encountering, the Emigrant

As they observe the great skies and waters from their promenade decks, most first class travelers also watch the third class emigrants from these places of privilege. In 1880 the Dutch newspaper *Algemeen Handelsblad* commissioned author Charles Boissevain to visit the United States for a report. In his *Van 't noorden naar 't zuiden* [From North to South] (1881-1882), Boissevain portrays himself as standing on the first class deck of the *Republic*, a White Star Line ship, from which he is able to observe the mother-of-pearl glistening fire of the sea and the "foaming ivory white stern-waves." In the foregoing paragraph, he has described himself as "looking down upon" the ship's 250 third class passengers, many of whom are emigrants. When the weather is fine, Boissevain notes, they sit down on coils of rope and on the hold's hatches, talking and playing. The men help the sailors with their work, whereas the women and girls have their red and gray shawls pulled over their heads and sit close to each other for warmth and comfort.[37]

Forty years later, in 1920, the Dutch scientist Marianne van Herwerden traveled to the U.S. with a grant from Utrecht University.[38] Like Boissevain, she looks down from the front deck of the *Noordam* and notes, in two consecutive sentences and in parallel fashion, both the splendid play of colors of the waves and the third class passengers wrapped in blankets. Suggesting her own disparity with the latter group, she states that when the wind becomes too fierce, she can no longer stay outside, but has to go in. When finally Long Island comes into view, and the first and second classes rejoice over their safe arrival, Van Herwerden does not hear anything from the third class. As a quiet sign of exodus, their deck only exhibits steeple-high stacks of trunks, their labels indicating addresses in various places in America. Van Herwerden concludes that all these people, from a great variety of backgrounds, status, and talents who had been huddled together during the days of travel, would now be dispersed all over the world. Very much like her new acquaintances in first class, so she assumes, many of these third class emigrants probably yearn for an upcoming reunion with relatives.[39] This is the only reference that suggests Van Herwerden's ability to establish some sort of connection among the otherwise so distinct passenger classes.

Of these two Dutch travelers, it is not the scientist but the journalist Boissevain who is able and/or willing to meet some of the emigrants in person. When a religious service is being arranged on board, led by the Anglican bishop from the Bahama Islands, the "emigrants," whom Boissevain clearly distinguishes from the "passengers," enter the first class salon in a long line. The women and girls have dressed up for the occasion, notes Boissevain, wearing hats with ribbons, coats, and gloves. However, their emigrant and class status is betrayed by their confusion when, struggling with the ship's rocking movements, they attempt to hold on to the first class chairs which have rotating backs. Still, although the emigrants are to sit apart from the other passengers, all join in the praying and singing. Moreover, after the service, accompanied by the bishop, Boissevain introduces himself to the emigrants. He has brought candy and dried prunes in order to be able to befriend the children, and he converses with an English laborer who tells of his ambition that, one day in America, his wife would wear a silk dress and his children would attend a good school.

We can safely assume that it is also – at least partially – Boissevain's assignment that induces him to inquire about the emigrants' treatment on board. After the interview he concludes that the men do not complain, which contrasts, Boissevain states, with the men of the first class, who grumble about the smallest issues. The author's impression of the English laborer as having a strong character is evoked when Boissevain one day steps down to the third class deck, where he befriends a little Canadian girl named Florence. Boissevain positively compares the girl's "civilized, simple" mother with "our Dutch mothers," who would not be so brave as to leave behind some of their children, travel by train for three days in a row, and then cross the Atlantic twice among the emigrants of the third class.[40]

Boissevain's acquaintance with Florence and her mother is paralleled in the aforementioned travel reports by Kuyper, Bouwman, and Pos, in which all three relate interpersonal encounters on board. Of the three, Bouwman's encounters with the ethnic or racial other are the most limited. He depicts life on board the *Rotterdam*, a steamship of the Dutch Holland America Line, as friendly. The hundreds of passengers, he states, regard each other as travel companions and friends. Most of them he calls approachable. Still, he only mentions mingling with his fellow first class passengers. When he discovers that, among the latter, many are not actively involved in a religion, he delights in the fact that many are, indeed, interested in matters of faith. He spends hours on end discussing the gospel with his fellow first class travelers.[41]

Mary Pos's extensive maneuvering room for associating with the cultural other is the most apparent of the three. Because of her special status as a journalist, like that of Boissevain, she shows a much broader interest in the ship's various passenger classes and a much wider reach of the ship's diverse spaces than do Kuyper and Bouwman. I discuss her explorations of the ship's boundaries as well as those of other observers in the following section. In the final section, I show how Kuyper mentally, if not physically, explores such boundaries during her two journeys.

Exploring the Ship's Boundaries

At first glance, Mary Pos appears to be the typical solo traveler. Her becoming one with the elements, which I have described above, occurs when fellow travelers are either seasick, are sleeping, or having their meals, and all decks are empty. On her way to America in 1949, standing on deck one evening and feeling exultant, she realizes how few people are conscious of such delight. Later, on her way back to Europe, she concludes that the atmosphere on board the *Westernland* of the Red Star Line is pleasant, yet she prefers to retreat to the ship's decks, bow, or poop, or to the gym and drawing room. She dines with her fellow travelers, but only hears their dancing music in the Lounge from afar. She prefers her contact with nature over the company of what she portrays as yawning and languid fellow passengers.[42]

Nevertheless, Pos explores the marginal spaces where Kuyper and Bouwman would never venture. Traveling back to Europe, she is allowed to descend into the 'black vaults' of the *Westernland* in order to visit the machine room, walking down the crew's greasy, slippery, and twisting iron steps. There she befriends the crew and joins them in their storytelling and dinner of beans.[43] Pos's suggestion, in her account, of her liminal position on board of the ship is repeated in her other writings. On her way to California in the early 1950s, where she is going to investigate the post-immigration lives of Dutch emigrants, Mary Pos travels on the *Westerdam*, which carries only first class passengers. Consisting of many Dutch emigrants but also German "displaced persons," this group is so varied that small cliques develop among individuals who feel drawn together.[44] Yet Mary Pos is the liminal figure who appears to be hovering above these diverse groups.

When the adult passengers become seasick or are otherwise unwilling or unable to take up childcare, she befriends many of the forty children on board by organizing activities and birthday parties and by giving them personal attention and Dutch licorice. Pos calls the Lithuanian parents of a small boy "apathetic." When no minister or pastor appears to be on the ship, Pos assists in setting up a Christmas celebration in which all passengers, despite their differences in nationalities and travel destinations, join the singing of Christmas carols – simultaneously in different languages and accompanied by a Viennese violin player and a Dutch emigrant who plays the piano. Later on, following a New Year's Eve celebration on board, she descends into the cavern-like spaces of the ship to celebrate with the crew, who otherwise are invisible for the passengers.[45]

In the years between the reports written by journalists Charles Boissevain (1881-1882) and Mary Pos (1949, 1953), several colleagues in the field took the liberty of exploring the various passenger classes of transatlantic ships. A first of three examples only indirectly refers to an anonymous journalist who, one evening in 1912, takes along on his trip down from the second class to the third class Peter Jacobus van Melle, a Dutch scientist and author in the field of horticulture. Although Melle is aware that the first and second classes of the *Rotterdam* had no "association," he repeatedly attempts to befriend passengers of the third class. Every morning he enjoys taking an egg, an orange, or some nuts to the "small Russians or Polaks," who quickly nip up the steps to receive the refreshments and kiss his hand by way of thanks. The ship's personnel does not approve of these contacts, as they may cause "squabbling" among the third class passengers.

However, guided by the experienced journalist, Melle that evening enters the full, hot, and hectic third class space. He describes the games being played, the women's songs, and promises the Dutch emigrants to organize a religious ceremony, as they are not allowed to join those arranged for the first and second classes. The ceremony he later holds attracts sixty to seventy emigrants who join him in the singing of psalms and hymns.[46]

Melle's guide may have been Taeke Cnossen, a Frisian journalist traveling to Canada in 1924 on the *Montroyal*. He spends more time "observing life in the third class," where the atmosphere is still good-natured, than hanging about the cabin department with its tourists. Cnossen enjoys the company of the Dutch, English, Polish, and Hungarian emigrants, who tell moving stories of leaving hearth and home, and hoping for a more comfortable life in America. Repeatedly, however, Cnossen notes his difference from the emigrants whose company he enjoys, when he portrays them as being ignorant of the difficult times ahead. They are unable to speak English and are utterly unaware of American labor conditions.[47]

A third and final example is offered by Jo van Ammers-Küller, a journalist of the *Haagsche Post* who, traveling first class on her return from a trip to the U.S., describes the third class of the *Nieuw-Amsterdam* as consisting of more than one hundred college boys and girls traveling to Europe. As the strict captain Van Walraven has prohibited all first class passengers from visiting the third class, Ammers-Küller is only able to hear the youngsters' jazz band from a distance and to listen to the captain's stories of the "exuberant joy" of the "young, free people."[48] However, when the first class celebrates the Fourth of July with the singing of national anthems and solemn speeches of "the greatness, the richness and 'brotherhood' of America," Van Ammers-Küller is allowed to leave and join the captain on an inspection tour of the hind of the ship, where the third class has organized a merry masquerade.[49]

Entering the "mysterious" quarterdeck, Van Ammers-Küller finds herself in the midst of a most crazy and cheerful revelry, which according to her description is a party of ethnic and gender transgressions. Using their own resourcefulness and fantasy, the American college girls are "parading" in male clothing and have become toreador, pirate, or apache. The boys are clad in kimonos and dressing gowns, and have transformed into sjeiks, Turkish robber chiefs, and a Dutch "Volendammer." One boy donning a satin robe-chemise and black silk stockings is mimicking a fashionable college girl. Thus, on the third-class quarterdeck, between the beams and on the bare wooden floor, this "queer company," as presented by Van Ammers-Küller, is able to celebrate the national holiday without the surveillance of parents, and without the curiosity of first and second class passengers. In that liminal space, which calls to mind Morrison's Rebekka and her tea party at the beginning of this article, Van Ammers-Küller is being told, this group "can take care of themselves."[50]

Thus, in addition to Boissevain and Pos, Melle and his journalist guide Cnossen and Van Ammers-Küller explore the ships' ethnic and socio-cultural boundaries. Henriëtte Kuyper never does so in person. However, when we closely read her two travel accounts, we can, very implicitly, find spaces of a subtle but stubborn undermining of the rigid social classification during her transatlantic voyages. This I will demonstrate in the following and final section.

Questioning the Ship's Stratification

Apart from her extensive personal reports of the sublime in her two books of travel, Kuyper also narrates at length the social aspects of her journey. Even before the *Potsdam* left Rotterdam harbor in 1906, Kuyper stood observing the other passengers, trying to identify with their states of mind. While the ship swarmed with passengers and everyone appeared to be mingling, Kuyper attempted to find some arrangement in what she is observing. She differentiates, first of all, between happy faces that laugh and talk, and sad faces that silently stare ahead of them. Realizing her lack of knowledge of what exactly the farewell ritual and journey may mean for the individuals around her, she rhetorically asks, "One journey, one ship, – but who knows which contradictions of the human fate are united here?" In addition, she points out a much deeper division between travelers of different "circumstances": those who believe in the "Heavenly Father" and those who do not.[51]

Kuyper's divisions between cheerless and joyful passengers and between the believers and non-believers, however, are done away with on the very same page. When the ship's bell tolls, Kuyper states, a feeling of solidarity has suddenly emerged among the passengers on the ship. Having left Rotterdam, the passengers have embarked on their journey and a new life has begun. However, only a few pages later, Kuyper continues her classification and differentiation of what she calls the ship's small world of people. Having acquainted herself with a group of nuns parading the deck clad in red and blue garb, Kuyper organizes her world in "us" Protestant Christians and Roman Christians.[52]

Her tendency to classify her fellow passengers is the more striking when we realize that she includes only very few references to the ship's class system in her account. This does not mean that her narrative turns the ship into a Turnerian liminal place where social and ethnic differences no longer count. She simply does not encounter many second and third class passengers. All of her references to the latter are mediated or secondary. First of all, she has heard from an unspecified source that eighty first-class passengers have become seasick compared to 400 in the second and third classes.[53] Secondly, she embarks on a captain-led tour of the ship, which brings her to the second and third class areas.[54] Finally, when the cello player Joseph Hollman and the Dutch singer "Mrs. D. who lives in Rochester" arrange for a concert on board, Kuyper notes that in the second class yet another "concert" is being held. "There they sing along with a harmonium. It sounds lovely over the water, and we enjoy listening to it."[55]

Kuyper's stubborn tendency to describe her fellow passengers in her own terms was still present in 1919, when the Dutch government sent her out as an advisor on the woman's question to visit the first International Labor Conference in Washington. In her *Tweede reis naar Amerika* [Second Journey to America], she continues to divide the passengers of the *Nieuw-Amsterdam* into alternative groups. Thus, she categorizes the passengers in first class as belonging to three "types": those who like to dress up and spend all of their days in the grand and beautiful salon, those who venture outside on the promenade deck and defy the cold, and those who, like Kuyper, spend their time on the boat deck where they confront the wind and the sun, but who have the most beautiful view over the ocean.[56] Immediately after that, on the next page, when describing the German American lady who shares her cabin and has brought her furs and silk dresses along, Kuyper relinquishes this classification and distinguishes between those of the Old World (including "Holländer" like Kuyper herself) and those of the New. Further, listening to the sermon led by an American minister, she ponders about the differences between religious groups and their ways of practicing God's will.

Finally, Kuyper sketches the dual nature of America that is represented on board. She mentions the idealist versus the materialist, as embodied by the "decent" and indecent girls on board, of whom the latter wear expensive dress and make-up. When the decked out young women do not appear at the dinner table, Kuyper sternly expresses her hope that the women are seasick.[57] Indeed, it is in a rare visit to the second class that Kuyper finds the simplicity that she concludes is lacking among the first class passengers. When she joins a group of Swiss passengers, she feels "so deliciously one with these simple people – and the more so I sense the rift that stands between me and the greater part of those on board."[58] With the latter she refers to those who are too dressed-up, materialistic, and indecent.

Thus, both of Kuyper's narratives appear to move beyond the confinements of the ship's class system and any social arrangement that is based on material wealth. Otherwise, her contact with the ethnic other on board is very tentative. However, whereas Kuyper appears to dispense with the transatlantic class system, this stance is only limited. When, during her second tour of America, she receives the message that her father is seriously ill, she informs those in charge of the *Mauretania* that she would accept any ticket available, even if it were for a "seat in the smoking room of the second class."[59] Consequently, before embarking on the return trip in 1921, she experiences feelings of class anxiety but is relieved when a first class passenger has canceled her trip and Kuyper is allowed to take her place.[60]

Conclusion

Enne Koops points out that historians "have focused primarily on the description of individual voyages." Instead of adding to what he calls "an incoherent collection of loose travel stories," Koops wishes to contribute to a "combined history of the changing experience of crossing the Atlantic Ocean."[61] My analysis necessarily is a collection of loose travel stories Koops refers to. These accounts are in no way representative of Dutch or European narratives of transatlantic travel. All of them are informed by the travelers' time of travel, their class background, their age at traveling and writing, their gender, their education, and the selected modes of travel. They also use a variety of genres to convey their stories – autobiography (Antin, Burlend), short stories (Yezierska), diary (Remeeus), journalism (Boissevain, Cnossen, Pos, Van Ammers-Küller), and travel account (Bouwman, Kuyper, Van Melle).

At the same time, I have indicated that very diverse, individual, or individualized expressions of transatlantic travel may include rather similar references to space, self, eternity, and one's decorated environment. My analysis shows how, in Dutch travel accounts, first class transatlantic voyages operate as crucial figurations of both existential bliss and of collective experiences, in which boundaries of class and status may be explored and crossed.

Notes

1. Toni Morrison, A Mercy (London: Chatto & Windus, 2008), 70, 80.
2. Morrison, A Mercy, 79-80.
3. Ibid. 80.
4. Ibid. 83.
5. Ibid. 80.
6. Ibid. 79.
7. Penelope Ironstone-Catterall, "A Morbid Principle in Terminal Space: Precarious Passages, Unsettling Viral Mobilities, and Other Anxieties at the Airport," Keynote Address held at the Conference 'Negotiating the Liminal,' York University and Ryersone University, 14-16 March 2008.
8. Morrison, A Mercy, 83; italics added.
9. Ibid. 71.
10. In an interview following the publication of A Mercy, Morrison explicates how she extensively "consulted migration patterns to find out who these people were, the average person who came to the colonies. Most of them were told to leave or go to jail." Morrison explains how her research was her "way of surrounding [herself] with the atmosphere and having a persuasive familiarity with more than just the story – the context." Christine Smallwood, "Black Talk: Toni Morrison," in: The Nation, 8 December (2008), 37. In addition, we know that Morrison's inspiration comes from other sources: first of all, "the presence of an ancestor," whose identity she does not explicate. Toni Morrison, "Rootedness: The Ancestors as Foundation," in What Moves at the

Margin: Selected Nonfiction (Jackson: University Press of Mississippi, 2008), 61. Secondly, she has explained that "The people in the work are the people who tell that it's right. I have to ask [the characters] is this the way it was? If they think or believe that I am bearing witness accurately, then I am content." Mustapha Hasnaoui, "Interview with Toni Morrison," Margaret Garner (LuFilms, 2007). Finally, in "The Site of Memory," Morrison explains that the "act of imagination," which is "bound up with memory," supports all of her writing. Toni Morrison, "The Site of Memory," in What Moves at the Margin: Selected Nonfiction (Jackson: University Press of Mississippi, 2008), 76-77.

11. Sarah Gilead, "Liminality, Anti-Liminality, and the Victorian Novel," ELH 53.1 (Spring 1986): 183-197; Susan Fanetti, "Translating Self into Liminal Space: Eva Hoffman's Acculturation in/to a Postmodern World," Women's Studies 34.5 (2005): 405-419; Jean H. Duffy, "Liminality and Fantasy in Marie Darrieussecq, Marie NDiaye and Marie Redonnet," Modern Language Notes 124.4 (September 2009).

12. Gilead, "Liminality," 183.

13. Fanetti, "Translating," 418.

14. Victor Turner, The Ritual Process: Structure and Antistructure (Chicago: Aldine Publishing, 1969).

15. Rebecca and Edward Burlend, A True Picture of Emigration, ed. Milo Milton Quaife (Lincoln and London: University of Nebraska Press, 1987 [1848]), 25.

16. Burlend, True Picture, 23-24.

17. Mary Antin, The Promised Land: the Autobiography of a Russian Immigrant (Princeton, NJ: Princeton University Press, 1985 [1911-1912]), 178-179; emphasis added. In "How I found America," one of the autobiographical pieces in Hungry Hearts & Other Stories (New York: Persea Books, 1985 [1920]), 260, Anzia Yezierska's narrator relates a very different dissociation from her fellow passengers: "Steerage – dirty bundles – foul odors – seasick humanity – but I saw and heard nothing of the foulness and ugliness around me. I floated in showers of sunshine; visions upon visions of the new world opened before me" (260). Unlike Antin's narrator, who emphasizes celebrations and comradeship that reach beyond nationality and ethnicity, Yezierska's narrator does not do so.

18. See, for instance, "Jacob Harms Dunnink to Harm Dunnink Family, September 1848," in Dutch American Voices: Letters from the United States, 1850–1930, ed. Herbert J. Brinks (Ithaca, N.Y.: Cornell University Press, 1995), 30; and "Klaaske Noorda and Onno Heller to Noorda Family 1891," ibid. 156.

19. Henry S. Lucas, ed., Dutch Immigrant Memoirs and Related Writings I and II (Assen: Van Gorcum, 1955), I, 189.

20. Ibid. 100.

21. Ibid. 97.

22. Remeeus in Lucas, Dutch Immigrant Memoirs, 92.

23. Ibid. 93.

24. Ibid. 97.

25. Ibid. 94, 97, 99.

26. Ibid. 96-97, 100.

27. Hans Krabbendam, "Rituals of Travel in the Transition from Sail to Steam: The Dutch Immigrant experience, 1840-1940," in From De Halve Maen to KLM: 400 years of Dutch-

American exchange, eds. Margriet Bruijn Lacy, Charles Gehring and Jenneke Oosterhoff (Münster: Nodus Publikationen, 2004), 283.

28. H. S. S. [Henriëtte] Kuyper, *Een half jaar in Amerika* (Den Haag: D.A. Daamen, 1907), 14.

29. Ibid. 14.

30. Ibid. 14, 12, 16, 38-39, 41; see also 15; author's translation.

31. H. S. S. [Henriëtte] Kuyper, *Tweede reis naar Amerika: Vier weken te Washington (Rondom de Eerste Internationale Arbeidsconferentie)* (Amsterdam: W. ten Have, 1921), 16-17, 20, 24, also 27.

32. H. [Harm] Bouwman, *Amerika: schetsen en herinneringen* (Kampen: Kok, 1912), 6.

33. Mary Pos, *Ik zag Amerika* (Amsterdam: Allert de Lange, 1941), 8-9, 15, 303. In another travel account, *Californië*, she refers to the pearly color of the water and the mother-of-pearl grayness of the sky. Mary Pos, *Californië: Dwars door Amerika op zoek naar Nederlanders* (Wageningen: Zomer & Keunings, 1953), 22-23.

34. Kuyper, *Een half jaar*, 37-38.

35. Bouwman, *Amerika*, 6-7.

36. Mary Pos, *Ik zag Amerika, en bezocht het opnieuw* (Amsterdam: Allert de Lange 1952), 9, 13-14.

37. Charles Boissevain, *Van 't Noorden naar 't Zuiden : schetsen en indrukken van de Vereenigde Staten van Noord-Amerika*, Volume I. (Haarlem: Tjeenk Willink, 1881-1882), 23, 36.

38. The grant was offered as a compensation by the Medical Faculty of Utrecht, which opposed the hiring of a female professor. Van Herwerden would later become the first lectrix in the Netherlands (at Utrecht University), and co-founder of the Netherlands Institute for Research in Human Genetics and Race-biology.

39. C. A. B. van Herwerden, *Marianne van Herwerden: 16 februari 1874-26 januari 1934* (Rotterdam: W. L. & J. Brusse, 1948), 67, 70; author's translation. Many of the travelers crossing the Atlantic in the first class observed emigrants from their privileged position. Scientist Hugo de Vries was one of them, as he states that all he noticed of the 800 or 900 emigrants on his ship, was their walking the deck below. Hugo de Vries, *O, Wies! 't is hier zo mooi!* (Amsterdam: Atlans, 1998), 52.

40. Boissevain, *Van 't Noorden*, 35-37; 49; 55.

41. Bouwman, *Amerika*, 246.

42. Pos, *Ik zag Amerika*, 14, 299, 301.

43. Ibid. 297-298.

44. Pos, 1953, 12.

45. Ibid. 9-12, 19; see also 204-205.

46. Ds. P. J. [Peter Jacobus] van Melle, *Reisindrukken: lezing gehouden te Nijkerk op 23 en 24 september 1912 na zijn terugkeer uit Amerika* (Nijkerk: n.p., 1912), 3-4. Many third class emigrants, of course, organized their own religious and other ceremonies. At times they joined emigrants of another faith in their rituals. See, for instance, John de Young's "History of Roseland" in Lucas 1955, 46; Johannes Remeeus's "Journey of an Emigrant Family" in: Lucas 1955 II, 94, 97-99.

47. T. [Taeke] Cnossen, *Dwars door Canada* (Amsterdam: N.V. Dagblad en drukkerij De Standaard, 1927), 16.

48. Jo van Ammers-Küller, *Mijn Amerikaansche reis* (Den Haag: Leopold's Uitgevers-Maatschappij, 1926), 145.

49. Ibid.

50. Ammers-Küller, *Mijn Amerikaansche reis*, 144-148.

51. Kuyper, *Een half jaar*, 10. Thus, Kuyper indirectly deconstructs a method used by the U.S. government of what she names "examining and sorting": before her departure, Kuyper had been unpleasantly surprised by a questionnaire sent to her by the Holland America Line on behalf of the American government: twenty-two questions investigating her status in terms of illiteracy, polygamy, anarchy, and a possible stay at a mental health institution or prison. Kuyper, 5-6.

52. Ibid. 10-11; 18-20.

53. Ibid. 21.

54. Ibid. 30.

55. Ibid. 20.

56. Kuyper, *Tweede reis naar Amerika*, 11.

57. Ibid. 14-15.

58. Ibid. 15.

59. Ibid. 116.

60. Ibid. 117.

61. Enne Koops, "From 'Floating Hollander' to 'Flying Dutchman': The Changing Experience of Dutch Immigrants on the Transatlantic Voyage to North America (1945-65)," in *From De Halve Maen to KLM: 400 years of Dutch-American exchange* eds. Margriet Bruijn Lacy, Charles Gehring, Jenneke Oosterhoff (Münster: Nodus Publikationen, 2004).

Competing Fictionalizations of the Lower East Side: Abraham Cahan's *The Rise of David Levinsky* and Michael Gold's *Jews Without Money*

Sostene Massimo Zangari

The Lower East Side holds a prominent place in the history of transatlantic migration. From the masses of Irish peasants escaping the Great Famine to the Puerto Ricans displaced by the industrialization program of post-WWII *Operation Bootstrap*, this New York neighborhood has been the first America for millions of immigrants. Emerging as a manufacturing hub shortly after the middle of the nineteenth century, the Lower East Side became the destination of choice for newcomers to the U.S., offering plenty of unskilled jobs and cheap, if unhealthy, lodgings.[1]

This multicultural past, however – reflected in a list of pet denominations spanning from German *Kleindeutschland* (1860s/1870s) to Puerto Rican *Loisaida* (1960s) – has been under threat of erasure, as an identification of the Lower East Side with the Jewish American community has prevailed in the popular imagination. Historian Hasia Diner noted that no other "ethnic group in America, with the exception of the African-American construction of Harlem, has so thoroughly understood, imagined, and represented itself through a particular chunk of space."[2]

This cultural construction not only downplayed contributions by other ethnicities to the history of the Lower East Side, it also imposed a "national" narrative of the Jewish American experience, a saga of progress from the fringes to the mainstream of American society, that silenced alternative accounts. After the Second World War, when a significant part of immigrant settlers left the neighborhood for other less cramped areas, what once was perceived as a slum – a transit point towards the affluence and well-being of suburbs – was turned into a shrine; it became the locale of cherished memories of a poorer, simpler and, most of all, more authentic Jewish life.[3]

Together with museum exhibitions, musicals, and movies, literature has been one of the channels of the post-war Lower East Side revival. Starting from the 1960s, a number of earlier novels, set partly or entirely in the neighborhood, were reissued. These books contained descriptions of crowded streets, peddlers, and holiday customs that fed the need for "authentic" American Jewishness. They also set forth the conflicts of gender, class, and religion that were an integral part of the Lower East Side experience and were under threat of being obliterated by its "rediscovery" and manipulation. Further, the study of ethnic literature, which concomitantly started to make headway into academia, revealed the "shocking" truth that the Jewish fictionalization of the East Side did not happen in a literary void but was part of a series of attempts, by immigrants as well as Americans, in English and in other languages, to come to grips with the new reality of a multi-ethnic immigrant ghetto.

Under the scrutiny of research, these texts were shown to be not neutral recollections of the neighborhood but complex acts of mediation, the products of a problematic positioning within the American literary scene. Authors had to take into account the expectations of the Anglo Saxon reading public, the availability of narrative languages, and the early twentieth-century debate on immigration. Sociologists and historians of the Jewish American experience were quick to use narrative material in their research on strategies of adaptation to a new environment, but the literary material itself was the result of adaptation to the American landscape.

Of the groups that arrived in the United States after 1880, East European Jews were the first to develop a literature in English. Before the 1940s, when it was still possible to apply the label of marginality to the group, Jewish writers had already articulated the experience of fellow immigrants. Sometimes referring to first-hand knowledge, they used a huge variety of forms and styles, with different locales as background. Naturally, the Lower East Side, as the center of Jewish culture in America, figured prominently in this body of work.

In order to expose some of the issues involved in representations of immigrant neighborhoods and the Lower East Side in particular, I consider two major works belonging to the Jewish-American canon: Abraham Cahan's *The Rise of David Levinsky* (1917) and Michael Gold's *Jews Without Money* (1930). *The Rise of David Levinsky* chronicles the social ascent of the hero from Talmudic scholar in the Russian Pale to prominent businessman in America. It depicts an immigrant community that is mostly apprehended as a collection of images, offering a picturesque background to the protagonist's route toward assimilation. *Jews Without Money*, by contrast, focuses on the daily negotiations of people in the neighborhood, assuming the viewpoint of those who didn't "make it" in America. The dissimilarity in narrative form is the result of a shift in balance between its two major dimensions – space and time. Cahan's book, describing the steps of Levinsky's adjustment to the New World and ultimate success, emphasizes the unfolding of events through time. Gold compresses chronology and privileges the exploration of space around the narrative focus.

SOSTENE MASSIMO ZANGARI

The range of narrative languages for the depiction of city and "slum" life was rather limited when Cahan entered the literary marketplace at the close of the nineteenth century. Then, the genteel tradition still dictated norms and conventions, while the bunch of innovators who embraced an aesthetics of realism was met with general disapproval. Magazine editors, in the name of respectability, routinely depreciated unvarnished renditions of the scandalous and immoral aspects of urban life. Cahan's *Yekl* (1899), for instance, elicited criticism from a contemporary reviewer who found the characters in the story too materialistic and selfish.[4] Gold, instead, came of age when Modernism was making a clean sweep of stuffy modes of representation – and unorthodox writing had an appreciative, if small, audience. Furthermore, Modernism had created a vocabulary of stylistic tools and devices to articulate the multiplicity of sights and populations of the urban milieu, a repertoire Gold keenly adopted.

A confrontation between the narrative constructions of the East Side experience developed in Cahan and Gold's books, far from being a mere exercise in memory, is connected to the question of immigrant authorship. When considered in the light of the literary vocabulary available, these two fictionalized versions of the Jewish community provide material to investigate the route traveled by minority writers seeking recognition and legitimacy within mainstream literature. This negotiation is part of the global process of immigrant communities adapting to a new environment, and in this respect adds to the study of the relationship between migrants and receiving societies.

Minorities and Literary Form

Richard Wright's essay "Blueprint for Negro Writing" offers a good starting point for a discussion of minority literatures. Published in 1937, in the short-lived militant journal *New Challenge*, the essay was meant to debunk the contemporary success enjoyed by a group of black writers among white audiences. Wright argued that such an achievement, however remarkable, depended mostly on the choice to represent black life through the medium of accepted mainstream (read: "white") models. As such, it was hardly a token of improving conditions and recognition for black Americans. On the contrary, by staying within the boundaries of convention, these works could not channel relevant facets of the African-American condition. Worse, this was yet another sign of the subordinate social standing of blacks. To make his point more compelling, Wright quoted Lenin's remark that "oppressed minorities often reflect the techniques of the bourgeoisie more brilliantly than some sections of the bourgeoisie themselves."[5] The use of this quote points to a paradox that reveals how pressing is the urge for minority writers to fit into accepted models.

Wright's preoccupations are by no means exclusive to the literature of the American black community. They provide a useful framework to examine Jewish-

American writers. Indeed, most authors who emerged from the early migratory waves of the 1880s and 1890s, like those berated in "Blueprint," produced work closely reflecting prevalent cultural norms and employed narrative styles then in fashion. The novels by Ezra Brudno (The Fugitive, 1904), Edward Steiner (The Mediator, 1907), Elias Tobenkin (Witte Arrives, 1916), as well as Mary Antin's autobiography (The Promised Land, 1912) express enthusiasm for America and its founding ideals of freedom and democracy. They firmly subscribe to the possibility of integration and success. Indeed, the very fact that Eastern European Jews had learned English, gotten an education and become writers testified to the prospects that the American system laid open for newcomers. Their fate was hardly typical. For most immigrants the new life in the U.S. meant adapting to grim and unhealthy ghetto tenements and labor in sweatshops.[6]

More nuanced versions of Jewish immigrant life were to follow. A full change came about in the 1930s, when a new generation of writers could not shake off a feeling of alienation. They were aware of lines dividing them from "real" Americans. Consequently, they were less keen on singing praises of the American system. The encounter with Modernism was crucial: Gertrude Stein's convoluted and rhythmic prose, James Joyce's symbolic apparatus and use of classical mythology, the fractured point of view employed by Sherwood Anderson, Francis Scott Fitzgerald, and John Dos Passos, as well as a keen interest in incorporating the physical features of the city into their work, provided a mode of writing that articulated both artistic aspirations and personal experiences of deprivation in the urban milieu.

Under the influence of Modernism, Jewish American fiction gradually abandoned narrative modes centered on mobility – the immigrant hero in the course of becoming American – to embrace stasis – synchronic accounts of life in the ghetto. With an emphasis on time, The Rise of David Levinsky follows the hero from childhood and youth in the Russian shtetl to full maturity in America. It thus constructs a complex geography where the East Side is placed within a network of locations connected by economic and social forces. At the same time, the neighborhood in Jews without Money exists as the only "real world." The wanderings of the protagonist and the other characters are confined to the streets of a few East Side blocks – a narrow spatiality suggestive of the forces that keep the population at the bottom of the social order. New York looms as a distant and alien space, the destination for exotic outings such as the family picnic to the Edenic setting of Bronx Park, or as the dwelling place of strange and mysterious people, either other ethnic groups or the rich Wall Street tycoons.

At the bottom of this divarication, then, stand competing conceptions of space. On the one hand, space is configured as map – a terrain of abstract knowledge and appropriation. On the other hand, it is habitat – a locus of active engagement with a physical landscape. This distinction lies at the heart of a conflict from which the American experience itself took form. In this article, I show how the

SOSTENE MASSIMO ZANGARI

choice to adopt one mode of spatiality over the other is part of a more complex web of relationships – with mainstream literature, tradition, the reading public, and the immigrant community – and their final configuration determines the authors' respective positioning within the American literary system.

Performing the Map: David Levinsky Retraces the American Mission.

The small popularity he had enjoyed with English-language stories of the East Side ghetto seemed to Cahan no better than a straitjacket. Convinced of the superiority of the Russian literary tradition, to which he felt he belonged, Cahan wanted to emancipate himself from local color sketches and attempt more complex narrative modes. The failure of The White Terror And the Red (1904), a tale about the Russian revolutionary movement, however, kept him away from major literary enterprises for almost a decade. Then he received a proposal to write a sketch for McClure's. The magazine was interested in reporting on the increasingly significant presence of Jewish immigrant entrepreneurs in the U.S. economy. The editors asked Cahan to contribute a piece detailing entrepreneurs' cultural backgrounds and offering some insight into their psyche. Cahan saw in the assignment an opportunity to reconnect with the American literary world. It gave him the idea for an epic story centered on an orphan who emigrates to the U.S. and there becomes a successful businessman in the garment industry. With Levinsky, Cahan attempted the "delineation of a great character" that he thought was lacking in American literature.[7] McClure published "Autobiography of an American Jew" in four instalments and later, in 1917, with some minor modifications, the story came out in book form under the title The Rise of David Levinsky.[8]

As suggested above, space in the book is seen mainly as a terrain of appropriation, connecting the successive stages of Levinsky's social ascent and the exploration of new chunks of American territory. Spatial knowledge of the country is understood as a consequence of the protagonist's business success. The plot of the novel, then, knits together the expansion of America and that of capitalism. At first, when the hero is still a sweatshop worker, his movements are confined to the ghetto, its cafés, shops, and synagogues. Later, as he starts his business enterprise, Levinsky acquires mobility. His activity needs designers, laboratories, potential clients, and investors, who are located in different parts of Manhattan. Then, in book X, "On the Road," Cahan describes Levinsky's attempts to find new customers for his products outside New York. The protagonist reveals that, "it became possible for me gradually to extend my territory as traveling salesman till it reached Nebraska and Louisiana."[9]

By progressively stretching the growing radii of his trips, Levinsky re-enacts the appropriation of territory through mapping which has been central to the American experience since its beginnings. From the Puritan interpretation of America as new Canaan to the eighteenth-century subdivision of land into a grid system, the virgin territory of the North American continent has been conceived of as a "blank spot" ready to be inscribed and consequently appropriated.[10] The map, however, conceals deeper implications, being functional to a vision of the geographical entity as a terrain of appropriation, persistently open to symbolic inscription. Cultural elites produced their new versions of the map, and its fate was to be superseded when newer discourses gained currency.[11]

This state of "constant revolution" – Sacvan Bercovitch singles out "conformity" as its distinctive feature – found a narrative representation in the rags-to-riches formula. This pattern of narration is organized around the successive stages in the life of a character that lead him/her through transformations to the achievement of a final goal/status. The self goes through a series of revolutions in order to "conform" to the established models or, better, to the "imagined" ideal. Its germs being already evident in early Puritan sermons, the rags-to-riches model has been an important line of development in American literary production. It has provided a prototype that was successively developed, accepted, adjusted, contested, and rewritten. In particular, marginals attempting to "find" place and legitimacy among the reading public saw its suitability as the medium for their tales of assimilation. Writers belonging to marginal communities, the above-mentioned Tobenkin, Steiner, and Antin, for instance, whose constructions of autobiographical selves are literary precursors of Cahan's Levinsky, interpreted their rise from "ethnic" obscurity to "national" prominence as a result of employing this narrative pattern.

By placing their stories within the boundaries of the rags-to-riches framework, these ethnic writers attempted to inscribe their experience in the grain of the dominant order. Much like the nineteenth–century European Bildungsroman, which Franco Moretti defines as a "mechanism able to reconcile [...] the two dominant economic classes of the epoch" – aristocracy and bourgeoisie – early twentieth-century ethnic American writing can be interpreted as a narrative mechanism reconciling immigrants and the Anglo-Saxon middle class, showing the former a route toward integration and the latter a way of neutralizing potential perceived threats from newcomers to national identity.[12] The cultural and political significance of such conciliatory efforts is the more evident when considering the contemporary debate on immigration: nativists complained that the loss of national identity would follow from unrestricted immigration, while its supporters argued that the American system, if working properly, was well equipped to transform foreigners into model citizens.[13]

Cahan was critical of the individualistic ideology embedded in the rags-to-riches pattern. His own cultural background as well as his role as editor of the Yiddish-language daily Forverts, where he oversaw the advice column to immigrants, gave him too much evidence to the contrary. Further, Cahan lamented in his literary criticism how American fiction too often lapsed into romance.[14] By adopting the rags-to-riches pattern, then, Cahan wanted to reconfigure some of its main features and develop an immigrant anti-hero. The story portrays Levinsky's transformation into an American not as a "conversion" to ideals of democracy and equality but merely as a surface transformation of speech and appearance.[15] Further, Levinsky's business success does not spring naturally from superior merit and fair play but owes much to cheating and opportunism. Finally, while the rags-to-riches hero is temperate and sexually restrained, Levinsky frequents prostitutes and conducts affairs with married women, one being the wife of a friend.

Nevertheless, the protagonist aspires to Anglo-Saxon respectability and gentility. He is forced to adopt patterns of thought and interpretations of the real that belong to the ideal he is pursuing. Language, in particular, is a problematic site. The Rise of David Levinsky is an account told in the first person and reflects Levinsky's story as an adult immigrant and a social climber aspiring to bourgeois respectability. As Jules Chametzky has noted, "Levinsky's language [...] is high-sounding and scrupulously literary." But like the language of people who have acquired it imperfectly, "it is controlled by clichés, stereotyped figures."[16] Irving Howe, likewise, considered The Rise a "dry, frugal work of a parsimonious imagination."[17] Cahan's is a narrative voice that, in Bachtin's parlance, emerges as dogmatic, i.e. authoritarian, absorbing the difference and plurality of experience. The Rise of David Levinsky reflects a hero struggling to conform to a middle-class, genteel standard.[18]

Some points in the narrative, for instance, betray a voice that seems unable to express complex feelings and emotions. In the two examples below, Levinsky uses a couple of cold, objective sentences to contain the reaction to episodes in which female characters cause him emotional distress:

> I went home a lovesick man, but the following evening I went to Boston for a day, and my feeling did not survive the trip.[19]

> A few days later the episode seemed to have occurred many years before. It did not bother me. Nor did Matilda.[20]

The first quotation comes after Levinsky discovers that Stella, a girl he loves, does not reciprocate his feelings. The second refers to the sense of humiliation provoked by an encounter with an old flame, who scorned his expensive clothes and refinement. This flavorlessness can be ascribed to Levinsky's construction of himself as a masculine, proactive individual. It is an effort that forces him to avoid elaborating on his emotional distress in order not to compromise the ideal of bourgeoisie manhood he wants to project.[21]

The same strategy surfaces in those instances when Levinsky deals with situations that would require from him an understanding of worldviews other than his own. Some comments made by Philip Joseph about a character in another work by Cahan, "The Imported Bridegroom," are a fit commentary on what happens to Levinsky. The character in question, Flora, "craved for a more refined atmosphere than her own." Her lofty aspirations, her desire to emancipate from the ghetto, distract her from the material circumstances of the ghetto itself.[22] Similarly, the middle-class outlook pursued by the hero throughout his social ascent endows him with an ability to detect, and satirize, the cultural pretentiousness of the newly rich Jewish immigrants, who flaunt knowledge of classical composers in the same way they show off their big diamonds and expensive jewelery.[23] But when Levinsky treads on other areas of life, this middle-class outlook proves useless. When he talks about his employees, he underlines their willingness to be paid non-union wages and work under a non-union regimen: "they could work any number of hours in my shop, and that was what my piece-workers wanted."[24] The treatment he grants to union activists, too, does not give the reader any insight into their motives, nor does it explain the reasons for their huge following in the neighborhood. "(T)he leaders of the Jewish socialists, who were also at the head of the Jewish labour movement, seemed to me to be the most repulsive hypocrites of all. I loathed them."[25] Although Levinsky was familiar with Dickens, he seems not to have gained any insight from him into how to look at the variety in the urban milieu.

Levinsky's single-minded pursuit of an American identity conceived as successful entrepreneurship distorts his relationship to the secondary characters. They are often seen as instrumental in achieving some benefit, be it financing, design expertise, advice, and so forth. But it is no wonder that these characters disappear once they have ceased to be useful to David. The lack of an ethical interest in people who shared the experience of dislocation means the hero is not interested in exploring life outside his own, and that blinds him to the conditions of the community.[26]

The higher Levinsky moves up the social ladder, the more he becomes estranged from fellow immigrants. This is further stressed by the author's depiction of the East Side Jewish community in terms of local curiosity, with panoramic view of cafés, synagogues, and the Yiddish theater, a bow to the dominant contemporary practice of depicting urban diversity as spectacle.[27] Much like magazine writing of the period, there is a predilection for images of the picturesque, as in the description of an evicted family with its furniture piled on the sidewalk. The reader is told nothing about the beyond that description.[28] Much later, the Babel of languages and political views in the Tevkin family are presented through a catalogue that sounds exotic though harmless. The episode is resolved within the outward dimension of the image. It omits any hint of historical reasons that might explain the "outlandish" scene, thus deploying a strategy of containment acceptable to the middle classes.[29] However debunked, the rags-to-riches pattern attaches a middle-class filter to Cahan's narrative. This device separates the indi-

SOSTENE MASSIMO ZANGARI

vidual from the crowd and consequently shuts off the possibility for a comprehensive testimony of the immigrant experience.

Philip Joseph suggested that Cahan, when choosing to write in English, "accepted some constraints in order to rid himself of others." In particular, Joseph focused on how English allowed Cahan the freedom to experiment with configurations of Jewish identities in the New World outside discourses accepted within the Yiddish press. In order to get published in American magazines, Cahan shaped his tales following dictates of local color. In *The Rise*, he added the middle-class outlook that was ingrained in the narrative form. This had the effect of privileging the point of view of the individual and highlights his attempts to transform the landscape to fit in with a vision of himself as a utopian being, i.e an American.

Performing the Body: Michael Gold and the Urban Mosaic

As William Boelhower has observed in *Through the Glass Darkly*, the abstract conceptualization of space through mapping by European settlers challenged and ultimately superseded the way aboriginals conceived and imagined their relationship with those surroundings. Natives did not understand space by means of abstract coordinates and measurement but through the concrete distinctive features of a territory, such as trees and creeks.[30] Curiously enough, this same focus on the body as organizational center of spatiality resurfaced in the works by Michael Gold and other ethnic writers of the 1930s.

This change of spatial organization was part of a larger trend in American literature. Post-World War I novel writers experimented with new narrative solutions to portray an increasingly complex and multi-faceted society. William Carlos Williams, among others, advocated an art form developed from material conditions of the locality where it originated.[31] The new conception of place created a subjectivity that, in order to reproduce the increasing diversity of urban life, gradually started to consider the city itself as a character. The city's features and their meaning took their place in the narrative. A favorite strategy was to push intradiegetic narrators to the fringes of the action and turn them into mere observers. This device granted unity to a kaleidoscope of physical perceptions. As Franco Moretti states:

A different style is required, in order to find one's way in the city of words; a weaker grammar than that of consciousness; an edgy, discontinuous syntax; a cubism of language [...] where the subject withdraws to make room for the invasion of things.[32]

This technique proved suitable to show and contain the many contradictory sides of ordinary lives in immigrant communities. Languages, cultures, and attitudes that survived the clash of Old World legacies and New World lifestyles began to co-exist. Henry Roth, for instance, identifies in Eliot's *The Waste Land* a vision of the real that is analogous to his own "made out of rags and patches ... a crazy quilt."[33] Another contemporary writer of Jewish origin, Daniel Fuchs, in his novel *Summer in Williamsburg* (1934), invokes a similar dissection of experience to make sense of the immigrant community: "(Y)ou must make a laboratory out of Williamsburg... you must pick Williamsburg to pieces until you have them all spread out on your table before you, a dictionary of Williamsburg."[34]

Gold's *Jews Without Money* follows the same lead. From early on, Gold had the idea of writing a novel based on his experience of growing up on the Lower East Side. This is evident in his piece published in *The Masses* entitled "Birth." However, no organic development of the tale followed, as Gold, busy with the editorial job at *The Liberator*, temporarily abandoned the project to concentrate on reporting strikes and reviewing and theorizing literature. New material based on recollections from his childhood appeared in sketches in *Menorah Journal* and *The New Masses*, starting from the latter part of the 1920s. This material, supplemented by other writings, was later included in *Jews Without Money*. The work showed a remarkable departure from the style of "Birth." This is how the fragment begins:

> I was born (so my mother once told me), on a certain dim day of April, about seven in a morning wrapped in fog. The streets of the East Side were dark with grey, wet gloom; the boats of the harbor cried constantly, like great bewildered gulls, like deep, booming voices of calamity. The day was somber and heavy and unavoidable, like the walls of a prison about the city. And in the same hour and the same tenement that bore me, Rosie Hyman the prostitute died, and the pale ear of the same doctor heard my first wails and the last quiverings of her sore heart.[35]

The piece replicated a then outdated nineteenth-century writing style. It centered around an I-narrator who imposes a point of view, both visual and moral, and provides the reader with those metaphors by which the setting is to be interpreted. The new beginning in *Jews*, instead, organizes narration as a collation of images and employs a prose that gives preference to short, coordinated sentences:

> I can never forget the East Side where I lived as a boy.
> It was a block from the notorious Bowery, a tenement canyon hung with fire-escapes, bed-clothing, and faces.
> Always these faces at the tenement windows. The street never failed them. It was an immense excitement. It never slept. It roared like a sea. It exploded like fireworks.
> People pushed and wrangled in the street. There were armies of howling push-

SOSTENE MASSIMO ZANGARI

cart peddlers. Women screamed, dogs barked and copulated. Babies cried. A parrot cursed. Ragged kids played under truck-horses. Fat housewives fought from stoop to stoop. A beggar sang.[36]

The development points to a relevant process of literary maturation, and some traces can be found in the reviews, manifestos, and editorials that Gold produced as editor of The Liberator and The New Masses.

In spite of a reputation as castigator of Modernists and harsh critic of their work, Gold had always been attentive to the literary experimentalism of the era. In his autobiography, Gold's long-time associate, Joseph Freeman, confessed that in the early days of The Liberator, the editorial committee was "still attached to the aesthetic ideas which we combated."[37] An important reference was Ernest Hemingway. Gold suggested that his "bare, hard style [...] precise and perfect as science," was a starting point for revolutionary writers of the future. The example of Hemingway, with his predilection for objective depiction of characters and places, taught Gold how strong effects could be achieved without explicit commentary – a rule he was not always able to follow in Jews. Nevertheless, the lessons from Hemingway can be seen at work in Gold's attempt at balancing the paragraph as an autonomous unit. In the following example, the images relating the suffering of the mother are encased within a repetition of the plain sentence reporting the tragic event:

Esther was dead. My mother had borne everything in life, but this she could not bear. It frightened one to see how quiet she became. She was no longer active, cheerful, quarrelsome. She sat by the window all day, and read her prayer-book. As she mumbled the endless Hebrew prayers, tears flowed silently down her face. She did not speak, but she knew why she was crying. Esther was dead.[38]

In a later piece of literary criticism, Gold would go as far as to acknowledge that "Hemingway and others have had the intuition to incorporate [a] proletarian element into their work" out of scorn for any "vague fumbling poetry." In the article, written in the mood of confidence following the publication of Jews Without Money, Gold outlines ten rules for writing what he calls "proletarian realism." He includes recommendations to use "as few words as possible," to avoid "straining or melodrama or other effects," and to attempt "cinema in words," concentrating on "swift action, clear form" and the "direct line."[39]

As to the organization of narrative material as a kaleidoscopic presentation of fragments of reality, Gold was inspired not only by John Dos Passos's Manhattan Transfer – which he enthusiastically reviewed in New Masses – but also by a year-long visit to Russia in 1925, where he familiarized himself with constructivist theater and the work of Vsevolod Meyerhold. Gold was particularly impressed by

Meyerhold's attempt to bring "the street onto the stage." Meyerhold reproduces an urban soundtrack of "horns, gongs, sirens, whistles" and divides the stage into a number of spaces where different actions were performed simultaneously.[40]

These narrative tools provided the instruments to give substance to Gold's global view of fiction, which he had expressed earlier in the visionary manifesto "Toward Proletarian Art." Published in the March 1921 issue of The Liberator, this programmatic pamphlet stated that art "is the tenement pouring out its soul through us," where the building is taken as symbol of the collective human fate of suffering and exploitation.[41] This point is reiterated in Jews Without Money when the narrator declares that "[i]t's impossible to live in a tenement without being mixed up with the tragedies [...] of one's neighbor." Gold makes clear that the commitment to the community is unavoidable.[42] The "tenement" compels Gold to assemble the small pieces that will provide the basis for reconstructing the neighborhood and the personal histories of its representative inhabitants.

Through the eyes of Mickey, the young boy whose conscience functions as the aggregating focus of the book, the reader is acquainted with significant aspects of East Side life, from home labor to prostitution, from the struggle to retain Jewish customs to the allure of American popular culture. Each chapter uncovers characters and situations that will contribute to a picture of the neighborhood that escapes the stereotypical collection of "ghetto types" and locations. The gallery of people is rich and varied. The narrator details the transformation of his aunt Lena, whose "rosy peasant cheeks and shiny black hair" have been turned pale and her eyes languid. He describes the last American on the street, Mary Sugar Bum, "as always drunk and disorderly." And he mentions Mrs. Cohen, the typical wife of a noveau riche who looks like some "vulgar pretentious prostitute."[43] The tragedies of the East Side include Reb Samuel, a pious Chasidic Jew whose heart fails when a rabbi, for whom the congregation has raised money for passage, leaves the East Side when he is offered a better salary elsewhere.[44] Or finally, the comedy of the tenement, where ancestral diffidence towards Italians and the Irish makes way for the recognition of a mutual destiny of suffering, as told in the chapter "Jews and Christians."[45]

Mickey's sensorial perceptions are exploited by Gold to lend texture to descriptions, and accordingly he incorporates the sounds of streetcars, the shapes of towering buildings, odors, and the constant feeling of overcrowding into the narrative. "Excitement, dirt, fighting, chaos! The sound of my street lifted like the blast of a great carnival or catastrophe. The noise was always in my ears. Even in sleep I could hear it."[46]

Through the objective style, Gold avoids overt sentimentality or forced interpretations – facile tricks that were part of a staple melodramatic and sensational representation of ghettos in the popular press. Gold wanted the facts to speak for themselves. His recurring allusions to long hours of toil, poverty, scarcity of food, and unsanitary housing conditions contribute to an indictment of capitalistic society while debunking the prevailing rhetoric of "getting-rich-quick," which is found to be illusory and alien to the fates of Eastsiders.

Gold writes of the adults in perennial arguments about money and work, gangs of children staging imitation battles to defend the borders of a street or to conquer a vacant lot, the sex market, the epidemic of dead cats, and the invasion of bedbugs. This recapitulation of the world of his youth constructs a vision of the Lower East Side as a capitalist hell. The neighborhood is identified with the ruins of Pompeii, projecting an image of decay that hints at America's failure to live up to its promise of prosperity.[47] In fact, the social stratus Gold is concerned with does not share in the fate of mobility impersonated by Levinsky, and none of the immigrants he writes about has the opportunity to leave ghetto life behind. Men and women in *Jews Without Money* seldom cross the boundaries of the neighborhood, entrapped in a way that is suggestive of their lack of social ascent. In this light, the call for a revolution that concludes the book, "O workers' Revolution [...] You will destroy the East Side when you come, and build there a garden for the human spirit" expresses a wish to break the vicious circle and open up the East Side to the opportunities of the city and of America.[48]

Conclusion: A Multi-Ethnic American Modernism

During the 1930s, other ethnic writers followed Gold in focusing on the daily negotiations between a narrator and his surroundings. James T. Farrell's *Studs Lonigan* trilogy (1932-35) and Richard Wright's *Lawd Today!* (written between 1936 and 1937), for example, explored the South Side section of Chicago from the point of view of Irish and African Americans respectively. They both dealt with protagonists whose desire for emancipation is frustrated by the inability to understand and therefore break the social dynamics of the ghetto as well as the deteriorating economic conditions of the Depression. This coupling of theme and form across ethnic boundaries testifies to a common perception of ghettos as privileged terrain to start a reconsideration of the historical processes and social mutations that America underwent during the era of mass migration: as Irving Howe argued, "what it (American Literature) has become is to a large extent what it has absorbed from alien intruders."[49]

The ruined cityscapes that populated the works of 1930s ethnic writers express an alternative vision of America that follows from the increasing diversity of its population. It is no accident that during the thirties, as Marcus Klein has maintained, the ghetto became a "root definition" of the American condition.[50] In fact, the literary production of the decade included many works that presented quasi-sociological surveys of ethnic neighborhoods at the expense of traditional plot arrangements. And the Lower East Side was one of those locales where this new vision of America took form.

Gold's trajectory was exemplary of a trend that rejected mainstream patterns and embraced modernist experimentalism. Shifting from a *mobile* approach to space – where plots unraveled through time – to a *static* one that allowed for richly textured renditions of city settings, the ethnic American writers broke free from the stylistic and ideological limitations inherent in traditional forms and constructed their own voice. It was a process that showed how literary forms dictate the range of possible meanings a writer can pursue, and how new meanings need new forms in order to be channeled.

The participation of ethnics in national culture occurred as part of the intellectual ferment in major cities such as New York and Chicago. Research conducted in the last decade has yielded insights into the relationship between ethnicity and Modernism, showing how the fact of being suspended between worlds and languages equipped so-called hyphenated American writers with a "modern" sensibility. A considerable number of them went further and appropriated modernist techniques in their work.[51]

In New York, for instance, a peculiar combination of bohemia and radicalism transformed Greenwich Village into a unique laboratory. There, art was seen as a means for individual and social revolt at the same time.[52] Village intellectuals and artists were open to the new ideas about literature and art that came from Europe but did not forget to include the immigrant workers earning their daily bread in the sweatshops nearby. When ethnics such as Gold and Roth abandoned the ghettos of their childhood, they found a cultural milieu where the artist's quest was viewed as a revolution against both cultural tradition and society, and in which intellectual work was a step toward the creation of a new order. Their literary production connects to the Modernist movement and represents those in that school who actively engaged with issues of class and marginality.

The Rise of David Levinsky and Jews Without Money, then, although participating in the dynamic of the 1960s cultural construction of the Lower East Side as site of Jewish American memory, resist the "national narrative." Instead, they promote a representation of the neighborhood as embedded in history. The Lower East Side thus emerged as the product of a complex act of weaving together literary forms and available stylistic vocabulary. Much in the fashion of realist authors, Cahan's representation of the neighborhood, and the whole city, is mostly a visual experience, where images and surfaces are central. What is hidden behind them is seldom revealed. The self is surrounded by "mirrors." Individual identity is carried out by constructing a social hierarchy measured in terms of outward appearance.[53] This mode of representation was replaced by new forms in which the individual hero is more actively engaged in the urban landscape. In fact, it is by a confrontation with people, social conditions, buildings, and architecture that the hero finds his own sense of identity. The reconstruction of the neighborhood in Jews Without Money responds to a primary need of the displaced hero to retrace his original self to a place other than that which he inhabits. By piecing together the

SOSTENE MASSIMO ZANGARI

fragments of what he has seen, heard, and suffered, the hero creates his own myth of origin. He constructs the neighborhood as the environment where the new American writer, a "wild youth of about twenty-two [...] the son of working class parents," developed quite unconsciously a writing that flows naturally from his experience. Gold outlined such a portrait in an essay, and it was to this image that he struggled to conform.[54]

Notes

1. Mario Maffi, *Gateway To The Promised Land: Ethnic Cultures on New York's Lower East Side* (Amsterdam/Atlanta, GA: Rodopi, 1994).

2. Hasia Diner, *Lower East Side Memories: A Jewish Place in America* (Princeton: Princeton University Press, 2000), 50.

3. Joanna Weissman Joselit, "Telling Tales: Or, How a Slum Became a Shrine," *Jewish Social Studies* 2 (1996): 54-63. See also Beth Wenger, "Memory as Identity: The Invention of the Lower East Side," *American Jewish History* 85 (1997 March): 3-27.

4. The review, published in *The Bookman*, saw in *Yekl* "not a gleam of spirituality, unselfishness, or nobility," "it is a hideous showing, and repels the reader". See Louis Harap, *The Image of the Jew in American Literature* (Syracuse: Syracuse University Press, [1974] 2003), 497.

5. Richard Wright, "Blueprint for Negro Writing" [1937], in *The Richard Wright Reader*, eds. Ellen Wright and Michel Fabre (New York: Harper and Row, 1978), 38.

6. See Sarah Blacher Cohen, "Mary Antin's *The Promised Land*: A Breach of Promise," *Studies in American Jewish Literature* 3 (1977): 28-35. For a general discussion of early Jewish-American authors, see Lewis Fried, ed., *Handbook of American-Jewish Literature: An Analytical Guide to Topics, Themes and Sources* (New York, Westport, CT: Greenwood Press, 1988). An example of Antin's enthusiasm for the United States can be seen in the following quote, where the author enthuses over the possibility that a girl of the slums gets to know a Senator: "How did I come by a Senator? Through being a citizen of Boston, of course. To be a citizen of the smallest village in the United States which maintains a free school and a public library is to stand in the path of the splendid processions of opportunity. And as Boston has rather better schools and a rather finer library than some other villages, it comes natural there for children in the slums to summon gentlemen from the State House to be their personal friends." Mary Antin, *The Promised Land* (Whitefish, MT: Kessinger Publishing [1912] 2004), 225.

7. See for instance the following comment by Cahan reported in Hutchins Hapgood's *The Spirit of the Ghetto*: "Now and then, indeed, I see indications of real art in your [American] writers – great images, great characters, great truth – but all merely in suggestions... You prefer an exciting plot to a great delineation of character... I love you all. You are clever, good fellows, but you are children, talented to be sure, but wayward and vagrant children in the fields of art". Hutchins Hapgood, *The Spirit of the Ghetto* (Cambridge, Mass: Harvard University Press [1902] 1983), 286.

8. Ronald Sanders, *The Lower East Side Jews: An Immigrant Generation* (Mineola, NY: Dover Publications, Inc., [1969] 1987), 417-18.

9. Abraham Cahan, *The Rise of David Levinsky* (New York: Random House, [1917] 2001), 311.

10. William Boelhower, *Through A Glass Darkly: Ethnic Semiosis in American Literature* (New York: Oxford University Press, 1987), 41-79.

11. Sacvan Bercovitch, *The Rites of Assent: Transformations in the Symbolic Construction of America* (New York, London: Routledge), 1993, 29-67.

12. Franco Moretti, *The Way of The World: The Bildungsroman in European Culture* (London: Verso, 2002), 63.

13. See John Higham, *Strangers in the Land: Patterns of American Nativism, 1860-1925* (Atheneum: New York, 1969).

14. See Philip Joseph, "Literary Migration: Abraham Cahan's The Imported Bridegroom and the Alternative of American Fiction," MELUS 27.4 (Winter 2002): 3-32.

15. See the following quotes from the book: "If I heard a bit of business rhetoric that I thought effective I would jot it down and commit it to memory. In like manner I would write down every new piece of slang, the use of the latest popular phrase being, as I thought, helpful in making oneself popular with Americans" [*The Rise*, 284], or "Bender [....] I would hang on his lips, striving to memorize every English word I could catch and watching intently, not only his enunciation, but also his gestures, manners, and mannerisms..." [*The Rise*, 125]).

16. Jules Chametzky, "Some Notes on Immigration, Ethnicity, Acculturation," MELUS 11.1 (Spring 1984): 49.

17. Irving Howe, *World of Our Fathers* (London: Phoenix Press [1976] 2000), 590.

18. See Mikhail Mikhailovic Bakhtin, *Rabelais and His World* (Bloomington: Indiana University Press, 1984), 121.

19. *The Rise*, 361.

20. *The Rise*, 376.

21. The prevalence of a 'dogmatic' attitude is all the more relevant when comparing *The Rise of David Levinsky* to Cahan's earlier short fiction. As a number of scholars have shown, Cahan was capable of using plurilinguism. See for instance Aviva Taubenfeld, "Only an L: Linguistic Borders and the Immigrant Author in Abraham Cahan's *Yekl* and *Yankel der Yankee*," in Werner Sollors, ed., *Multilingual America: Transnationalism, Ethnicity, and the Languages of America* (New York: New York University Press, 1998), 144-165.

22. Philip Joseph, "Literary Migration: Abraham Cahan's *The Imported Bridegroom* and the Alternative of American Fiction," MELUS 27.4 (Winter 2002): 3-32.

23. Levinsky's effectiveness as critic of the newly rich can be seen in this description: "I noticed, for instance, that Auntie Yetta, whose fingers were a veritable jewelry-store, now and again made a pretense of smoothing her grayish hair for the purpose of exhibiting her flaming rings. Another elderly woman, whose fingers were as heavily laden, kept them prominently interlaced across her breast. From time to time she would flirt her interlocked hands, in feigned absent-mindedness, thus flashing her diamonds upon the people around her. At one moment it became something like a race between her and Auntie Yetta." [*The Rise*, 357]

24. *The Rise*, 265.

25. Ibid. 370.

26. The extent of Levinsky's single-mindedness can be appreciated by comparing how one narrative situation – in this case a trip on the Elevated – is exploited differently by two different narrators. Levinsky: "While the Elevated train was carrying me uptown I visioned an avalanche of new orders for my shop and a spacious factory full of machines and men. I saw myself building up a great business." [*The Rise*, 229] Instead, in William Dean Howells's *A Hazard of New Fortunes*, the Elevated is a pretext for an outward projection of the narrator: "At Third Avenue they took the Elevated for which she confessed an infatuation. [...] He said it was better than the theatre, of which it reminded him, to see those people through their windows: a family party of work-folk at a late tea, some of the men in their shirt-sleeves; a woman sewing by a lamp; a mother laying her child in its cradle; a man with his head fallen on his hands upon a table; a girl and her lover leaning over the window-sill together. What suggestion! what drama? what infinite interest." William Dean Howells, *A Hazard of New Fortunes* (Oxford: [The World's Classics] Oxford University Press [1890] 1990), 63.

27. Keith Gandal, *The Virtue of the Vicious: Jacob Riis, Stephen Crane and the Spectacle of the Slum* (Oxford: Oxford University Press [1997] 2006).

28. *The Rise*, 94.

29. Sabine Henni, "Visual and Theatrical Culture, Tenement Fiction, and the Immigrant Subject in Abraham Cahan's *Yekl*," *American Literature* 71. 3 (September 1999): 493-527.

30. Boelhower, *Through A Glass Darkly*.

31. Marcus Klein, *Foreigners: The Making of American Literature, 1900-1940* (Chicago: University of Chicago Press, 1981), 85.

32. Franco Moretti, *Modern Epic: The World System from Goethe to Garcia Márquez* (London: Verso, 1996), 134-5.

33. Henry Roth, "Itinerant Ithacan," in *Shifting Landscape* (New York: Saint Martin's Press, [1987] 1994), 211.

34. Daniel Fuchs, *The Brooklyn Novels* (Boston: Black Sparrow Books, 2006), 11.

35. Michael Gold, "Birth" in *Michael Gold: A Literary Anthology* (New York: International Publishers, 1972), 44.

36. Michael Gold, *Jews Without Money* (New York: Carroll and Graf, [1930] 1996), 13.

37. Joseph Freeman, *An American Testament* (New York: Farrar & Rinehart, 1936), 325.

38. *Jews*, 288.

39. Gold, "Proletarian Realism," in *Michael Gold*, 207-8.

40. Richard Tuerk, "Michael Gold's Hoboken Blues: An Experiment that Failed," *MELUS* 20.4 (1995): 3-15.

41. Gold, "Toward Proletarian Art," in *Michael Gold*, 65.

42. *Jews*, 30.

43. Ibid. 131, 134, 178, 217.

44. Ibid. 204.

45. Ibid. 156-173.

46. Ibid. 14.

47. Ibid. 40.

48. Ibid. 309.

49. Howe, *World*, 585

50. Klein, *Foreigners*, 36.

51. See Werner Sollors, *Ethnic Modernism* (Cambridge, Mass: Harvad University Press, 2008).

52. See Malcolm Cowley, *Exile's Return* (London, New York: Penguin, [1956] 1994), 66.

53. Paula E. Geyh, "From Cities of Things to Cities of Signs: Urban Spaces and Urban Subjects in *Sister Carrie* and *Manhattan Transfer*," *Twentieth Century Literature* 52 (2006 Winter): 413-444.

54. Gold, "Introduction," *Michael Gold*, 8.

Kishinev Redux: Pogrom, Purim, Patrimony

Nancy K. Miller

> *Rise and go to the town of the killings and you'll come to the yard and with your eyes and your own hand feel the fence and on the trees and on the stones and plaster of the walls the congealed blood and hardened brains of the dead.*
> Hayim Nahman Bialik, City of the Killings

What I believed as a child: we came from Russia. Russia: a vast, faraway, almost mythical kingdom, ruled by bad Czars, filled with mean peasants, who lived in the forest with wolves, and even meaner Cossacks who, when they weren't riding horses, or maybe while they were riding horses, specialized in physical attacks on Jews called pogroms. Overall it was a place one left, if one was a Jew, as soon as possible. The fairy-tale like simplicity of this geography and its inhabitants did not include a longing to return. No one ever talked about going back there, wherever 'back there' actually was.

Before I traveled to Eastern Europe, I would have been unable to locate the city of Kishinev on a modern map. Kishinev itself was a place name that came belatedly, when I was already a middle-aged adult, as an overlay to my childhood vision of the Russian empire. It wasn't yet Chisinau, the capital of Moldova, consistently referred to in the media as the poorest country in Europe, known for sex trafficking, the illegal sale of bodily organs, and Twitter-assisted post-Soviet political turmoil. But why was I going to Kishinev, and why did I think that we – my father's side of the family, the Kipnis side – came from there?

Not long before his death in 1989, my father gave me a few monogrammed forks and spoons, which he described as "silverware from our family in Russia." Around the same time, he also gave me a photocopy of the articles index to the *New York Times* with references to the 1903 Kishinev pogrom checked in the margins, as well as a map of Bessarabia with Kishinev circled in red. I do not remember asking my father directly where his parents came from, nor do I recall ever hearing accounts of their immigration to the United States. And so when he died, the matter of where we were from remained just that: a fixed, generic, third-generation Jewish template – a classic American narrative of immigration followed by assimilation. For the next ten years, as had been true of my life before his death, I was not particularly interested in knowing more. I had the vague sense that the *where* in Russia we were from was Kishinev.

I probably would have remained locked in my ignorance about the specifics of my Eastern European origins if an enterprising real estate agent had not, in 2000, reached my sister and me with the news that we had inherited property in a village on the outskirts of Jerusalem from our paternal grandparents. The property amounted to two dunams – two tiny plots of one-quarter acre each, bought in my grandmother's name. This startling information led to an encounter with the other heir to my grandmother's dunams, my father's nephew, his older and only sibling's son, who was living in Memphis, Tennessee. In 2000, I met my cousin Julian Kipnis for the first time, as well as his daughter, Sarah Castleberry. Through Sarah, who had already become fascinated with family history, I discovered a website devoted to our family name that included the ship's manifests for a multitude of Kipnis immigrants. On the manifest for my grandparents and uncle, under the category "last permanent residence" was written by hand: Kishiniew. With that click, I was instantly hooked by the possibility of finding out more about this family, the Kipnises, whose existence had always been shrouded in a kind of dark silence.[1] The encounter with my newly met cousin sent me back to the haphazard collection of objects and ephemera that I had taken from my parents' apartment after my father's death and that I had saved without quite knowing why. Now I had someone with whom to share notes.

Sorting through my father's papers, I found a formal portrait of his parents and older brother. The name of the studio and its location in Kishinev were prominently identified on the front and back of the image. Based on what I took to be the age of the little boy – my uncle, whom I had never met – standing between my grandparents, I guessed that the photograph had been taken in 1903, which was also the year of the pogrom. Widely reported throughout the world, the Kishinev pogrom stood as a turning point in Jewish history, not only in Russia.[2] Perhaps, I thought, these ancestors of mine had actually witnessed the event as immortalized in Bialik's famous 1904 poem, 'City of the Killings,' and Israel Zangwill's 1908 play, remembered now mainly for its title, The Melting Pot.[3] My grandparents and uncle left Russia for America in 1906.

Although only a handful of biographical facts about the trio had been transmitted to me, the photograph, the newspaper references to the pogrom, and the map led me to link the Kipnis family name with Kishinev. There was something uncannily suggestive about the way the names of the family and the city seemed to mirror each other, the resemblance carried by the initial letter K, and the overlapping sounds of the syllables (Kip/Kish/nis/nev). I began, largely unconsciously, to identify the family enigma with the history of the city and to wonder whether the place itself could reveal what my father had failed to put into words. I began to feel that the pogrom belonged to me.

NANCY K. MILLER

In the spring of 2008, almost impulsively, I decided to make the trip that would bring me to the city where my grandparents had resided before their emigration, despite the fact that I knew I was not likely ever to learn exactly where and how they lived or to meet anyone who had known them. The photograph no longer satisfied my longing to know more about them, nor did the ship's manifest. By the time I made the pilgrimage to the site of the pogrom, large numbers of third-generation descendants of the vast emigration from Russia at the turn of the twentieth century had, like me, begun looking for the towns their ancestors had left, and Web-based organizations like Jewishgen.org had set up Internet engines to facilitate the journey of return. Indeed, it was through a reference from www. Jewishgen.org that I found my guide Natasha.

Initially, I resisted calling my journey a "roots-seeking trip," as Natasha always referred to the persona animating the itinerary, "Amerikanka looking for babush-ka," but I cannot deny that the category fit my desire.[4] I had become not just curious but consumed with curiosity to see for myself the part of the world my father's parents – and his brother – had left behind, and to follow the path of the pogrom. By email, Natasha explained to me that if I wanted genealogical informa-tion from the Moldovan archives, I would have to engage a specialist. Even before I arrived in town, the archivist she recommended had already found records for one of my great-grandfather's cousins in Kishinev – his marriage and profession – as well as a document about a dead child who had lived only three days before dying of convulsions, the son of Refuel (my grandfather's name) from Tulchin, a small town now in Ukraine. This was more evidence that I, we, they somehow were from there, from this corner of Bessarabia, as it was called then.

I immediately located the position of this cousin on a branch of the tree that an American genealogist with Kipnis ancestors had made for me years earlier, and looked again at the ship's manifest that I had already downloaded from Ancestry. com. The man, his wife, and his children left for New York from Odessa, a few weeks after my grandparents had left Kishinev, on the same ship from Rotterdam, and were headed for the home of my grandfather Raphael Kipnis at 96 Allen Street in New York. 96 Allen Street no longer exists, but at the time the building shared a courtyard, back to back, with 97 Orchard Street, the current home of the Tenement Museum of the Lower East Side.

I went to Kishinev and followed the path of the pogrom as described in Bialik's poem, but it was only the *second* trip I made to the city – the one that could prop-erly be called a return – that helped me understand my puzzling compulsion to make the first journey, a compulsion shared by thousands of fellow questers across the world, and abetted by technology; descendants of immigrants for whom, like me, the image, the screen, and the archive do not seem to be enough. We seem to want, though we might not put it that way, the real thing.

Not long after getting back to New York in May 2008 from my first trip to Kishinev, Aleksandar Hemon published *The Lazarus Project* and, at the same time, my sister handed over an album of photographs from Russia that had belonged to my grandmother.[5] Together, these unexpected occurrences illuminated both the meaning of my individual quest and the wider phenomenon expressed in rites of return: the genre, as it were, of the experience and the modes by which we return, think we return, and think about returning. The book and the album sent me back for a closer look.

Lazarus Averbach survives the 1903 pogrom in Kishinev and emigrates to the safety of America, only to be murdered a few years later in Chicago. In the novel, Brik, the narrator, tries to unravel Lazarus's story, and embarks on detective-like travels to Eastern Europe in order to reconstruct the immigrant's pogrom past. When Brik and his travel companion, Rora, a photographer – both Bosnian like the author, neither Jewish – arrive in Moldova, they set out to research the pogrom: "the two of us who could never have experienced the pogrom went to the Chisinau Jewish Community Center to find someone who had never experienced it and would tell us about it." I was overcome with a sense of anxiety. Here was my own private adventure somehow scooped and transformed into literature through an artful postmodern scrim. What was the novelist doing to my pogrom? Naturally, Brik and Rora's guide is a Philip Rothian character, a beautiful if slightly bored young woman, pale with "deep, mournful eyes."[6] The two men ask her about the pogrom, which she dutifully recounts, and then are led to an adjacent room where they gaze in horror at a display of photographs: "bearded, mauled corpses lined up on the hospital floor, the glassy eyes facing the ceiling stiffly: a pile of battered bodies; a child with its mouth agape; a throng of bandaged, terrified survivors...."[7] The description seemed familiar. I'd seen many of those same images online, illustrating the historical event. But I did not see them on my visit. What I saw on display about the pogrom that I too was researching as a character in my own story was an arch in the one-room museum around which collaged photographs had been pasted. The strongest image I remembered was that of young men clutching the Torah scrolls desecrated during the rioting. Had my guide failed to show me these other photographs? Had I seen them and forgotten?

As I raced through the pages of the novel, I had the uncomfortable sensation that Hemon's fiction was challenging my memory and even my sense of reality. In the novel, for instance, the two characters leave the display of pogrom photographs and move further into the room. Behind an alcove, they see "a couple of dummies in Orthodox Jewish attire, positioned around an empty table, their eyes wide open, their hands resting on the table's edge."[8] I traveled back in my mind, looking at the photographs I had taken, and coming up blank. I started to distrust my reliability as the narrator of my memoir. I sent Natasha a frantic email, telling her about the novel and asking her whether we had seen these rooms. How could I have missed the pogrom exhibit? Surely I would have noticed these "dummies" meant to represent, the novel's guide explains, "a Jewish family from the time of

NANCY K. MILLER

the pogrom."[9] But maybe my panic was misplaced. After all, this was a novel –
fiction, not memoir. Maybe Hemon had invented the whole thing. I hated myself
for being so literal-minded. I was a professor of literature and knew about genre.

Natasha wrote back about the dummies: "Yes, and Purim figures. It's in the
JCC, with the library where Olga [the librarian] showed you around ..." Natasha
attached two pictures she had taken of our visit: "Please see yourself and the
puppets." But these puppets are Purim figures, Queen Esther and King Aha-
shuerus, not dummies dressed as Orthodox Jews. Did Hemon and I visit the
same place? I turned to Olga, laying out my confusion. "Aleksandar Hemon is
correct in his description," the librarian began. And the dummies? "The dummies
in Orthodox attire just symbolized the atmosphere of an average Jewish home,"
she said. I held my breath, stunned by this confirmation of my memory lapse.
Finally, toward the end of her long, detailed message, Olga explained that before
2005 – presumably when Hemon had visited the city – the museum and therefore
the exhibit were located across the street from its current location: "So you
couldn't have seen the described artifacts." I had missed not only the dummies,
but also, Olga added, the "exposition devoted to the Pogrom with map, names of
the victims, and a large picture of Torah Scrolls damaged by the looters." I
couldn't have seen what I didn't see! My heart exploded with relief.

A few weeks later, Olga sent me photographs from the exhibit Hemon described. I see the dummies, I see a beautiful young woman who might have been
the guide in the novel, pointing to the photographs of the pogrom. The dummies.
The husband is dressed in a long, black gabardine coat, like a Hasidic Jew. His
large hat, much too big for his head, is scrunched down around his ears, in front
of which curl significant side locks; his bushy, untrimmed beard and full mus-
tache complete the representation of the Orthodox Jew, his gaze resolutely turned
away from modernity. His wife's hair is covered with a black shawl knotted
around her shoulders; dressed in a full, white blouse, a knitted vest, and long,
full flowing skirt with an embroidered pattern around the hem, she looks like a
Ukrainian peasant.

Compared to the dummies, the photograph of my grandparents taken in Kishinev shows a couple that has distanced themselves from the styles of Bessarabian
Orthodoxy. My grandfather has trimmed his beard and poses hatless, in street
clothes. My grandmother does not cover her hair and is wearing a fitted blouse
and elegant taffeta skirt. The couple looks European, Victorian.

In my grandmother's album I found two studio cards from Kishinev photography studios. These were portraits of friends, who have inscribed across the back
of their portraits messages of farewell in Russian, dated a few months before my
grandparents' departure from Kishinev. In posture and affect, the friends resem-
ble the characters in period representations of Chekhov. One reads: "To my dear
friend R. Kipnis with his wife, from G. and E. Frein. May you remember us
fondly." I know nothing about these people, but what their faces, fashion, and

words tell me is that far from the caricatures of the dummies, Rafael and his wife belonged to a circle who knew there was a future beyond the pogroms. Three months later, my grandparents would sail for America. My grandmother was pregnant, or about to be, with my father.

The photographs from the dear friends, their gesture of farewell, confirmed to me what I had traveled to find the first time but hadn't: something beyond the ship's manifest and beyond the family portrait. My second trip to Kishinev was to see not just the site of the pogrom again but to see for the first time the place that my grandparents had left as members of what I had since learned was a vast middle class of petit-bourgeois Jews. The tenements of the Lower East Side must have been something of a comedown for the upwardly mobile Bessarabian Kipnises, if they lived anywhere near their friend Mr. Samuel Grigory Traub, "in his private dwelling house... in the upper, newly built part of the town." Or perhaps they lived near the photography studio located, it says on the card stock, "near the water pump house."

In my return to Kishinev, I was following an impulse I could not fully explain to myself, but it was hard to resist the self-diagnosis that I had succumbed to Freud's account of the "repetition compulsion" in *Beyond the Pleasure Principle*.[10] In the *fort/da* story, Freud famously describes how a child tries to master an anxiety over loss through a game, a game that allows him to repeat through a symbolic act a feeling – the fear of his mother's absence, of losing his mother – that threatens his sense of security. Repetition in this sense is a pleasurable way for the child to master the terror of loss beyond his control. For those of us for whom the past is often what novelist Kiran Desai named "the inheritance of loss," returning to the scene of where something important was lost can feel comforting.[11] As adult returnees, like the child playing with the spool, we try to fool ourselves with time travel. We can't really recapture the past with its losses, but we can go back to its places. Playing with loss becomes a way to deal with one of the crucial features of these rites of return, and that is a confrontation with what we are missing. Sometimes this is something literal: trying to see, find, discover what we have missed – that is, overlooked. But also something symbolic: recognizing what's irretrievably missing.

I wanted to know where they lived. I'm not going to know that. But because of the studio cards on my return I'm going to walk past the street where one of the city's two water pumps was located. I'm going to walk past the street where the water pump is no more but where the friends who were already missing my grandparents had their photograph taken. On my repeat pilgrimage, I'm going to follow the poem more carefully because now I finally understand the route the *pogromchiks* took and that I had walked through in a daze the first time, overwhelmed by the strangeness of the topography in which I had found myself. I'm starting to understand what is next to what, what is far, what is close. The river

Byck that marked the border of the poor section of town at the time of the pogrom in 2009 is barely a rivulet, and often entirely dry.

With the screen of the novel doubled by images from the exhibit I hadn't seen, my effort to fathom the city's past sometimes felt like a replay of childhood trips to the Museum of Natural History where we were instructed to gaze at dioramas of lost worlds and foreign peoples. But when I crossed the threshold of the Jewish Cultural Center, something felt immediately different, even though the exhibits had not changed. As I walked through the rooms with Olga, I experienced the pleasure of familiarity, repetition. I could double-check some of the details for my book, but I was at ease – not even taking photographs.

Toward the end of our time together, Olga mysteriously left the small performance space for the children's theatrical productions we had revisited, saying she would be back, saying something, I thought, about "doors." I waited. When she returned, she was carrying three dolls (the "doors"): Hemon's dummies and, in fact, hand-made puppets the size of small children. Olga quickly reconfigured the scene that had been the centerpiece of the exhibit I had missed, seating the puppets on chairs around a small table, which was covered with a festive Sabbath cloth, set with candlesticks and a ceremonial kiddush cup, all against the background of a painting representing a Kishinev streetscape from the era of the pogrom. In this reconstructed, improvised version, husband and wife are joined by their daughter, Ora. Olga danced with the daughter doll to show me how the puppets could be used. I don't know what I would have made of this scene had I encountered it on my first visit. I wasn't put off, though, as were the characters in Hemon's novel, by the sight of these figures in an earlier choreography, "a couple of dummies," awkwardly positioned in their chairs.

Instead, on this return visit to the tiny museum setting, I was moved by what I perceived as the affect driving the curatorial decisions: the twin effort to touch the visitor from abroad, but at the same time to engage the small children living in the city who participate in the Center's activities. In a minor, miniature key, the Kishinev Jewish Cultural Center echoes the efforts made by museums of conscience like the Tenement Museum in Manhattan to reproduce the material setting in which earlier generations lived.[12]

Through many layers of remove and mediation, the props, the puppets, and domestic artifacts all rehearse the holidays that by definition recur in a kind of perpetual present tense: the weekly Sabbath, the annual Purim. When Olga the librarian danced with Ora the doll, I felt the poignant, physical effort to keep alive through ritual something important that was irremediably past, except as remembrance, or as symbolic performance. You can play in the rooms that contain the local exhibits, as the children do, reenacting the story of Purim – Purim as the story of a pogrom averted – but the adults are summoned to remember the pogrom as tragic history. Those who remained were not rescued, Queen Esther notwithstanding.

Looking at the puppets on the stage, I suddenly collapsed inside like the balloons wilting on the stage behind the dolls, a whoosh of intensely held in breath that I could finally let go. It struck me that I had been working too hard at all of this, my compulsion to document, to find the exact spot, to keep returning until I got it right. These were the rites. By their stylized artifice, the puppets forced me to realize that the historical people they stood in for would be real to me only as actors in shared rituals, celebrating a long history of survival, as well as loss, a history that extended to all the descendants who wished to see themselves as part of it. Maybe as a good daughter of Freud, my anxiety subsided on this visit because the puppets brought me back to a childhood memory of relation to a Judaism already lost to me, through assimilation and Americanization over two generations. Maybe what I had been trying to find was a way to compensate for my indifference to the narrative that I'm now starting to see has shaped me all along. Let's say that's part of it, searching for the path of a lost history whose effects nonetheless remain embedded in me. But how much can this process of return give meaning in retrospect to all that I didn't know, and don't know still?

On this second visit to Kishinev, a broader uncertainty that had accompanied me throughout my quest also began to ease, and this was a troubling anxiety about the story itself that I was constructing to put in the place of my ignorance. I had experienced this uncertainty both on the site, as it were, and as I carried out the research on my lost family at a distance, in my head and on paper, as a kind of dissatisfaction, or dissonance: insufficient information, or approximate pieces of knowledge. I sometimes called this feeling by a term from mathematics that had captured my imagination early on. Asymptotic: not meeting, not falling together. As plotted on a graph, an asymptote is a line that a curve forever approaches. The curve and the line look as though they will ultimately meet, but in the end, they never touch. Nicely for me, the word symptom shares the root of this term, which makes a kind of circular logic. My symptom was my frustration at what would not fall together. But given the nature of my quest, the failure to coincide with the thing itself was inevitable.

How close, then, was close enough? I wanted to discover my grandparents' records in the archive; instead I had to make do with their second cousin, the way in nineteenth-century novels the protagonist has to tolerate poor relations. On this return visit, I began to internalize this information differently: the second cousin offered lateral confirmation, a side bar of evidence, but confirmation all the same, of my family's passage in this city, good enough, to use the comforting language of object relations, close enough to begin repairing the loss, rebuilding lost knowledge.

On our final walk through the pogrom area, Natasha and I stopped to buy water at the little grocery adjacent to the dwelling known as "House Number 13," a place singled out as a scene of violence by Vladimir Korolenko's newspaper reportage in 1904.[13] On my previous visit I had been frustrated not to be able to enter the courtyard of the building, a site described by an Israeli researcher who had visited Kishinev on the 100th anniversary of the pogrom.[14] Natasha asked the young clerk if he had access to the courtyard and scribbled the phone number of his boss, the grocery store owner, in her notebook. But we both knew without saying that it was too late. I would have to accept the evidence of the many neighboring courtyards I had already seen. Much as I longed for particulars, I was going to have to be satisfied with the markers of collective, not individual, identity – with approximation. This should not have been surprising. All along I had been able to piece together the Kipnis puzzle, my patrimony, only through the lateral bonds that tied these family members to others of their generation, and to the conditions of their emigration, to the collateral domain of what I call the transpersonal.[15] Wasn't that what the museum exhibits were designed to represent, "an average Jewish home" at the time of the pogrom, a community, moreover, that revealed something important about my grandparents by their difference from its rules?

This lesson of the second visit was not lost on me. A door had literally closed – the door to the yard of House No. 13. Gentrification had begun in the pogrom area; more of the old buildings were bound to disappear. The exhibits at the Jewish Center had changed and would no doubt change again. The monuments to the pogrom and to the Holocaust would remain, but the city would reconfigure its shape and architecture around them. In yet another rescripting of historical borders, the impoverished country of Moldova itself might soon merge with its neighbor Romania and fly a new flag. As myth, however, Kishinev would linger in the metaphors of the "City of the Killings," and in collective Jewish history.

Would this be my last return? As we headed for the airport at Chisinau, I felt that something had settled in me, the compulsion had loosened its hold. I knew so much more than when I had begun, and yet there was so much I would never know. The exertion of the voyage had been absolutely necessary, but so was acknowledging its limits. And yet, I've come to relish the pleasures of vanishing knowledge: a photograph of my grandparents taken in a photography studio that no longer exists, and a home address, not theirs but that of their friends, friends whose relationship is established, after the fact of their separation, in a handwritten farewell inscribed on the back of yet another photograph taken at another photography studio that no longer exists. Most of the rest of what I wanted to know will take that form of removal – the equivalent of the psychic distance, and yet relatedness, of second cousins – and of puppets.

In a conversation I moderated among Saidiya Hartman, Eva Hoffman, and Daniel Mendelsohn about their memoirs of return, Mendelsohn recalled an event with Leon Wieseltier in which Wieseltier challenged him about the expression "going back." How could you go back to where you had never been, Wieseltier wanted to know? Mendelsohn answered that when you grow up in an immigrant family, you constantly hear about "the country of origin. So it does feel like going back."[16] In my case, I had not heard enough growing up to feel that I was going back to a specific place in the "old country" – and in particular, when I visited, on the heels of my first trip to Kishinev, the town in Ukraine where my paternal grandfather and great-grandfather were born (as I had discovered searching through the archive of immigrant papers in New York), I definitely did not feel that I was returning there or that my roots lay there, even though, literally, by blood line and genealogy, I knew this to be true.

Instead, the second trip to Kishinev persuaded me that this was where I might have and wanted to have, come from. Through the literary history of the city, the traces of the archive, and the photographs of my grandparents and their stylishly dressed friends, I was moved to an act of "affiliative self-fashioning," a chosen identification created by the journey.[17] Returning to Kishinev had forced me to understand that while this place was the scene of a historical experience that I needed to see, a place where history had happened to the people who came before me, much of what I wanted from the past would continue to elude me. No matter how concrete, how referential the way a photograph refers to the object in front of its lens, this place of the past lacked the story I was seeking, but it was the origin of the story I would write.

Notes

1. I identify this triggering moment for my inquiry into the immigration history of my family in the epilogue to But Enough About Me: Why We Read Other People's Lives (New York: Columbia University Press, 2002). A version of this essay appears in Rites of Return: Diaspora Poetics and the Politics of Memory (New York: Columbia University Press, 2011), eds. Marianne Hirsch and Nancy K. Miller, and in my family memoir, What They Saved: Pieces of a Jewish Past (Lincoln: University of Nebraska Press, 2011).

2. Beginning on 6 April 1903, the last day of Passover and the first day of Easter, a determined horde of local perpetrators launched a violent two-day attack on the Jewish population of the town of Kishinev, the capital of Bessarabia. Men, women, and children were beaten and murdered; women were raped; businesses and homes were looted and devastated. For a succinct account of the pogrom and its historical aftermath, see Edward H. Judge, Easter in Kishinev: Anatomy of a Pogrom (New York: New York University Press, 1992).

3. 'City of the Killings', Songs from Bialik: Selected Poems of Hayim Nahman Bialik, trans. Atar Adari (Syracuse: Syracuse University Press, 2000). The poem's title is alternately translated as 'In the City of Killing' and 'The City of Slaughter.' Bialik was sent by the Jewish Historical Committee in Odessa to write a report based on victim testimony; instead, he wrote a poem. The hero of Zangwill's play is described as a 'pogrom orphan,' who still bears the scars of the attack on his face [The Melting Pot, Drama in Four Acts (New York: Macmillan, 1932)]. Zangwill published a children's story version of his drama as "The Melting Pot: A Story of True Americanism," in From the Tower Window of My Bookhouse, ed. Olive Beaupré Miller (Chicago: The Bookhouse for Children, 1921).

4. The archive of the experience has been inventoried and canonized in a now out-of-print, door-stopper size volume, *Jewish Roots in Ukraine and Moldova: Pages from the Past and Archival Inventories* published by Miriam Weiner and her 'Routes to Roots' foundation in 1999. On the move from the web to the journey, see Marianne Hirsch and Leo Spitzer, "The Web and the Reunion: <czernowitz.ehpes.com>" in *Rites of Return*, eds. Hirsch and Miller. I describe my two trips more fully in *What They Saved: Pieces of a Jewish Past*.

5. Alexander Hemon, *The Lazarus Project* (New York: Riverhead Books, 2008).

6. Ibid. 229.

7. Ibid. 230.

8. Ibid. 231.

9. Ibid. 232.

10. Sigmund Freud, *Beyond the Pleasure Principle*, trans. James Strachey (New York: W.W. Norton, 1961).

11. Kiran Desai, *The Inheritance of Loss* (New York: Grove Press, 2006).

12. On the affect generated by visits to the Tenement Museum, see Liz Sevcenko, "Sites of Conscience: Activating Historic Sites for Adressing Contemporary Issues," *Rites of Return*, eds. Hirsch and Miller.

13. V. G. Korolenko, "House No. 13: An Episode in the Massacre of Kishinev," *Contemporary Review* 85 (February 1904): 266-280.

14. Dan Laor, "Kishinev Revisited: A Place in Jewish Historical Memory," *Prooftexts* 25 (2005): 30-38. As Laor's title suggests, every visit to Kishinev *after* Bialik's poem, which itself performs a return and an invitation to bear witness, could also be considered a return. But Laor also closely followed the itinerary recorded in Bialik's notebooks of testimony. On the relation of the testimony to the poem, see Mikhal Dekel's "'From the Mouth of the Raped Woman Rivka Shiff,' Kishinev, 1903," *WSQ* 36.1-2 (Spring/Summer 2008): 199-207.

15. See my article "Getting Transpersonal: The Cost of an Academic Life," *Prose Studies* 31.3 (December 2009): 166-180, where I develop the concept of transpersonal as the activities of "identification and disidentification [that] take shape in the connective tissue that binds together language, custom, practice, cultural memory, and the archive. The transpersonal is a process through which the self moves into and out of the social, psychic and material spaces of relation." It is the "transaction between singular and collective" identities (168).

16. "Memoirs of Return," in *Rites of Return*, eds. Hirsch and Miller. The three writers identify the role played by inherited stories of injury and loss in the formation of their desire to understand the past and its shaping role on the present. The development of innovative technologies and Internet archives has popularized as it has facilitated the widespread practice in the United States, but also in the United Kingdom, of making a journey to sites of historical atrocity. This twenty-first-century need to return and to redress still damaging injustices and to retrieve lost stories is the subject of the essays collected in *Rites of Return*.

17. Term coined by Alondra Nelson in "Bio Science: Genetic Genealogy Testing and the Pursuit of African Ancestry," *Social Studies of Science* 38.5 (October 2008): 759-783. "Whereas objective self-fashioning highlights the epistemological authority of re-

ceived-facts that become resources for self-making... such as the lab or the courtroom, affiliative self-fashioning attends as well to the weight of individual desires for related-ness, for 'communities of obligation'...." (771). In other words, kinship entails an act of voluntary identification as much as a result of evidentiary authentication.

Contributors

Gur Alroey is professor of Jewish history in modern times at the University of Haifa, Israel. He is also the author of *Immigrants: Jewish Immigration to Palestine in the Early Twentieth Century* [in Hebrew]; *The Quiet Revolution: The Jewish Emigration from the Russian Empire, 1875-1925* [Hebrew]; *Bread to Eat and Clothes to Wear: Letters from Jewish Migrants in the Early Twentieth Century*; and *Seeking a Homeland: the Jewish Territorial Organization and its Struggle with the Zionist Movement, 1905-1925.*

Cecilia Alvstad is associate professor in Spanish at the University of Oslo. In 2011 she was a visiting researcher at the Institute for Interpretation and Translation Studies at Stockholm University. Alvstad's current research interests include translational relations between Scandinavia and the Americas as manifested in literary translations, migrant letters, and travel writing. Her Ph.D. dissertation was a target culture analysis of all translations published for children in Argentina in 1997. She has published articles in *Target* and *Meta* on translation and ambiguity with reference to Swedish and Spanish translations of Hans Christian Andersen's tale about the steadfast tin soldier. Alvstad is a member of the research group "Norwegians in Latin America, 1820-1940" and the head of the international research group "Voice in Translation," which explores the concept of voice in translation studies and employs empirical research on translations. Alvstad is vice president of the European Society for Translation Studies (EST).

Babs Boter is affiliated with the department of gender studies at Utrecht University, where she explores European travel accounts of North America (1870-1950). In particular, she studies the ways in which female and male visitors of the U.S. position themselves vis-à-vis America's marginalized (and gendered, racialized) subjects. Her dissertation, which she defended in 2005, is entitled: *Fabrication of Selves: Girls of Color Coming of Age* (Amsterdam School for Cultural Analysis, University of Amsterdam). She teaches at Utrecht University, University College Utrecht, the Free University of Amsterdam, and Emerson College, Castle Well in Limburg.

Michael Boyden is assistant professor of American culture at the faculty of translation studies of Ghent University College in Belgium, where he specializes in translation issues in Atlantic migration literature. In this capacity, Boyden has worked as a research consultant for the Red Star Line Museum in Antwerp. Prior to his appointment, he was a post-doctoral researcher at the University of Leuven, a fellow at the German Historical Institute, and a Fulbright scholar at the Harvard University Longfellow Institute, a center dedicated to the multiple linguistic traditions of the United States. He received his undergraduate and doctoral degrees from the University of Leuven in a program that included periods of study at Queen's University Belfast, the University of Edinburgh, and the University of British Columbia in Vancouver.

Frank Caestecker read history at the University of Ghent, and after his undergraduate studies he worked at the University of Brussels, the University of Warsaw, the University of Osnabrück, and the University of Wisconsin-Madison. He completed his graduate studies at the European University Institute in Florence where, in 1994, he defended his Ph.D. entitled "Belgian Alien Policy, 1840-1940. The Creation of Guest Workers, Refugees and Illegal Aliens" (Berghahn Books, 2000). Together with Bob Moore, he edited the volume *Refugees from Nazi Germany and the Liberal European States, 1933-1939* (Berghahn Books, 2010). He is now affiliated with the University of Ghent and University College Ghent.

Ron Geaves holds a chair in the comparative study of religion in the theology, philosophy, and religious studies department of Liverpool Hope University,and is the director of the Centre for the Applied Study of Muslims and Islam in Britain. His research interests focus upon the transmigration of Hinduism, Sikhism, and Islam to the UK. He began his work on the study of contemporary Islam and its diverse religious groups in 1990, when he embarked on postgraduate research at the University of Leeds focusing on the newly created Community Religions Project. His publications are numerous, including student texts on the study of religion. His recent publications include *Islam Today* (London: Continuum, 2010) and *Abdullah Quilliam: The Life and Times of a Victorian Muslim* (Leicester: Kube Press, 2010). He is currently working on an edited collection entitled *Transformations and Trends in British Sufism* and *The Collected Works of Abdullah Quilliam: A British Muslim of the Nineteenth Century*, both due for publication in 2012.

Hans Krabbendam is assistant director of the Roosevelt Study Center in Middelburg, the Netherlands. He holds degrees from Kent State University (M.A. 1989) and Leiden University (Ph.D. 1995). His main interest and expertise is in American history – specifically in the history of Dutch immigration to the United States – and U.S. religious and diplomatic history. He has published widely on these subjects and co-edited a number of volumes on European-American (and Dutch-American) relations, among them *Freedom on the Horizon: Dutch Immigration to America 1840-1940*.

Nancy K. Miller is distinguished professor of English and comparative literature at the Graduate Center, City University of New York. Her most recent books are *But Enough About Me: Why We Read Other People's Lives*, the co-edited anthology *Picturing Atrocity: Photography in Crisis*, and the family memoir *What They Saved: Pieces of a Jewish Past*.

Yannis G. S. Papadopoulos holds a Ph.D. in history from Panteion University in Athens, a Master of advanced Studies in anthropology from the École Pratique des Hautes Études in Paris, an M.Phil. in cultural information systems from the University of Crete, and a B.A. in history and archeology from the University of Ioannina. He teaches modern history at Panteion University in Athens. His Ph.D. dissertation is entitled "Greek Orthodox Immigrants from the Ottoman Empire to the USA and the Foreign Policy of the Greek State from 1890 to 1927". His research focuses on issues of migration, ethnicity, conceptualization of identifications among immigrants, and the repercussions of the Eastern Question in the United States of America.

Ute Ritz-Deutch received her doctorate in history from the State University of New York at Binghamton in May 2008. Her dissertation is entitled "Alberto Vojtěch Frič, the German Diaspora, and Indian Protection in Southern Brazil, 1900-1920: A Transatlantic Ethno-Historical Case Study". Her research interests are in ethnohistory, trans-Atlantic history, the German diaspora in Brazil, nation-building processes, the history of anthropology, human rights, indigenous rights, and immigrant rights. She teaches history courses at State University of New York at Cortland and at Tompkins Cortland Community College in Dryden, New York. She is also active in the Ithaca chapter of Amnesty International and the Tompkins County Immigrant Rights Coalition and gives frequent lectures on human rights and immigrant rights issues.

Liselotte Vandenbussche is assistant professor of Dutch at Ghent University College. She studied Germanic languages and literature at Ghent University and literary theory at Leuven University. She obtained her Ph.D. in 2006 at the Center for Gender Studies with a dissertation on liberal women writers in Flemish literary and cultural journals (1870-1914). Vandenbussche is the author of *Het veld der verbeelding. Vrijzinnige vrouwen in Vlaamse literaire en algemeen-culturele tijdschriften (1870-1914)* (Ghent: Royal Academy for Dutch Literature and Linguistics, 2008). It was awarded the Jozef Vercoullie Prize 1998-2006, the Provincial Prize for History 2008, and was nominated for the Frans van Cauwelaert Prize 2008. She has published in journals such as *Tijdschrift voor Nederlandse Taal- en Letterkunde*, *Nederlandse Letterkunde*, *Spiegel der Letteren*, and *Yang* and contributed to several books with articles on gender, literature, and translation in nineteenth- and early twentieth-century Flanders. Vandenbussche's postdoctoral research focuses on literary translators in Flanders between 1830 and 1914.

An Van Hecke studied Romance philology (French-Spanish) at KU Leuven. She obtained a Master's degree at the Universidad Nacional Autónoma de México in Latin American Studies and a Ph.D. in literature at the University of Antwerp (Belgium) with a dissertation on the Guatemalan author Augusto Monterroso. She is assistant professor of Spanish at the sub-faculty of language and communication at Leuven University and Lessius University College in Antwerp. She has published articles on Mexican, Chicano, and Guatemalan literature and has presented papers at numerous conferences in Europe and the United States. Her main areas of interest are translation, displacement, intercultural relations, national identity, and intertextuality. Her current research deals with (auto)translation, bilingualism, and code-switching in Chicano literature. She coedited El artista caribeño como guerrero de lo imaginario (Frankfurt-Madrid: Vervuert-Iberoamericana, 2004). Her book, Monterroso en sus tierras: espacio e intertexto, has been published by the Editorial de la Universidad Veracruzana (Xalapa, Veracruz, Mexico, 2010).

Elisabeth Vik is a Ph.D. student at the Institute of Literature, Area Studies and European Languages at the University of Oslo. She has a cand.polit. degree (advanced MA) in social anthropology and has earlier worked on social processes and discourse analysis within development aid and microfinance in Bolivia. She is currently researching the history of Norwegians in Argentina between 1880 and 1940. Her study is part of an ongoing project called Norwegians in Latin America 1850-1940. The project is managed at the University of Oslo, Norway and has participants from other Norwegian universities as well as in Argentina and Brazil.

Adam Walaszek is professor of history at the Institute of American Studies and Polish Diaspora, Jagiellonian University in Cracow, Poland. He has worked on the history of international migrations, the history of Polish ethnic groups in the United States, and U.S. social history. He is currently director of the Institute. Some recent publications include: Migracje Europejczyków 1650-1914 (Kraków: Wydawnictwo Uniwersytetu Jagiellońskiego, 2007), Życie na pograniczu i 'życie pomiędzy'. Polacy w zagłębiu antracytowym w Luzerne County, Pensylwania z innymi grupami w tle (1753-1902) (Kraków: Wydawnictwo Uniwersytetu Jagiellońskiego, 2012), "Diaspora," in The Palgrave Dictionary of Transnational History. From the mid-19th Century to the Present Day, edited by Akira Iriye and Pierre-Yves Saunier (Palgrave-Macmillan Publ., Houndmills-New York, 2009), "Migrations from a Galician Village: Babica before World War I," in European Mobility. Internal, International, and Transatlantic Moves in the 19th and early 20th Centuries (Transkulturelle Perspektiven), edited by Annemarie Steidl et al. (Göttingen: V&R unipress, 2009); "Zum Brot: Osteuropaer auf dem Weg nach Amerika," in Aufbruch in die Fremde. Migration gestern und heute, edited by Diethelm Knauf and Barry Moreno (Bremen: Edition Temmen, 2009); "Do Ameryki za chlebem: Central Eastern Europeans Cross the Atlantic," in *Leaving Home. Migration Yesterday and Today*, edited by Diethelm Knauf and Barry Moreno (Bremen: Edition Temmen, 2010).

Sostene Massimo Zangari has a Ph.D. in English from the University of Milan, Italy. He has conducted extensive research on Herman Melville and ethnic American literature and has published articles in *The Black Scholar*, *PAAS Journal*, and *Enthymema* as well as contributing essays to collective volumes on Herman Melville and Richard Wright. He is currently working as a teaching assistant in the department of English at the University of Milan.

Index

German Brazilians 16, 135-138, 140, 142-143
Luso-Brazilians 17, 136-138, 140-141
Bremen (Germany) 46, 61, 69, 83, 85-86, 92-95, 108, 112
Brinkmann, Tobias 59
Brinks, Herbert J. 182
British Muslim Association 168
Brody (Poland) 34
Brudno, Ezra 200
Brussels (Belgium) 69
Budapest (Hungary) 29, 33
Buenos Aires (Argentina) 15, 37, 84, 108, 115, 121-129, 155
Bujak, Franciszek 29, 33-34
Bukowski, Jan 29, 40
Burlend, Rebecca 181-182, 184-185, 192

Caestecker, Frank 13
Cahan, Abraham 21, 156, 197-205, 210
Calcutta (India) 171-172
California (USA) 188
Canada 36-37, 39, 64-65, 69, 123-124, 127, 187, 189
Cardiff (United Kingdom) 165, 167, 173-174
Carpentier, Alejo 154, 157, 159
Catholics 36, 129
See also Ukrainian Greek Catholics
Cape Town (South Africa) 122
Cardiff (United Kingdom) 165, 167, 172-174
Chametzky, Jules 203
Chekhov, Anton 151-152, 157, 159, 219
Cherbourg (France) 46
Chicago (Illinois, USA) 29, 66, 71, 209-210, 218
Children 13, 54, 61, 64-66, 69-70, 89-92, 94, 103, 128, 141, 150, 154, 156, 187-188, 209, 217, 221

Chile 128, 158
China 53, 61, 168
Chişinău, see Kishinev
Cholera 62, 67, 84
Christians 38, 46, 167, 169, 190, 208
See also Catholics, Greek Orthodox, Protestants, Puritans
Churches 11, 15, 29, 36, 127-131
Class 18-20, 53, 71, 87-88, 95-96, 126, 131, 141, 153, 166-170, 174, 180-181, 184-192, 198, 202-204, 210, 220
Cleveland (Ohio, USA) 36
Club Europeo 129
Cnossen, Taeke 189-190, 192
Collectives 15-17, 20-21, 45, 52-53, 105, 121, 131, 149, 156, 180, 183, 192, 208, 223
Colonists 16, 135, 136, 138, 140, 165-166, 174
Columbus, Christopher 18, 152-154, 157, 159
Consulates 13, 48, 63, 125, 130
Cork (Ireland) 59, 82
Cortázar, Julio 153
Cortes, Hernan 18, 152, 154, 159
Crescent, The (newspaper) 19, 167, 169, 171-172
Croatia 31, 33, 35
Cronin, Michael 14, 105-106
Cuba 150, 152-154, 157
Cunliffe, Obeid-Ullah 170
Czar Alexander II 38
Czech Republic (migrants from –) 30-32

Danish-Argentine Association 130
Decision-making in migration process 12, 15-16, 30-31, 39, 59, 81, 96, 121-122, 126-132
Deeke, José 136, 140
DeHaan, Kathleen 136
Denmark (migrants from –) 15, 29, 32, 123-124, 127, 129-130
Desai, Kiran 220